The Mature Student's Guide to Writing

Palgrave Study Skills

Authoring a PhD
Business Degree Success
Career Skills
Critical Thinking Skills
e-Learning Skills (2nd edn)
Effective Communication for
  Arts and Humanities Students
Effective Communication for
  Science and Technology
The Exam Skills Handbook
The Foundations of Research
The Good Supervisor
How to Manage your Arts, Humanities and
  Social Science Degree
How to Manage your Distance and
  Open Learning Course
How to Manage your Postgraduate Course
How to Manage your Science and
  Technology Degree
How to Study Foreign Languages
How to Write Better Essays (2nd edn)
IT Skills for Successful Study
The International Student Handbook
Making Sense of Statistics
The Mature Student's Guide to Writing (2nd edn)
The Personal Tutor's Handbook
The Postgraduate Research Handbook (2nd edn)
Presentation Skills for Students

The Principles of Writing in Psychology
Professional Writing (2nd edn)
Researching Online
Research Using IT
Skills for Success
The Study Abroad Handbook
The Student's Guide to Writing (2nd edn)
The Student Life Handbook
The Study Skills Handbook (3rd edn)
Study Skills for Speakers of English as
  a Second Language
Studying the Built Environment
Studying Business at MBA and Masters Level
Studying Economics
Studying History (3rd edn)
Studying Law (2nd edn)
Studying Mathematics and its Applications
Studying Modern Drama (2nd edn)
Studying Physics
Studying Programming
Studying Psychology (2nd edn)
Teaching Study Skills and Supporting Learning
Work Placements – A Survival Guide for Students
Writing for Nursing and Midwifery Students
Write it Right
Writing for Engineers (3rd edn)

Palgrave Study Skills: Literature

General Editors: John Peck and Martin Coyle

How to Begin Studying English Literature
  (3rd edn)
How to Study a Jane Austen Novel (2nd edn)
How to Study a Charles Dickens Novel
How to Study Chaucer (2nd edn)
How to Study an E. M. Forster Novel
How to Study James Joyce
How to Study Linguistics (2nd edn)

How to Study Modern Poetry
How to Study a Novel (2nd edn)
How to Study a Poet
How to Study a Renaissance Play
How to Study Romantic Poetry (2nd edn)
How to Study a Shakespeare Play (2nd edn)
How to Study Television
Practical Criticism

The Mature Student's Guide to Writing

Second edition

Jean Rose

palgrave
macmillan

First edition published 2001
Second edition published 2007 by
PALGRAVE MACMILLAN
Houndmills, Basingstoke, Hampshire RG21 6XS and
175 Fifth Avenue, New York, N.Y. 10010
Companies and representatives throughout the world

PALGRAVE MACMILLAN is the global academic imprint of the Palgrave
Macmillan division of St. Martin's Press, LLC and of Palgrave Macmillan Ltd.
Macmillan® is a registered trademark in the United States, United Kingdom
and other countries. Palgrave is a registered trademark in the European Union
and other countries.

ISBN-13: 978–1–4039–8995–6
ISBN-10: 1–4039–8995–8

This book is printed on paper suitable for recycling and
made from fully managed and sustained forest sources.
Logging, pulping and manufacturing processes are expected to
conform to the environmental regulations of the country of origin.

A catalogue record for this book is available from the British Library.

Library of Congress Catalog Card Number: 2006052970

10 9 8 7 6 5 4 3
16 15 14 13 12 11 10 09 08

Printed and bound in China

Contents

Part Four: Moving On

Acknowledgements

The author would like to thank the following:

BBC Radio 4 for permission to quote from Anthony Giddens's BBC Radio 4's Reith Lectures 1999 – *Runaway World*.

The Daily Telegraph for permission to quote from 'Tory tipple more compassionate and hangover-free' by Andrew Gimson, 1 March 2006.

Devon Life for permission to quote from the following features: 'Class Glass', 'The Trading House', 'The Rich Earth' and 'A Plant Phenomenon'.

A. C. Grayling for permission to reprint 'Why a high society is a free society', *Observer*, 19 May 2002.

Pan Macmillan Ltd for permission to quote the poem 'Tea' from *Rapture* by Carol Ann Duffy.

Penguin Group (UK) for permission to quote from *The Psychology of Perception* by M. D. Vernon.

All the adult students I have taught (without whom this book would not have been written), and especially students who were kind enough to let me use some of their work here. All names have been changed.

Every effort has been made to trace all the copyright holders, but if any have been inadvertently overlooked the author and publishers will be pleased to make the necessary arrangements at the earliest opportunity.

Who Is this Book For?

This book is for adults. You are likely to be a mature student, but you might be studying anything from IT to drama or from business studies to building construction. Perhaps you're about to begin a full-time course in higher education – or you might be studying part-time or be enrolled on an Open University course, or even be taking an on-line course. Maybe you're starting an Access to Higher Education programme. You might be a science student who has always found English baffling or someone whose first language is not English, so you want really clear and easy-to-understand explanations of the techniques you need to master. Perhaps you are not a student at all, but you just want to brush up your skills. Whatever you're doing, you'll find lots of tips here to help you with writing well and improving your style.

If you're having difficulties with your written English, but can't work out what's wrong, this book will prove invaluable. If you missed out at school or have forgotten some of the basic rules of good writing, you'll find help here. You may have tried looking at books that give grammatical rules but then found that you couldn't relate these to your own situation. This book explains things in the context of the kinds of writing you might be required to do, and most of the explanations and examples have been kept simple in order to make the process as stress-free as possible.

How to Use This Book

There are a number of different ways you can use this book. What you do will depend very much on your individual circumstances – on how much you remember from your previous education, for instance, or on what particular assignments you have to cope with. You'll probably find that there are some things you just need to brush up on and others that you need to look at more carefully. You might find that you will need to cover one or two issues immediately and others as they arise in relation to your course or other work.

Let's suppose you've just begun an Access to Higher Education course. Perhaps you have been asked to write a letter for an assignment. You are likely to want to look at chapter 6, in Part Two, so that you can get the main structure right straight away. When your tutor has seen and commented on the letter, you may find that you need some help with understanding how verbs work. That will be the time to turn to chapter 12 on verbs. This chapter will show you how to use verbs accurately in your sentences.

If you just need to brush up on your knowledge of verbs, you might like to scan the introduction in chapter 12 and then turn straight to the summary at the end of the chapter to see if it makes sense to you. If it rings bells and you feel fairly confident, you could turn back to the activities and try one or two to test yourself. This might be all you need. If, however, things are not coming back easily, or if an item is quite new to you, you'll probably want to work through the whole chapter. It would be a good idea to take one section at a time when you have a spare 20 minutes or so, rather than trying to do too much at once. This way, you won't overload yourself with new information.

You can also use the book as a quick reference tool. Perhaps you want to know what an adjective is, or how to use a semicolon. Just turn to the index and this will refer you to the page you need.

Always give new information time to sink in. Learning to improve your writing is not like learning a set of dates. You will need to practise each skill that is new to you. So don't be alarmed if you continue to make mistakes for a little while. Expect to improve gradually. When your tutor marks an error in your writing, go back to the rules so that you understand *exactly* what went wrong. It is through fully understanding our errors that we are able to make most progress.

Each chapter begins with a brief introduction. This is followed by explanations and, sometimes, activities for practice. At the end of the chapter, you'll find a summary of the main points you need to remember.

PART ONE

When you return to study, the thing that's likely to be uppermost in your mind is submitting your first essay. It might be years since you wrote one, and you're probably aware that more will be expected of you now. Chapter 2 will take you slowly through the process, explaining everything you need to do and how to do it. In order to write the essay, however, you're going to need to have written some notes. So chapter 1 helps with this and shows different methods for note-taking. Essay-writing also involves giving references, so chapter 3 will talk you through the process.

PART TWO

This part covers particular writing tasks you are likely to be doing. Chapter 4 on style forms a basis for each of the others. Besides giving you some general techniques on improving your writing in general, it contains important material on how to adjust your writing for different types of assignment.

If, for example, you need to write a letter about a faulty freezer, you'll need to include specific details of the fault and of where you bought the item. If, however, someone writes an article comparing several freezers, it will be likely to include details of performance and may also give background information on the process of refrigeration and on market trends. But if a freezer features in a detective novel because it contains a corpse, the emphasis will be on the horror of the situation. Whatever we write, we need to be clear on the purpose of the piece so that we can write in a suitable mode and include relevant information. Chapters 5 to 10 explain what's necessary for a variety of purposes.

PART THREE

You may need to refer to items in Part Three at any time. It's full of rules on grammar and punctuation. So dip into it whenever you are unsure of something or whenever your tutor comments on a process that you need to revise. You can, of course, work through these chapters in full if you want to, but it's better not to overload yourself with too many rules all at once. Part Three is especially important, however, because it shows you how to be sure that your writing is easily understood. An essay that is full of good ideas can fail to get a high mark if it's difficult to follow.

PART FOUR

This part of the book looks beyond your life as a student to give you help with applying for jobs. You are likely to be making applications from the spring of your final academic year onwards. You might, however, want to use it while you are still in the early stages of your course. You might want to look for part-time work to help with the cost of studying, or you might want to gain some valuable experience (whether paid or unpaid) in your chosen field. Chapters 15 and 16 will show you how to construct a really useful CV and how to approach application letters. Writing a CV can be a time-consuming process, but the good news is that once you've got a CV together, it can be changed and updated as you go along. It will be with you for life.

If You Think You May Be Dyslexic . . .

There are many forms of dyslexia. As well as causing problems with writing, these can affect various other activities, particularly your ability to organise your work. It's possible, of course, that you are not dyslexic at all. Sometimes, well-meaning friends can suggest that a person is dyslexic just because his or her spelling is not good. If you are at all concerned, contact the student services section at your college or university and arrange to see an expert who will be able to discuss the issue with you.

Most colleges and universities are keen to do all they can to help. Even students in some evening classes can get help if they are studying for an exam. Sometimes, notes and handouts can be provided in a special format for those who are dyslexic, and sometimes a laptop computer can be obtained for your personal use. Extra time can be allowed in examinations, and sometimes a student can be allocated someone to help take notes in class sessions. All this takes time to organise, however, so it's important to speak to your tutors as early as possible in the academic year – or as soon as you are accepted on a course. If you leave this too late, help may not be available, or you may have fallen so far behind that it's difficult to catch up.

If it turns out that you are dyslexic, you will need to ask a dyslexia specialist how you might make use of this book. It is unlikely that you will be able to work through it in the same way as a student who is not dyslexic. So make sure that you take advice. This book does *not* contain any specific help with dyslexia.

Part One
The Big Picture

1 Taking Notes

INTRODUCTION

If you're not used to taking lecture notes, you're likely to try to fall back on what you did at school. This generally means writing at great speed in order to try to take down almost everything a speaker says. This is better than nothing, of course, but it's not going to serve you very well. You won't be able to learn as much from the lecture as you would if you spent less time writing and more time thinking about what's being said; and your notes won't be easy to use for writing essays and revising. Changing old habits isn't easy at first. But the benefits of using a good system are invaluable. So it's well worth persevering to make changes. It will pay dividends.

Note-taking from written materials involves a different procedure because you're likely to be doing it as preparation for writing an assignment. You'll be focusing on specific aspects of a text (a piece of writing), aiming to draw out of it just those things that will serve your purpose. So you'll be starting to analyse what's been written. There's a section on analysis in this chapter. Reading and writing skills go together. The better you become at understanding how a text functions, the better you'll become at both discussing it on paper and at constructing your own essays.

NOTE-TAKING IN LECTURES AND CLASS SESSIONS

Your first problem is likely to be knowing how much to write down. You will probably find that some of the other students end up with writer's cramp because they write all the time, and some seem to sit through a whole session and write down practically nothing.

Neither of these methods is likely to be much help to you in the long run. In any class or lecture session, you need to spend some time considering what's being said, so if you spend all your time writing, you will have missed out on mulling over ideas as they come up and on taking part in any discussions. If, on the other hand, you write down very little, you will have to rely heavily on your memory, and few of us have memories capable of retaining a lot of new facts and ideas in one go.

What you need are notes that give you outline information in a very readable format. So notes written in sentences are not going to make things easy for you. Not only do they take too long to write, but they take too long to read as well. It makes sense, therefore, to develop a method that's going to save you time while still recording what you need.

Watch, first of all, for the way a class session or lecture is structured. Some tutors start with an introduction in which they tell you what will be covered; so if you know there will be three sections, mark them out as you go along. This will help you to feel in control of the situation. Your **syllabus** may also give you some clues as to which are the important areas to concentrate on, so check the relevant section of it before the lecture and listen out for key topics. You may be given a handout that shows the main areas of the day's lecture. This is an invaluable guide. There may even be spaces for you to fill things in as you go along.

Quite often, the way a person speaks can give a clue to important points: a tutor's voice may rise, he or she might stress certain words very strongly, might pause before an important point, or might even repeat a phrase or two. Aim to jot down names, dates, technical terms and other key words. You might like to underline or ring key words as you go. Alternatively, you could do this after the lecture. You'll probably want to leave out extras such as descriptions and full details of examples.

It's possible to use your page rather like a drawing board, ignoring the printed lines if you find that easier. Spreading your notes out and leaving space on each page is especially important. After the lecture, or even weeks later or when you're revising, you might come across something else you need to add. It's infuriating if there's no space. Not only that – a cramped page can be a scary prospect when you come to revise. If every line is filled with full sentences, revision can become overwhelming because there's so much to read.

Look now at the following transcript of the opening to a lecture given by Professor Anthony Giddens in 1999 for the Reith lecture series broadcast on Radio 4 on the subject of globalisation:

> A friend of mine studies village life in central Africa. A few years
> ago, she paid her first visit to a remote area where she was to

carry out her fieldwork. The evening she got there, she was invited to a local home for an evening's entertainment. She expected to find out about the traditional pastimes of this isolated community. Instead, the evening turned out to be a viewing of *Basic Instinct* on video. The film at that point hadn't even reached the cinemas in London.

Such vignettes reveal something about our world. And what they reveal isn't trivial. It isn't just a matter of people adding modern paraphernalia – videos, TVs, personal computers and so forth – to their traditional ways of life. We live in a world of transformations, affecting almost every aspect of what we do. For better or worse, we are being propelled into a global order that no one fully understands, but which is making its effects felt upon all of us.

Globalisation is the main theme of my lecture tonight, and of the lectures as a whole. The term may not be – it isn't – a particularly attractive or elegant one. But absolutely no one who wants to understand our prospects and possibilities at century's end can ignore it. I travel a lot to speak abroad. I haven't been to a single country recently where globalisation isn't being intensively discussed. In France, the word is *mondialisation*. In Spain and Latin America, it is *globalización*. The Germans say *globalisierung*.

The global spread of the term is evidence of the very developments to which it refers. Every business guru talks about it. No political speech is complete without reference to it, yet as little as 10 years ago the term was hardly used, either in the academic literature or in everyday language. It has come from nowhere to be almost everywhere. Given its sudden popularity, we shouldn't be surprised that the meaning of the notion isn't always clear, or that an intellectual reaction has set in against it. Globalisation has something to do with the thesis that we now all live in one world – but in what ways exactly, and is the idea really valid?

Now have a look at my notes (below) for the opening of that lecture. They are possibly shorter than you might expect, and you might feel that the layout is a bit strange. I've tried to record just the key concepts and to leave out background information. I've made links between key points by drawing lines instead of taking up time by writing extra words.

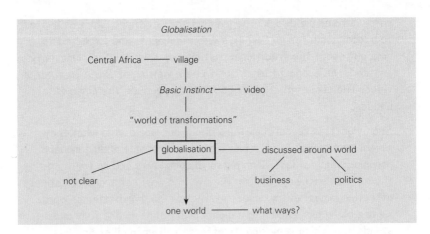

If I had been prepared to add to my notes after the lecture in order to fill in any gaps, I could have written even less:

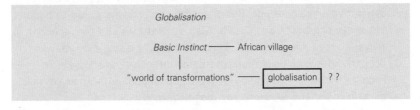

Here's how Helen might have begun to make notes from a lecture on the Founding Fathers from her course on American Studies. The notes are written along the line, as you might normally expect to write.

Founding Fathers – America

Country gents / upper class / those in commerce – had influence & power –
   e.g. Thomas Jefferson (7,500 acres) & wife (11,000 acres).
The colony was governed separately from Britain – the Governor
   appointed by the Crown.
Governor app. a Council. Council app. local assemblies.
There was more representation of the people than in Britain because
   more land available.
N. States – 75% males voted
S. States – 50%   "   "
Most colonists were loyal to the British Crown. When there were
   difficulties, they blamed Parliament (not the King).
There were some tensions over taxes. Britain passed acts to
   recoup expenses – e.g. for British troops in N. America – to
   protect against Indians & French.
Colonists resisted the Stamp Act and the Townsend Act (which
   led to problems in Boston).

Below, however, you can see what Helen actually did, because, by the time she took these notes, she'd had bit of practice in using a clearer layout.

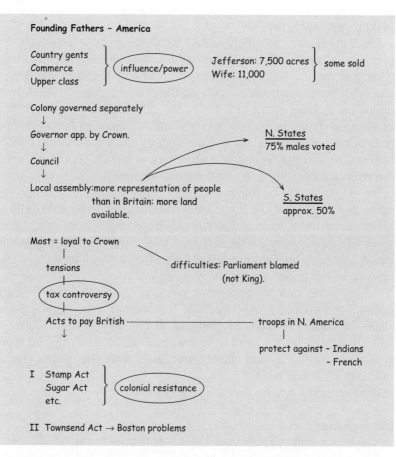

The main things to notice here are:

- only a few key words are written down
- lines are drawn to link points
- there's space to add more later
- these notes are very easy to read

Another method of taking notes is to draw a mind map (see below and chapter 2). With this method, you start by putting the title of the lecture in the middle of the page and then draw a straight line each time you want to note something down. Use capital letters to make things stand out. You can add bullet points or lists. You can also colour-code points after the lecture to make things stand out. If you are good at drawing, you can even add small pictures since visual cues are good memory-sparkers.

Mind maps are extremely useful in some areas – especially for preparing essays and revision notes – but my own feeling is that they work less well in lecture situations. This is partly because links are so crucial: it's tricky, when you come to the end of a page, to know how to link the following page to it. For this reason, I favour Helen's method of working down the page. It's important, however, to find a method that works for you in relation to the course you're on and the type of lectures you attend. Trying out some new methods should help you discover what's going to be quickest and clearest for you.

There will always be things you miss. So go over your notes on the same day as your lecture if you can. You are likely to be able to fill in extra points while your memory is still fresh. This is one of the best ways of helping to make the material stick in your mind. If you can make time for a brief study session with a friend, you'll probably come up with all the important points between you.

Taking notes can be quite hard work, and you'll probably find it easier if you adopt a good posture. If, for example, I'm listening to the radio for Budget changes that will affect me, I have little trouble in hearing exactly what I need to know because I'm so alert. The more you are interested in your subject, the easier it will be to spot crucial points in what you hear.

Here are some tips for surviving a lecture:

beforehand:
- check your syllabus to see how this lecture fits in
- do some reading on the topic
- write down three questions before the lecture starts
- talk to other students about likely topics

during:
- note key headlines on any handouts provided
- pay special attention to the introduction
- listen for words or phrases that are stressed

afterwards:
- debrief with other students

- discuss any contentious points
- add items you missed

Devising specific questions before going into a lecture can be especially helpful for focusing your mind on what's to come and getting your brain in gear. It may not matter too much if the lecture doesn't provide specific answers. The object of the exercise is to get your brain alert and moving. You can always follow up various issues later if you need extra information.

When going over your notes, you can add colour-coding for different topics or processes. Aim also to put in headings and sub-headings to show the main topic areas. All of the following are great for helping things stick in your mind:

- patterns
- colour
- pictures
- diagrams
- lists
- highlighting
- underlining
- boxing
- ringing
- arrows for linking

The important thing is to find the method of note-taking that is quickest, easiest, and that suits you best. However you do it, make use of as many abbreviations as you can because these are great time-savers. Here are a few I use all the time:

therefore	∴
because	∵
is	=
isn't	≠
nineteenth century	⒆
twentieth century	⒇
more than	>
less than	<

It's a good idea to get into the habit of making your own simple short forms for words you use often. Here are some of mine:

history	hist.
literature	lit.
psychology/psychological	psych.
tradition	trad.

If you need to get in some practice in note-taking before starting a course, you might try listening to a radio programme on a subject linked to your course. Go for radio rather than TV programmes if possible so that you won't be distracted by pictures.

ANALYSIS: UNDERSTANDING A TEXT

Obviously, you'll have more thinking time when you take notes from books. When you are faced with a chapter or article to read and absorb, there are various strategies you can use to make the process easier.

Before you begin reading anything, it's a good idea to ask yourself some questions about what is likely to be in the text. Try to think up three or four, such as:

- Will I find out about x?
- What details will there be on y?
- What is the writer's view on z?

It doesn't matter if your questions don't seem particularly penetrating. The object of the exercise is just to get your brain in gear. Asking yourself any kind of question will help because this will start to focus your brain on the topic area you are going to be reading about.

The next thing to do is to scan the material very quickly. Look at headings, sub-headings, diagrams, graphs and any other illustrations. This will help to make you feel more comfortable because your brain will be starting to become familiar with the material. If you are facing something that looks difficult, just covering the ground in this brief manner will start to make the task seem less daunting.

Then you can skim. Read just the first and last sentences of each paragraph. This is another way of familiarising yourself with the subject matter. It's a way of tricking the mind into thinking that it knows all about what's coming. Doing this will almost automatically make a difficult piece of material seem more accessible. You will see below that those first and last sentences can be particularly revealing.

After this, you can do a slower reading in order to work out in detail what's being said.

In order to work through the following section, please now read the article 'Why a high society is a free society' by the philosopher A. C. Grayling (originally published in the *Observer*). This is not dense material. I've chosen something reasonably straightforward so that you can quickly follow some analysis of it. The paragraphs have been numbered so that you can refer to things easily.

Why a high society is a free society
A. C. Grayling

1   One measure of a good society is whether its individual members have the autonomy to do as they choose in respects that principally concern only them. The debate about heroin, cocaine and marijuana touches precisely on this. In my submission, a society in which such substances are legal and available is a good society not because drugs are in themselves good, but because the autonomy of those who wish to use them is respected. For other and broader reasons, many of them practical, such a society will be a better one.

2   I have never taken drugs other than alcohol, nicotine, caffeine and medicinal drugs. Of these, I have for many years not taken the two former. I think it is inimical to a good life to be dependent for pleasure and personal fulfilment on substances which gloss or distort reality and interfere with rationality; and yet I believe that heroin, cocaine, marijuana, ecstasy and cognates of these should be legal and available in exactly the same way as nicotine and alcohol.

3   In logic [there] is no difference between legal and currently illegal drugs. Both are used for pleasure, relief from stress or anxiety, and 'holidaying' from normal life, and both are, in different degrees, dangerous to health. Given this, consistent policy must do one of two things: criminalise the use of nicotine and alcohol, in order to bring them in line with currently illegal substances; or legalise currently illegal substances under the same kinds of regime that govern nicotine and alcohol.

4   On civil liberties grounds the latter policy is preferable because there is no justification in a good society for policing behaviour unless, in the form of rape, murder, theft, riot or fraud, it is intrin-

sically damaging to the social fabric, and involves harm to unwilling third parties. Good law protects in these respects; bad law tries to coerce people into behaving according to norms chosen by people who claim to know and to do better than those for whom they legislate. But the imposition of such norms is an injustice. By all means let the disapprovers argue and exhort; giving them the power to coerce and punish as well is unacceptable.

5   Arguments to the effect that drugs should be kept illegal to protect children.fall by the same token. On these grounds, nicotine and alcohol should be banned too. In fact there is greater danger to children from the illegality of drugs.

6   Almost everyone who wishes to try drugs, does so; almost everyone who wishes to make use of drugs does it irrespective of their legal status. Opponents say legalisation will lead to unrestrained use and abuse. Yet the evidence is that where laws have been relaxed there is little variation in frequency or kind of use.

7   The classic example is Prohibition in the USA during the 1920s. (The hysteria over alcohol extended to other drugs; heroin was made illegal in the USA in 1924, on the basis of poor research on its health risks and its alleged propensity to cause insanity and criminal behaviour.) Prohibition created a huge criminal industry. The end of Prohibition did not result in a frenzy of drinking, but did leave a much-enhanced crime problem, because the criminals turned to substances which remained illegal, and supplied them instead.

8   Crime destabilises society. Gangland rivalry, the use of criminal organisations to launder money, to fund terrorism and gun-running, to finance the trafficking of women and to buy political and judicial influence all destabilise the conditions for a good society far beyond such problems as could be created by private individuals' use of drugs. If drugs were legally and safely available through chemist shops, and if their use was governed by the same provisions as govern alcohol purchase and consumption, the main platform for organised crime would be removed, and thereby one large obstacle to the welfare of society.

9   It would also remove much petty crime, through which many users fund their habit. If addiction to drugs were treated as a medical rather than criminal matter, so that addicts could get safe,

regular supplies on prescription, the crime rate would drop dramatically, as argued recently by certain police chiefs.

10   The safety issue is a simple one. Paracetamol is more dangerous than heroin. Taking double the standard dose of paracetamol, a non-prescription analgesic, can be dangerous. Taking double the standard medical dose of heroin (diamorphine) causes sleepiness and no lasting effects.

11   A good society should be able to accommodate practices which are not destructive of social bonds (in the way that theft, rape, murder and other serious crimes are), but mainly have to do with private behaviour. In fact, a good society should only interfere in private behaviour in extremis.

12   Until a century ago, now-criminal substances were legal and freely available. Some (opium in the form of laudanum) were widely used. Just as some people are damaged by misuse of alcohol, so a few were adversely affected by misuses of other drugs. Society as a whole was not adversely affected by the use of drugs; but it was benefited by the fact that it did not burden itself with a misjudged, unworkable and paternalistic endeavour to interfere with those who chose to use drugs.

13   The place of drugs in the good society is not about the drugs as such, but rather the freedom and the value to individuals and their society of openness to experimentation and alternative behaviours and lifestyles. The good society is permissive, seeking to protect third parties from harm but not presuming to order people to take this or that view about what is in their own good.

autonomy	freedom to determine one's own actions
inimical	unfavourable, hostile
cognates	related things
analgesic	pain killer

► **Key sentences**

Within any piece of writing, the paragraphs will show how the writer has broken down the main subject. Everything in a paragraph is likely to revolve around one topic (or possibly a group of minor but related topics) and every paragraph will contain a key sentence – that is, the most important statement in the paragraph. Once you have found this key sentence, understanding meaning becomes a lot easier.

Look at Grayling's first paragraph – his introduction. This is the point where a writer is likely to make clear what the text is going to be about. Grayling's first sentence prepares the reader with the words 'good society' and 'autonomy'. We begin to get the message that he has a particular ethical stance and that he is in favour of the freedom of the individual. Sentence 2 gets straight to the main topic: drugs. Then, in sentence 3, he gives an immediate clue that this is the core of the paragraph by saying, 'In my submission'. He's clearly going to set out his stall here:

> In my submission, a society in which such substances are legal and available is a good society ... because the autonomy of those who wish to use them is respected.

Notice that I've omitted the comment, 'not because drugs are in them- selves good'. I've done this because it's an aside – interesting, but not part of Grayling's main statement. Sentence 4 makes an additional point but it's clearly not part of Grayling's main drift at this juncture.

The key sentence in paragraph 2 is the long one beginning 'I think ...' The first two sentences are merely personal information. In the third and final sentence, Grayling starts to develop his ideas. (Note that in an essay, you won't generally mention yourself – see chapter 2.)

In paragraph 3, the key sentence is the first. It forms the basis on which Grayling's argument (set out in the third and final sentence) rests in this paragraph – that society must either criminalise nicotine and alcohol or legalise illegal substances.

In paragraph 4, the key sentence is again the first. It explains which of the possibilities put forward at the end of paragraph 2 should be chosen and why. The remaining part of this paragraph gives further elaboration and explanation of this statement. In paragraph 5, the key sentence is the first and in paragraph 6, it's the last. Before reading on, note down which you think is the key sentence in paragraph 7.

Generally speaking, explanation in a paragraph will be secondary to the key sentence, and anything in brackets is clearly not the main focus of the writer's ideas. The opening sentence here points us to Prohibition without making any statement about it. The final sentence sets out the situation. The key sentence is 'Prohibition created a huge criminal industry.' This overturns the idea made by the opponents of legalisation that was put forward in the previous paragraph. Don't worry if you didn't get this right. If you've not done this kind of thing before, just focus on picking up the general idea. You'll improve by leaps and bounds with a little practice.

In each of the paragraphs 8–13, the key sentence is the first. This is clearly a typical position for it. A paragraph will then elaborate on its initial statement and frequently be tied up neatly at its end by a sentence setting out the writer's particular angle on that statement – his or her argument (see chapter 2). Things can get a little tricky here. The key sentence will be the logical base on which the paragraph rests and will help you to understand its meaning; but it might not be the one that interests you most in relation to the assignment you're working on (see 'Selecting information', below).

Whenever you are faced with reading a complex text, following the punctuation can be a help towards understanding. Sentences are a paragraph's building blocks and a writer will be expecting you to absorb the meaning one sentence at a time. Even watching for commas can help you with picking out meaning, as they mark off different parts of a sentence, showing which sections fit together (see the section on commas in chapter 14).

▶ Implication, suggestion and bias

It's important to be alert for attempts to sway your judgement in things you read – for statements that result from a writer's bias, or that just don't hold water. Seemingly simple things like repetition or the use of a term as though it had academic significance can also be used to sway readers.

Grayling repeats the phrase 'good society' a number of times, and he uses it as though it has a specific meaning that we can all agree on. But your definition of a good society may not be the same as his – or mine – even though we'd probably agree that such a society would be founded on sound ethical principles. He is a very experienced writer, so this repetition cannot have occurred by chance. It's been done for a reason. When he comes to his conclusion, Grayling subtly strengthens the effect by changing from the non-specific '*a* good society' (my italics) to the specific '*the* good society'. He has not only given the term prominence by repetition but has finally enforced its validity with the word 'the'.

Explicit language says exactly what it means:

The train for Brighton leaves at 1500 hours.

Implicit language contains some kind of suggestion that is not actually stated:

> "We're told that the train for Brighton leaves at 1500 hours."

That sentence is not so straightforward. By beginning it with the words, 'We're told', the speaker suggests that the information might not be accurate – that in this case, there might be some delay. There's a further possible implication that trains to Brighton are often late. So there's an implied criticism of the service on this line – or possibly of the whole rail network.

Look at this sentence:

> Easton's MP has been seen lunching with high-ranking members of the Opposition on three occasions in the last fortnight.

What's the implication? It's that the MP in question is about to leave his party and defect to the Opposition. But this wasn't stated outright, so if a sentence like this appeared in a newspaper, there could be no accusations of libel. The writer has stuck to observable facts, but has put them forward in such a way that readers will draw the conclusion that defection is imminent.

▶ Things that writers omit

When a writer wants to put forward a particular view, he or she will frequetly omit to mention facts and arguments that might detract from that view. It's essential to be on your guard for this. A. C. Grayling's piece on heroin was written for a newspaper (the *Observer*) and is an 'opinion' piece. This means that he did not need to include detailed evidence or give references for his assertions. The article is useful, therefore, as a means of discovering Grayling's views and as a way, perhaps, of broadening our perspective on the drug issue. What it does not do is provide much material on the current state of heroin use that could be used to prove an academic argument in one of your own essays.

NOTE-TAKING FROM WRITTEN SOURCES

There are various ways you can make notes, and what you do will depend partly on the subject you are studying and partly on what the notes are to be used for. People also find that particular methods suit them better than others, so you need to take account of your own personal preferences.

You will be guided, in part, by the task or assignment you've been set. You're almost certainly going to be either writing an essay or preparing to give a short talk or a seminar paper. It's a good idea to have a note of the task in front of you so that you focus your reading and note-making clearly on the required area and so prevent yourself from wasting time on things that aren't relevant. *Never* spend time on books that are only vaguely related to your subject; and never make notes on a whole chapter unless it is brimfull of ideas and data that are relevant to your assignment. Pick and choose the things you need and those that will be useful for you.

If you own the book you're working from, do underline things and make brief notes in the margin. Some people feel that doing this would deface the book. Books you've bought for your studies, however, are your tools. They are there to help you get a qualification. So make them work for you. If you use pencil, you can always rub things out later. It's best not to use a highlighting pen since highlighting can't be changed if you find you've made an error.

We all develop our own methods of note-making. There are, however, several things you will need to do. Always take a fresh sheet of paper and copy carefully at the top:

- the title of the book or journal (underline this)
- the full name of the author
- the publisher
- the date and place of publication of a book, plus edition (if relevant)
- volume number, plus first and last page numbers of the article for a journal

Many of us learn this the hard way, finding that we have scraps of paper containing disconnected notes and no reference to where they came from. You can't use ideas or quotations in your assignments without saying where you got them. So without names and titles, your work would be wasted.

You need to record the relevant page numbers for both points you note and for quotes. It's a good idea to put this in your left-hand margin. Page numbers are essential for:

- referencing (see chapter 3)
- finding your way back to a point you might want to check or expand on later

If you have ideas of your own or want to note down a comment on what the writer says, be sure to use a consistent method of showing this in your notes, otherwise it may be hard to differentiate your own observations from what the writer actually wrote. I generally put my comments in square brackets and add my initial.

Wherever possible, make notes in your own words rather than copying the original. This helps you to fully understand what you are writing about and will be useful for essays where you will need to prove that you understand a topic. It's fine, however, to copy occasionally where the writer has put something especially well or when it would be particularly difficult to change the way something has been expressed. When copying, quotation marks are essential (see chapter 3).

▶ Full notes

If you were to make full notes on A. C. Grayling's article, they would probably look something like those below. These would be useful if you were either having to write specifically on Grayling or make a detailed summary of 'Why a high society is a free society' (see chapter 5). There are paragraph numbers down the left-hand side. If you were taking notes from a book, this is where you'd be putting in page numbers.

1 Soc. where all drugs legal = gd. because: freedom of individual.
2 Grayling believes: a) 'good life' shd. not depend on 'substances which ... distort reality' b) hard drugs shd. be legal.
3 Legal/ illegal drugs used for: pleasure, stress relief, escapism. Both = 'dangerous to health'.
4 Only practices that harm soc. or 'unwilling third parties' shd. be illegal. Letting those who 'claim to know ... better' than others to make laws = wrong.
5 Same applies to children. Kids more at risk when drugs illegal.

6 Drug-taking not prevented by laws. Relaxation of law doesn't change no. of users.
7 Prohibition in USA caused increase in crime.
8 Organised crime = threat to society: money-laundering, terrorism, vice rings, buying political influence. Ans. = controlled sale of drugs in chemists.
9 If addicts got supplies on prescription, petty crime wd. lessen.
10 Dangers of overdose on prescription = small.
11 If a practice isn't dangerous to soc., it shd. not be illegal. A 'good society' restricts 'interfere[nce] in private behaviour'.
12 Some people will suffer from misuse, but hist. shows little damage to soc. as a whole from drug use.
13 Freedom of individuals to choose lifestyles = essential in 'good society'.

▶ Selecting information for a particular essay

In most situations, you won't want to take notes on a whole article or chapter. Let's suppose you've been asked to write an essay with the following title:

Heroin should be legalised. Discuss.

Your essay would look at facts on drug use, examples, and the views of various professionals and commentators. So if you wanted to mention Grayling, you'd need just his main ideas. You might make the following notes from his article:

1 A 'good society' protects freedom of the individual.
5 Children more at risk when drugs illegal.
6 Prohibition in USA exacerbated crime problem.
8 Legal availability through chemists wd. reduce organised crime.
11 Gd. soc. restricts 'interfere[nce] in private behaviour'.
12 Hist. shows little damage to society as a whole from drug use.

You might, however, prefer to make your notes in the form of a mind map, like the one on the following page.

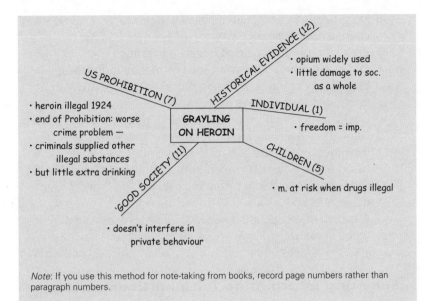

Note: If you use this method for note-taking from books, record page numbers rather than paragraph numbers.

At some point, you might like to have a look at *The Mind Map Book* by Tony and Barry Buzan. You'll see how a map can hold a large amount of information and become a valuable tool in your learning process.

Yet another way of organising your information is to put it in the form of a table – something like this:

Grayling on heroin

'Good Society'	Children	Historical evidence
individual autonomy (1)	more at risk when drugs illegal (5)	lifting Prohibition (US) left: • worse crime problem • no extra drinking (7)
protects third parties (4)		little damage to society from wide use of opium (12)
doesn't interfere in private behaviour (11)		

Note: The numbers in brackets refer to paragraphs in the article.

Your essay would be likely to contain a number of facts on heroin use and on medical issues as well as the views of various commentators, and you'd also need to come to a conclusion on the best policy to adopt. If you were in favour of legalising heroin, you might note the reasonableness of Grayling's position and stress his points on less damage to children and the lack of historical evidence showing any harm to society.

If, on the other hand, you became convinced by your reading that heroin should not be legalised, you might still want to refer to Grayling's article because, in order to 'discuss' the proposition on legalisation, you'd need to show a range of views. So you might suggest that there are issues where freedom of the individual must be curtailed and that Grayling's concern about 'interfere[nce] in private behaviour' is misplaced.

SUMMARY

This chapter has covered:

Note-taking in lectures
- how to prepare for a lecture
- techniques for note-taking
- what a page of lecture notes might look like

Analysis
- ask yourself questions
- scan the material
- find key sentences
- look for the argument

Note-taking from written sources
- recording the source
- using your own words
- taking full notes
- choosing points relevant to a specific essay
- linear notes, mind maps and tables

2 Writing an Essay

INTRODUCTION

Writing your essays on an academic course is likely to be a time-consuming process at first, and many people become extremely worried about submitting essays. Sandra, one of my students, was afraid that I would think her work was childish. Another student, Bill, felt that if he didn't get everything right first time that there was no hope for him.

Neither student need have worried. Sandra needed to realise that everyone has something useful to say, even if at first they have difficulty expressing their ideas on paper, and Bill soon found out that we learn to write essays through practice. Your tutors are not likely to expect you to be able to submit competent essays from the word 'go'.

At college or university, you are likely to find that things are rather different from what many of us did at school 5, 10, 20, or more years ago. When we were given the title for an essay, we usually went away and wrote as much as we knew on the subject. Now, you will be given a very specific question. This means that instead of writing all you know on a topic, you will need to select information that is relevant to that particular question. Selection is a key part of academic work.

Writing an essay is a *process* that contains different stages. It concerns time spent in gathering information, in working out what we think about various aspects of what we've studied, and in finding out how best to get the crucial issues on paper. Essays grow. You'll almost certainly find that some stages go well, while at others you feel you're wading through treacle. The answer is to address one issue at a time. So aim to give yourself space to work on your essay (sometimes for quite short periods) over a week at least – more if possible.

Different subjects have different ground rules. For example, if you are studying history, there will be great emphasis on evidence, on when this evidence originated, and on various accounts by later commentators of the period you are studying. In sociology, the emphasis is likely to be on theories about society and on surveys of different societies. If your subject is English literature, you will have found that you need to analyse language very closely and to consider looking at a text from different angles. If you are studying a science subject, you will be aware that you will need to focus on data, to show clear results, and to demonstrate how these are arrived at. It would be a good idea, therefore, before going any further, to jot down a list of what you know of the important criteria for writing on aspects of your subject area. This will get you thinking along the right lines.

Writing an essay is a very personal process. With a little practice, you will find your own ways of approaching the different parts of the work. Use this chapter to begin to find out what works for you, and feel free to adapt things to your own needs. You may find that, as you work, the stages I've outlined start to overlap or even change places. The crucial thing is that you submit a satisfactory assignment. How you get there is of less importance. At the end of the chapter, you'll find two examples of good student essays.

I PREPARATION

▶ Analysing the question

Why do essay questions look so difficult?
Sometimes, people are put off by the question itself. Essay questions often seem very complicated. Most of them turn out to be a lot less complex than they at first appear, but if you are already feeling nervous, a difficult-sounding question can seem like the last straw.

Questions often look difficult because they are written in rather formal language. There are two possible reasons for this. The first is that the tutor has probably tried to be as precise as possible and to write something that cannot be misunderstood or read two ways. S/he is actually trying to be helpful. The other reason is that the question will have been set out in such a way as to put boundaries on what you do. If the topic is not restricted like this, you could end up doing much more work than necessary. Oddly enough, it sometimes turns out that questions which look easy prove to be harder to answer than those which appear more complex. A tightly structured question will help to keep you on track.

Underlining the key words

Many people have learned the hard way that it is absolutely essential to *underline the key words* in an essay question before you do anything else. It's crucial to the whole enterprise. If you get things wrong at this stage, all your work could be wasted. Never, ever, try to omit this stage. There are two reasons for this: you need to understand *exactly* what is wanted and you want to eliminate the possibility of making errors that would send you off in the wrong direction. It's so easy to misread a word or even to answer the question that you hoped you would be asked. This can sometimes happen with a topic that you're particularly interested in. The mind plays tricks, and you think you see the question that you want to answer, rather than the one that's actually been asked.

Underlining will help to get you started and to get your brain focusing on the main topic areas and make sure that you address every issue that your tutor will be looking for. It will also help prevent you from getting carried away and starting to write about personal interests or on a topic that you know a lot about but which is not related to the question.

Let's suppose that you have been asked to write an essay with the following title:

Discuss the case for having increased censorship in the media.

Here are my underlinings:

<u>Discuss</u> <u>the case</u> for having <u>increased censorship</u> in the <u>media</u>.

You'll notice that I've underlined nearly everything. This often makes people feel that it would be quicker to underline the whole title and be done with it. But that would defeat the object which is to break up the question into its separate parts. As you can see, however, it's sometimes reasonable to keep certain words or phrases together.

It's important to be clear on what is *not* asked. The question does not, for example, ask for a full survey of current censorship. So to do that would result in the award of a low mark. Nor does it ask for a historical analysis or a detailed analysis of practice in one area. Either of those two approaches could lead to an equally nasty grade. All three of these ideas, however, may be useful. A very brief survey might help to give background information; one or two references to what has happened in the past might be relevant; and some analysis will be essential – though to confine this to one area alone might be a mistake.

The process of writing essays is a process of training the mind to think clearly. A good essay is one which sticks like a limpet to the key issues in the question and so does exactly what was asked. If, by any chance, you cannot make sense of the question, go back to your tutor for help. Never begin a piece of work until you are quite clear on what's wanted.

You may sometimes need to use a dictionary for accurate definitions of certain key words in the question. Be careful, however, over technical words that may have specific meanings for your subject. Technical words are not likely to be defined sufficiently fully in a non-specialist dictionary, and you can easily be misled by brief definitions. For these words, you might need a dictionary that is subject-specific. This type of dictionary is available for most subject areas. It's likely, however, that the words you need are explained in a handout you've been given or that they've been defined in a class session. Never copy definitions into your essay, however. Your tutor will not be impressed. You don't have to prove the meanings of words anyone can find in a dictionary.

Following the instructions in an essay question

It was important to underline the word 'Discuss' in the essay title above because this gives the instruction on how to angle the essay. You will often be asked to *discuss*. This means that you need to set out, explain, and give some analysis of both sides of a question – or more if more exist, and then make your own judgement on which is/are the more reasonable. Underlining the instruction will highlight the way you need to deal with the content of the essay. Here's a list of different instructions you might be given:

analyse	pull a topic apart to show its constituent parts and criticise these in detail
argue	make a case for something, using evidence and examples, and draw a clear conclusion
assess	weigh something up and consider how valuable it may be
comment	explain something, giving a brief judgement, with reasons
compare	show the similarities and differences between two items or ideas
contrast	show the differences between two items or ideas

criticise	show the good and bad points of something, looking at any implications
define	give the precise meaning of
describe	give a detailed account of
discuss	explain and analyse various sides of a topic, showing which is most reasonable
evaluate	explain the worth of something, giving reasons
explain	make clear with reasons, showing any implications
explore	examine thoroughly from different viewpoints
illustrate	give fully explained examples of something in order to make it clear
interpret	explain, showing key features and implications
justify	give good reasons why something has been said or done, answering possible objections
outline	give a broad description of the main issues of something
review	give a general survey, noting key features and commenting on their value
trace	set out the history or development of something, explaining the stages
verify	check out and report on the accuracy of something

▶ Making a mind map

The next stage is to construct a mind map. Don't worry, it's OK to be in a state of confusion at this stage. The whole point about all these activities is to get you going and keep you going – even though you may still feel that producing this essay is completely beyond you. You might be surprised, however, at what emerges in a mind map.

In this book, the term *mind map* is used to refer to two different processes – getting ideas and making notes. Here, we're looking at the process of getting ideas. A mind map is said to mimic the way our brains work, making connections that look more like a web or net than a straight line. So a mind map can frequently be more useful than a list. Constructing a mind map is a way of trawling for ideas in order to see what needs to be done next. The steps for this are:

- take a sheet of A4 paper and turn it sideways (landscape)
- write the essay question in the centre and draw a box round it
- as each new topic comes to mind, draw a straight line from

the box, and write the topic on this line in capitals, if possible in one word

The reason for using capital letters is to make things stand out. It prevents us from starting to write sentences and so getting bogged down. It's important to think in broad terms at this stage. What you want here is the big picture. Here's my map for the censorship essay (mentioned above):

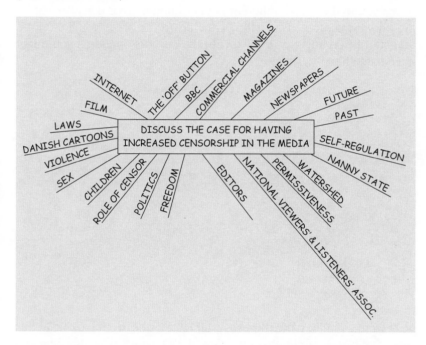

The important thing is to put down all your ideas – the useful ones, the useless ones, and the totally crazy ones. The thing is to keep your thoughts moving and not to censor anything at all. Censoring can result in putting your brain on a 'go-slow' or causing you to start worrying. What you are after here is free flow, positive thinking, and confidence. Seemingly daft ideas can sometimes lead on to really good ones that have been lurking in your subconscious. So be creative.

A word here for tidy people: there are times when tidiness is highly valuable, but this is not one of them. Creativity won't occur when you are busy dotting i's, crossing t's and using a rubber. Mind maps can, however, be used for note-taking or revision, and then you will want to work tidily.

Making decisions

At this point, you are going to need to decide on the main areas you'll cover. You can't cover everything. In your *introduction* (see below), you can explain how your essay will focus on particular topic areas in order to answer the question.

You'll want, as far as possible, to go for areas that interest you, that you know something about (though not enough yet, obviously) and that you can use in a useful discussion of the essay question. You might now want to draw up a different kind of mind map or diagram, focusing on your choices. This will narrow down the areas you'll work on and start to organise your ideas. For the censorship essay, you might have something like this:

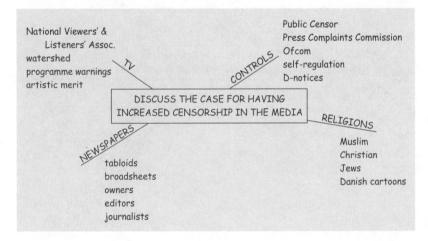

National Viewers' & Listeners' Assoc.
watershed
programme warnings
artistic merit

TV

CONTROLS

Public Censor
Press Complaints Commission
Ofcom
self-regulation
D-notices

DISCUSS THE CASE FOR HAVING INCREASED CENSORSHIP IN THE MEDIA

RELIGIONS

NEWSPAPERS
tabloids
broadsheets
owners
editors
journalists

Muslim
Christian
Jews
Danish cartoons

If I were going to write this essay, I might decide, from looking at this map, that I'll have enough for the essay by focusing on newspapers and that I can omit TV altogether. I'd need to check with the tutor, however, that this would be acceptable.

▶ Gathering information

Your next job is to gather together any class notes, lecture notes, photocopies and handouts that will be relevant to the essay. You should now have a rough idea of what topics you are going to need to read up on.

When you do background reading for an essay, you will be looking for **evidence** and examples that can be used to back up what you write.

You'll also be wanting to find out what key writers have said about your topic. It's probable that your tutor has given you a bibliography of the titles of useful books. In that case, you can stick to looking at things from this list. If you have no bibliography, ask your tutor to recommend something; if this fails, see what you can find in the college or university library. You'll generally be able to find a friendly librarian to help you if you're stuck. Don't, however, go home with a great pile of books. You won't have time to read them and the mere sight of the pile is likely to make you despair. You are not even going to read one book from cover to cover. Use **contents** and **indexes** to get straight to relevant sections.

You'll undoubtedly want to make use of the Internet as this is so useful for finding articles that have been printed in reputable newspapers and journals. These can be extremely useful for evidence (and for saving you time), but confining yourself to using the Net is no substitute for learning to work from books that have been put together with the benefit of lengthy research. Newspaper articles, while interesting, may have purely temporary interest and a limited viewpoint as well as lacking a firm basis in research.

You'll be looking for relevant ideas and theories, for facts, figures and proof, and for explanations of areas that have confused you. Facts and figures will comprise much of the evidence you will use to prove the points you make in your essay. If, however, you are working on a literature essay, you won't be looking for figures, and your facts are likely to be the comments made by other writers and critics. Don't be fooled, however, into assuming that writers and critics in any field are always right. When you are sure of your ground, it's quite acceptable to challenge their ideas in your essays.

It's important to get plenty of notes together before you start to write (see chapter 1). This will give you material to choose from and will also ensure that your essay has depth because your understanding of the topic area will be more developed. You may use only a small proportion of your notes, but you will have a good overview of the topic and you'll be able to choose just the most fitting items. Notes that you don't use for your essay may well come in handy at exam time, so don't feel that your work has been wasted.

▶ Planning and structuring

When you have read up (and made notes on) the main areas you will be covering, it's time to make a rough plan of how you are going to construct your essay. This will give you a framework to work to. Careful planning is one of the keys to good essay-writing. It's also very often the hardest part. One of the great things with planning, however, is that it puts you in control. Perhaps a stronger inducement is that you'll almost certainly get higher marks for carefully structured work.

Whatever the topic, your plan will fall into three broad sections:

Introduction (one paragraph)
- indicate the main issues
- state what ground your essay will cover
- give very, very brief background information

Main body
- show the topics and theories, etc.
- number your sections

Conclusion (one paragraph)
- sum up your main points
- note what you see as the most reasonable conclusion(s) to draw

The meat of your plan lies in the middle section, and you will need to think carefully about the order in which you set out the topics you deal with. Don't worry if your introduction is blank to start with. You probably won't have a clear idea of what goes in it until you have completed the middle section.

Your plan will be a working document: you'll almost certainly need to adjust it as you work on writing the essay itself. If your plan turns out to be restrictive or unhelpful in any way, change it. Sometimes, students feel that there's no point making a plan in the first place if it's likely to be changed. But it's only when you have created a structure that you can begin to find out what does and doesn't work. In other words, you have to begin somewhere.

Below is the basis of Pete's plan for his censorship essay, showing just one way of structuring it. There are many ways to write a good assignment. What you do will depend on your own interests and experiences as well as on the topic and your individual way of working. There are three basic rules, however, for writing up a plan. It needs to:

- fit on one side of A4 paper
- be set out in single-line spacing (the essay itself will be in double)
- be written in note form.

Discuss the case for having increased censorship in the media

PLAN

Introduction

democracy & the media

censorship is alien to democracy

the problem of events

1 Privacy rights of the individual

anonymity of offenders

place of the legal system

human rights

2 Self-regulation

media can self-regulate where necessary

TV warnings of disturbing material

Watershed

3 Public opinion as regulator

a free press is not without restrictions

reaction to Danish cartoons of Muhammad and

   Jyllands-Posten's apology

Conclusion

media must be free to make mistakes

legal frameworks & self-regulation are sufficient

public opinion is the ultimate regulator

It's often helpful, when you've decided on the main structure of an essay, to colour-code the sections you want to use from your notes, handouts, and so on relating to the main sections on your plan. This can save a lot of time because it means that you can easily find items you need when your mind is otherwise engaged on the writing process.

If you happen to be one of those people who not only finds planning an excruciating business but also writes easily 'off the top of your head', there's another way of approaching the making of a plan. Whenever your ideas are running, write down whatever you have in your head. You'll probably end up with a number of separate paragraphs. Leave your writing for a day or so, and then go back and look at what you've written. Note the topics you've covered and then have a go at roughing out a plan, thinking about where in the essay your paragraphs would best fit. It's great to be able to write easily, but it's also essential to be able to impose a logical structure on your essays.

▶ The argument

A good essay will contain a clear line of argument. That doesn't mean that you need to get heated. It means that you need to look at the evidence, set out what you feel is the most valid interpretation of the issues involved, and comment clearly on the topics you raise as the essay progresses.

One thing you want to avoid is telling a story. If, for example, you are writing a history essay, focusing on past events, you will not need to recount them all. Aim to pick out just those that you can use for a discussion of the essay question. You will be graded on the way you interpret, analyse and discuss, not on your ability to reproduce a vast mountain of facts. If you are studying a science subject, however, do be guided by your tutor over the amount of factual information you will need to include in an assignment.

You need to explain to the person reading your essay what you want him or her to *think* about the material you cover. It is possible for two students to cite similar evidence and yet draw different conclusions from it. Your tutor needs to understand your particular angle on the material. If you think for a minute about a court of law, you'll see what I mean: counsel for the prosecution and counsel for the defence will give completely different views of the evidence in their summing-up. What you as an individual make of the material is likely to be the key to getting good marks. An especially important point to remember here is that every point you make needs to address the essay question in some way. In other words, make sure that everything you write is relevant to that question. Then back up your points with **evidence**.

Putting argument into your essay means writing persuasively (see also chapter 4). Everyday life is full of persuasion, but we generally engage in it orally. If, for example, you have a 13-year-old son or daughter who wants to become a regular whisky drinker, you're going to want to show that this wouldn't be a good idea. Teenagers can be very persuasive themselves, of course, so you'll need a good argument. You'll probably trot out some facts: selling alcohol to under-18s is illegal; an early drink habit can lead to alcoholism; too much in the way of spirits can damage the liver. We could plan out your line of attack like this:

1 the law
2 alcoholism
3 other health issues

As you mention each topic, you'll argue your case:

1 the law:	the law is for your protection/law-breakers often go to prison
2 alcoholism:	this could ruin your life – your job, relationship and home could be at risk
3 other health issues:	it's important to look after your body

Let's suppose it's a good day and you're feeling calm. You might introduce your argument by saying something like this:

"There are lots of reasons why I can't let you drink whisky. Let me explain ..."

You might conclude by saying something like this:

"So I'm sorry but I really can't let you to do this because it's my duty to protect you."

That, in a nutshell, is the shape of an argument: there's an introduction, key topics are covered, comment is given on each and there's a conclusion that sums up your position. Persuading a teenager not to drink whisky is, of course, rather one-sided. In this instance, you probably wouldn't want to put forward any evidence for an alternative viewpoint. In your essays, however, you're generally going to need to look at things from more than one angle. Including other viewpoints can even be a way of strengthening your own stance because you can show what's wrong with what other people have said.

People sometimes try to reduce an essay to two sections – points for and points against – but this method generally has problems. It forces you to put everything in one section or the other without allowing for grey areas and a full discussion. It can also result in two huge, unwieldy sections – or worse, one tiny and one enormous one. Splitting the essay up by topic areas and commenting on each as you go along will result in a much more balanced and effective piece of work.

Before reading any further, have a look back at the discussion of key sentences in A. C. Grayling's article on heroin. These key statements carry much of his argument, and you can see how he advances it at every stage of the article. Do be aware, however, that Grayling has written an article – not an assessed essay. This means that he has had more leeway to advance his personal views than is possible in an essay.

While you are working on your plan, aim to fill in some very brief notes on the **evidence** you'll use and on the argument you'll put forward. This will give your tutor a very clear idea of where the essay is coming from before s/he starts to read it. At the end of this chapter, you'll find two essays with very detailed plans.

II STARTING TO WRITE

Many people find that the hardest part of writing an essay is actually getting started. Well, the good news is that you don't have to start at the beginning. People often leave writing the introduction until last because, until you've actually written an essay, it can be tricky to explain what it's about – especially since you may have fresh ideas as you write.

So you can, if you wish, start by working on the section that interests you most or that you find easiest. Your enthusiasm will then have a spin-off effect and you'll find it easier to do things you'd felt were more difficult. You might like to think of your essay as a jigsaw puzzle. It can sometimes be easier to use separate pages for different aspects of the topic so that you can rearrange them as necessary. The main thing is to cover the ground – to get the whole thing on paper *somehow* without worrying about making it look perfect.

It doesn't even matter if you're not quite sure what you think before you begin writing. One of the functions of essay-writing is to force us to think and to clarify things in our own minds. We often don't know what we really think until we've tried to express it on paper. As you work on your assignment, you will almost certainly find that your ideas become clearer.

If you are really stuck, start by writing down something that your tutor – or another student – has said on the topic. You can always cross this out later. What you will be doing is tricking your mind into getting started. It doesn't matter what your first effort looks like. If you are hand-writing the essay, use one side of the paper only. You will see the importance of this when you come to redrafting (see below).

By the way, don't fall into the trap of thinking that, because your tutor knows the subject inside out, you don't need to spell things out. The only way for him or her to find out whether *you* understand the topic fully is for you to write it down. The fact that you were able to discuss the issue competently in a class session will not count. Marks can be given only for what you actually put on paper.

▶ Paragraphing

A paragraph splits up a piece of writing into separate topic sections. The idea is to make for easy reading. Knowing what to include in one paragraph, however, or when to change to a new one are problems that worry lots of students. You have probably been told to start a new paragraph when you change to a new topic, but you may still not be too sure of where to make a break.

Constructing a paragraph

Generally speaking, a paragraph will focus on one topic only. Occasionally, it will focus on a group of minor but related topics. It also needs to show how each topic relates to the essay title. As we've seen with A. C. Grayling's article (in chapter 1), a paragraph will always contain a key sentence – that is, a sentence that sets out the main point being made in that paragraph. It is very often the first sentence, and, in order to make things easy on yourself, you might like to use that format with each of your own paragraphs. The rest of the paragraph will elaborate on that key sentence and is likely to contain evidence that will bear out what that key sentence states. The final sentence in a paragraph generally pulls together the points in that paragraph and explains to the reader what he or she should make of the evidence you've set out.

You might, however, need several paragraphs to cover one topic. If you are discussing an issue that has several aspects, you might want to have a paragraph for each aspect. It depends in part on how much material there is to cover. Here's how Jim has split up his points on germ theory in an essay with the title, 'Discuss Louis Pasteur's value to society':

> Pasteur became increasingly aware that infection was spread by doctors and nursing staff from sick to healthy patients. He impressed on these doctors that avoidance of microbes meant avoidance of infection and slowly the practice of employing antiseptic medicine and surgery became the rule and continues today. Even in filthy conditions, an individual can, to some extent, protect him or herself from disease by giving attention to the water that is drunk. As Pasteur discovered from researching fermentation and the souring of wine, by heating solutions to a high temperature and then pasteurising, bacteria would be eliminated and no longer pose a threat to health. For example, in the Philippines, the orthodox Chinese who had retained the ancestral habit of drinking nothing but tea made from boiled water remained free of cholera during epidemics which killed the Filipinos who did not boil their drinking water.
>
> Pasteur's germ theory led to a more accurate understanding of the circumstances in which host and parasite come into contact and paved the way for the formulation of disease control policies and practice which proved to be more effective than other measures used before. Understanding and improved knowledge of the properties and behaviour of infective micro-organisms often suggested a way to attack them either before or after they had reached the human body. This is the key to the practice of immunisation which involves establishing resistance against a disease by exposing the body to the infective agent. The science of immunity is one of the most direct outcomes of Pasteur's germ theory. Getting immunity to an invading parasite is, in many ways, one of the most extraordinary discoveries in life.

Jim's first paragraph centres on Pasteur's discoveries on avoiding infection. His second paragraph looks at immunisation. A paragraph could be said to be a bit like a mini-essay. It has an opening, a middle, and an end which often ties up that particular section. The reader needs to understand exactly what the writer feels about the relation of the topic in that paragraph to the essay question. It's just a case of spelling things out. Jim tied up his first paragraph with a clear example that bears out his points on Pasteur's theory on avoidance of infection. His second paragraph ends with a comment on the high value of immunisation.

Paragraphs that are too long

Like punctuation, paragraphing helps the reader to understand your meaning. It sorts a piece of writing into sections and breaks it up into manageable chunks. If there's too much going on in one paragraph, a reader may start to get bogged down. So aim to cover just one topic – or, perhaps, one aspect of a longer topic in a paragraph. If you have a handwritten paragraph that is a page or more long, check to see whether it contains more than one issue or whether it can helpfully be broken down into smaller chunks. The same goes for a word-processed paragraph of more than about twelve lines.

Have a look at the following paragraph from an undergraduate essay on subjective views of class structure. It would be much better split into two paragraphs. Where would you make the break? (Answer below)

The authors [of a particular survey] state that aspirations for status-raising through friends was negligible – friends who had interesting work, a good education or 'a bit of class'. Considering the wording of that last phrase, it is surprising that anyone admitted to agreeing with it. There is a case here for using methodology from psychology to structure questions and interpret replies. It is likely that people who choose friends according to their social standing are unaware of what they are doing, and would therefore not agree that they chose people who had 'a bit of class about them'. The specific questions on residence and occupation would probably yield data on whether or not a respondent associated with people from a different social background. However, the question of why they had associated with them would still be unanswered. The terminology itself is restricting and provides added restraint on answers over and above the highly structured nature of the interviews. The section on residence shows the same problems. For those who wanted to move house, respectability of area was said to be more important than somewhere 'select'. In each case, respondents were asked for one answer, unlike Hillier's [a sociologist] method of taking into account secondary conceptions. For the Luton sample, who were highly geographically mobile, and therefore lacked the support of kin, respectability might be quite likely to be their first priority. However, further data and analysis may well have shown up other (and possibly equal) priorities, particularly if respondents had been encouraged to formulate their own responses.

My answer comes after the next section, **Linking**.

Paragraphs that are too short

If a paragraph covers only two or three lines or is composed of only one or two sentences, it's almost certainly too short. There are two possibilities here: it may fit better as part of the preceding or the following paragraph, or it may need expansion. It's most likely that it needs expansion. You've almost certainly raised a new idea that now needs explanation, examples and comment. The fact that you've written very little on it may indicate that you know less about this than other issues covered in your essay. It's no good, however, raising an issue and then leaving it hanging in mid-air. If you've got no clue on how to expand a short paragraph and it won't fit into the preceding or following one, you're going to have to be ruthless and cut it out.

▶ Linking

Clear linking of one paragraph to the next is essential. Anyone reading an essay needs to be shown how one point leads to another. This is very closely linked to argument. Throughout your essay, everything you write must relate to the question and you must spell out this relationship. Good links are vital for this process. A well-structured piece of writing will be put together in such a way that each section follows smoothly from the one before in a logical manner. You might do this by the use of specific linking words (see the list below) or by referring explicitly to an aspect of your previous paragraph.

A. C. Grayling's article is a particularly good example of linking. He spells out his links clearly throughout the entire piece. This is very good practice, and the process is so important for your own work that its worth looking at links throughout his article.

Paragraph	Method of linking
2 linked to 1	By the simplest means. Grayling re-uses a word from his introduction early in the first sentence: 'drugs'.

3	2	By the use of the word 'legal'. He has just been talking about making substances legal.
4	3	Through the phrase 'the latter policy'. At the end of 3, he has given a choice of policies. Now he refers to one of them.
5	4	With the phrase 'by the same token'. This refers specifically to what he's just mentioned – the argument that good laws protect the vulnerable and bad ones merely adhere to dogma.
6	5	Less obvious. He moves in this paragraph to consideration of the opposing position to his own. The word 'legalisation' links to the whole of his argument up to this point, and the introductory sentence brings the argument from theory into practice.
7	6	Very neatly by giving an example of what he means. The words 'the classic example' make that link clearly.
8	7	With the word 'Crime' – the topic that was mentioned at the end of 7.
9	8	By using the word 'also'. In 8, he shows how serious crime figures might be improved. In 9, he moves on to petty crime. The word 'also' forces the reader to make the link.
10	9	Implicit. Paragraph 9 mentions 'medical' matters. The 'safety issue' is obviously relevant here.
11	10	Implicit. Paragraph 10 plays down the effects of heroin. Paragraph 11 goes on to state that the effects do not damage society as a whole.
12	11	By giving an example – in this case, from history.
13	12	The opening reference to society – the topic that has been central to paragraphs 11 and 12.

Here are some more useful words and phrases for making links at the start of a paragraph:

- conversely
- in addition
- despite the above
- in contrast
- as a result

- similarly
- besides
- therefore
- the above shows that
- although
- notwithstanding
- moreover
- it follows from this that

My answer to the paragraph-breaking question

I'd break that paragraph after 'structured nature of the interviews'. That sentence would form a good conclusion to the first paragraph, which centres mainly on status-raising through friends. The second paragraph will then focus on areas of residence. Note that the phrase 'the same problems' forms a good link in what will be the first sentence of the second paragraph.

▶ Introductions

As explained earlier, it's often easiest to write your introduction after you've written the rest of the essay. You will need to:

- identify the issues your essay will cover
- outline how your essay will deal with these issues
- give *very brief* background information that will set the scene for the essay

Here's how Jeff opened an essay:

Discuss the value to society of one historical figure

Mohandas Karamchand Gandhi lived from 1869 to 1948. During his lifetime, he confronted racism, prejudice, discrimination and dictatorship and invented Satyagraha, the policy of non-violent resistance. He abolished laws that discriminated against Indian people, developed new rights for the untouchables and played a large role towards India gaining and surviving in independence from British rule. Gandhi affected the lives of a great number of different people around the world and still does, even today. This essay will look at Gandhi's value to society during his lifetime, looking at the value of his campaigns and the effects of them, good and bad, and whether the effects were important to the people's lives he helped to change. By also looking at the contributions and legacies Gandhi gave to his fellow Indian people and by looking at the influence he had on the rest of the world, this essay will discuss the enduring value to society of Mohandas Karamchand Gandhi.

This introduction is a little on the long side, but it clearly states what the essay will be covering and it gives a neat and interesting introduction to Gandhi's life.

It's perfectly reasonable to put boundaries on your essay. You can't cover everything. Of course, you will need to make sure that you don't omit anything vital, but, generally speaking, as long as you address the topics from the question and make clear in your introduction what your essay will cover, there should be no problem.

► Conclusions

A conclusion is where you sign off, so to speak, by underlining your main points and tying up your argument. You will need to:

- summarise your main argument
- state your general conclusion(s)
- mention why this is important
- relate your conclusion to the essay question

There are a couple of things here that you must *not* do:

- don't introduce any new material
- don't use quotations at this point

Here's Jeff's conclusion to the essay on Gandhi:

Thousands of people attended Gandhi's funeral, testifying to how much of an impact he had on the Indian people; he was 'the Mahatma'. The things he achieved during his lifetime helped progress not just in his own country but around the world, providing it with a philosophy of non-violence that was of extreme value to everyone. Gandhi's way of protesting without violence has lived on

> long after his death and is used all over the world. Gandhi lived in a time when there were two world wars and acts of mass murder and where weapons of mass destruction had been invented. To come out of the era and provide the world with tactics of fighting injustice without violence shows the value to society of Mohandas Karamchand Gandhi.

This ties up the essay well. The only thing I'd be inclined to change would be to omit the reference to the funeral because this is new information.

▶ Language and clarity

When you write the final draft of your essay, you'll need to be sure not to write just as your thoughts flow. It's essential to move from thinking to writing grammatical sentences. Good essays are those which make the writer's ideas really clear to the reader – in this case, your tutor. It makes no difference that he or she may have been teaching for 20 or 30 years and knows the subject inside out. S/he needs to be helped to understand *exactly* what *you* are getting at.

You don't need to try to sound like a textbook; just aim to write in a simple and straightforward manner. It's a good idea to keep in mind that your work should be understandable to an intelligent reader from a *different* subject specialism. This means that you'll use technical terms only when necessary, that you'll explain your ideas fully, and that you'll be as precise as possible (see chapter 4, Style).

Academic writing is logical and unemotional, factual and precise. Because of the need for precision, we have to be especially careful not to state that something is the case if there is the least chance that it might not be so. A good way of getting around this sometimes is to say things such as:

> It is *likely* that X is the case

or

> X *seems* to be the case

Saying things in this way allows you to show both that you know the possibilities and that you are aware of the pitfalls. Don't overdo this trick, however. You don't want your tutor to complain that you always sit on the fence.

▶ Writing impersonally

Nowadays, some tutors are happy to accept essays containing the word *I*, but your work will be more sophisticated if you learn to write impersonally. Some people feel that they *must* write in the first person. "I must admit that the views in the essay are mine", they say. The simple answer to this is that if an essay has your name on it, it is very clear that the views in it are yours. Don't worry about sounding authoritative. Your tutors are looking for essays that show strength of purpose. An essay that does not contain the word *I* actually comes across much more forcefully. Notice how the statement:

> Education for adults is essential

seems somehow to have more validity than the statement:

> I think education for adults is essential

The words *I think* introduce an element of doubt. They seem to imply that you feel that maybe you've got things wrong and that anyone who holds opposing views to yours must have a reasonable case. The first statement is adamant, although it contains no obvious emotion.

It's also best to omit the word 'you' from essays. It can often be helpfully replaced by the word 'people'. So, instead of writing:

> You want a good education for your children.

put:

> People want a good education for their children.

▶ Writing objectively

It's very important, in academic writing, to omit personal views and to give evidence for your argument. Look at the following emotive piece of writing:

> Fox-hunting is a cruel and barbaric sport. It is undertaken by upper-class types who don't care about hurting an animal. People who lose their jobs get what they deserve.

The views contained in those three sentences could be put across much more persuasively by omitting emotion and including some factual material:

> Fox-hunting is considered by some people to involve cruelty. The fact that the sport is traditional should not be a reason to ignore any pain suffered by foxes. Links to a network of rural employment, however, make the issue of banning fox-hunting more complicated. The answer is diversification. Farmers, for example, have frequently boosted their incomes by developing nature trails and other leisure pursuits that bring tourism to an area. There are numerous ways in which declining rural economies can rejuvenate themselves; those who have relied on occupations directly allied to fox-hunting need to reinvent their working lives.

▶ Clichés and slang

Clichés can be a problem for new writers because we all start by expressing what we want to say in the words we've picked up from TV, newspapers, and whatever else we've heard and read. Clichés are over-used, worn-out phrases that have lost their bite - such as *in this day and age, tried and tested, the bottom line,* and so on. Whenever you can, say things clearly in your own way. I've almost certainly used a few clichés in this book, but I'm not writing a strictly academic work. Since I want to chat to you, a few clichés are bound to have crept in. It's also important to avoid *slang*. This is language that is often felt to be inappropriate or not polite, and whose meaning is not sufficiently specific, such as *dead cert, dodgy, loaded*. Slang can spoil the texture of your work and even make it look as though you are not thinking clearly.

▶ Tense

Changing **tense** (see chapter 12) by mistake is another common problem. If you are discussing a topic in the past tense, don't change to the present; if you are discussing it in the present, don't change to the past. You will find out whether you've done this if you look for it specifically when you proofread (see below). It's a particular issue for those who are studying literature. When talking about a character in a book, it's fatally easy, for example, to swap back and forth between *she did* and *she does* without realising what we are doing.

▶ Abbreviations

Generally speaking, abbreviations should not be used in essays. Things like *i.e.* and *e.g.* are not admissible. You may, however, be given some assignments in which particular abbreviations are acceptable, especially in science or technology. Check with your tutor. It's also the case that you can use capital letters for an institution if you give the initials in brackets immediately after your *first* use of the institution's full name. For example, if you write the following in an essay:

> The Royal National Institute for the Blind (RNIB) grew from the British and Foreign Society for Improving the Embossed Literature for the Blind

you can subsequently use the initials RNIB throughout the essay. You won't need to give the full name again.

▶ Raising questions

Some people feel that formulating questions can be a useful means of drawing attention to particular arguments. When giving a talk, this is fine, but in written work, it can end up being more trouble than it's worth. And you are likely to find that your tutor is not too keen on you putting questions in your essays. Assuming you've remembered to use the question mark itself (see chapter 14), there are further problems to negotiate. Asking questions rather than making statements can give the impression that you don't really know what you are talking about. But that's not all.

When you are writing an essay, you are already grappling with a question you've been given. That's usually a hard task in itself. Raising more questions can just make the whole thing more complicated because once you've asked a question yourself, you really need to try to answer it – or you can appear to be less than clued-up.

Technically speaking, raising questions can get you into a real minefield because of difficulties with grammar and construction – both of individual sentences and of the essay itself. Students sometimes tie themselves in knots trying to answer extra questions that they've raised themselves while still struggling to answer the main essay question.

Sometimes, however, you will need to talk about questions that other people have raised about various issues, and it's important that you set these out really clearly. For this, you need to understand *the difference between the question itself and a statement of this question.*

Let's assume that you have been asked to write up a report on a seminar discussion on the subject of poverty in the Third World, and that during the discussion, one student, Tom Rush, said, "How can governments co-ordinate a global approach?"

When you write your piece, you *could* merely repeat Tom's question:

> One student said, "How can governments co-ordinate a global approach?"

But that may look a little simplistic. A better way of doing it would be to *report* what Tom said (see the section on reported speech in chapter 15). This means that you will rephrase the question so that it becomes a statement – like this:

> One student raised the question of how governments might be able to co-ordinate a global approach.

Notice that when I've used the student's *actual words,* I've added a question mark, but that when I've *reported* his question, I've used only a full stop. This is very important. A question mark should be used *only* after a question, never after a statement or report of the question.

One thing you want to avoid at all costs is *combining* a question with a statement. This is bad practice:

> One student said how would governments be able to co-ordinate a global approach to the problem of Third World poverty?

Either use the exact question (with speech marks and a question mark) *or* report it (*without* speech marks or a question mark).

Now you may be feeling that it is essential to mention questions that frequently come up in relation to certain topics. You might want to show that you are aware of these. Or you might want to show that a particular view is not foolproof and that questions *should* be asked about it.

You might cope with this in a similar way to the reporting of Tom Rush's question. Suppose you are writing an essay on the current state of secondary education in Britain. You have mentioned the relevant Acts of Parliament and various other government initiatives, and you have looked at classroom practice. Now you want to conclude your essay by asking the following questions:

1 Why isn't more money spent on education?

2 Why are parents not expected to be more involved in schools?
3 Why doesn't Britain try to learn more from European education systems?

You can turn those questions into statements – like this:

> The most useful measure that government could take to improve education in our secondary schools would be to spend more money. If parents were then routinely involved much more closely in their children's education, the public would become far more aware of the cost of good systems and would accept the inevitable increase in taxes. Finally, it is clear that Britain could learn a good deal on structuring an education system from its near neighbours, France and Germany.

That simple process has transformed the questions into a forceful conclusion.

III THE FINISHED PRODUCT

▶ Drafting and redrafting

Occasionally, at the beginning of a course, tutors will ask you to submit both an essay itself *and* your rough drafts. What they'll be looking for is evidence that you have moved through a *process* – beginning with ideas that may well be vague and a draft that is probably messy and even rather incoherent – to a finished product which is clear and neatly organised. This is the process through which any serious writer will go. No published book or article arrives on the author's desk fully formed. Everybody adds things, deletes, makes changes, and puts whole sections in the bin. This particular chapter, for example, has been moved from a different part of the book, been completely reorganised, and had scores of additions, deletions, alterations and corrections.

Nowadays, some departments in colleges and universities refuse to accept handwritten work, so if you don't already use a computer, it would be good to take a short course on the basics as soon as possible. Whether you hand-write or submit word-processed work, however, it's a good idea to leave a line between paragraphs in your final draft. It makes your work look really neat, enables anyone reading it to see clearly where paragraphs start and end, and gives tutors space to add comments. I'd suggest you actually write this way from the start – even in your early drafts. You are likely to find that the extra space is handy for additions as you go along.

Some people like to write a first draft really quickly, getting all their ideas on paper before settling down to look more carefully at various items. Others work best in a slower, more reflective manner, thinking things through as they go along. You will soon find what works best for you.

When you have completed the first draft, it's a good idea to leave it on one side for a day or two if you have time. Then when you return to it, you will look at it with a fresh eye. First of all, you'll need to look at structure. You want to check that each section follows clearly from the one before, and that anyone reading the essay would find it easy to follow. Then check for sufficient evidence and argument.

You might find that you need to reorder things. But being able to change what you've written can give you a feeling of control over your work as you take charge of the editing process. Restructuring is easily done if your work is on computer, but if you hand-write, life will be a lot easier at this stage if you have used only one side of the paper for your draft because you can cut the thing up and stick it together in a revised order. If you use a computer, it can help to work from a print-out rather than trying to do the whole job on screen. As you scroll up and down, it's easy to overlook things that are hidden as you focus on the section that appears in front of you. If you have access to a computer but are new to using it, do get someone to show you how to save your drafts on a disk or CD. It can be agonising to lose work that you've spent many hours putting together. Keep your printouts, too, until you've submitted the final draft. You might want to retrieve something you've deleted on screen.

My own method for any kind of work is to write a first draft in pencil. When I have completed a section, I put it on the computer and print it off. This gives me a sense of progress and allows me to see clearly what I've written. When I've got the whole thing on computer and I have a full printout, I can begin to see the wood for the trees, so to speak. I make alterations on the printout until it's starting to get messy, and then I go back to put these on the computer. Then I do a second printout. This process goes on until either I'm happy with the result or I've run out of time and am forced to stop.

When redrafting, keep an eye out for anything that doesn't specifically answer the question – such as background information or details of another topic that you happen to be good at but which doesn't actually fit the essay. Unrelated information is likely to lose you marks because it suggests that you are not thinking clearly. Aim to put yourself in the reader's shoes.

▶ Proofreading

Your final draft needs to be checked for spellings, grammatical problems, and other minor errors. It's often easiest to do a separate read-through for each type of error so that you can concentrate on one at a time. You will focus much more easily if you are looking for just one thing. Some people find that it helps at this stage to read their work aloud.

You will want your work to read smoothly, but you may find that you have some long, unwieldy sentences that don't seem to say quite what you mean. You might sort this out by splitting the sentences up into shorter ones. Each sentence might cover one small stage in a process or one step in an argument.

▶ Learning from feedback

Your tutor's comments on your work are specific to you and designed to help you to progress. You will sometimes find that s/he has also added factual items and useful analysis. This might come in handy for your exams. So aim to treat comments as valuable information rather than as harsh criticism. If you can't follow what's been said on your work, do ask for explanation. Understanding what has been written may be crucial for your next assignment. Tutors are always pleased to find that a student is making good use of comments on an essay.

As your course progresses, keep a note of tutors' comments on your work and of the errors that you've made. You are very likely to find that you keep making similar mistakes. This is quite usual, but it will go on happening until you address the particular issues consciously. So make yourself a list of problems that keep cropping up. Stick it on a piece of card and have this by you when you work. That way, you'll progress really fast.

If there are an awful lot of corrections on your work or if you've got a bad grade, even though you've worked hard, try not to despair. It really is all part of the learning process. I once nearly gave up all my studies quite early on over a bad grade. I'm very glad I didn't. There are gurus in the business world who state categorically that if you are not making mistakes you are not likely to make progress. They are far happier to see employees working creatively and getting some things wrong than playing safe and never opening up new horizons. Getting things wrong is the first step to getting them right.

▶ Student essays

Here are two very good essays written by students. They take rather different positions on the question given them. I've included a very detailed plan for each one so that you can see what to aim for. I've omitted their bibliographies as all aspects of referencing are dealt with in chapter 3.

Here is Sadie's essay:

Discuss the case for having increased censorship in the media

PLAN

Introduction
newspapers:
   power of owners
   tabloids stretch truth
   self-regulation
this essay will argue:
- increased censorship necessary for religious beliefs/privacy
- freedom of reporting necessary otherwise

	Evidence	Argument

1 Danish cartoons of Muhammad
Muslim response
European reprints
results: Muslim
   demonstrations &
   boycott of goods
	deaths
	£millions lost
	Hamshari's threat
	Guardian: Tabish
	   Khair
		- respect for others
		  is essential

2 Journalists' concerns
defence of freedom
causing offence
 	
intruding on privacy
	Reporters Without
	Borders
	Guardian 2006
	British Govmt.
	   response
	Kate Adie 2002
	Seirestad 2004
		
		- regulation could
		  have prevented
		  extreme response

3 Privacy of the individual
Human Rights Act
 	
possible problems with
censorship
	
	2000
	Jonathan Aitken –
	Mass Media: Press
	Complaints
	Commission 2006
		
		- benefits of
		  increased
		  censorship

4 Demand for sensational reporting
increase in newspaper sales
journalists under pressure
		
		- appropriate
		  censorship would
		  end pressures on
		  journalists

Conclusion
Increased censorship would:
   prevent problems re. religion & privacy
   alleviate pressure on journalists

Discuss the case for having increased censorship in the media

Newspapers in Britain are owned by a small group of formidable corporations that have power over a large market. We all obtain information and entertainment via these newspapers which convey to us the values, opinions and codes of behaviour considered necessary for us to fit into our society. While we have a free press that can operate without government interference, we also have some of the most notorious tabloid papers in the world, known for publishing controversial material and for their stretching of the truth, especially concerning people in the public eye. Newspaper owners have power without responsibility, a view often expressed today. The British press has more freedom than their broadcasting equivalents, being self-regulatory, with voluntary codes of practice which are often reinterpreted or ignored. This essay will argue that increased press censorship is necessary in order to deal with the sensitive, contentious issues of religious beliefs and privacy, while on the other hand accepting that the press also need freedom to work openly to report the truth.

Respect for religious beliefs has rarely troubled the mainstream press. Recent caricatures printed in a Danish newspaper, mocking the Prophet Muhammad, caused a furore among Muslims who repeatedly asked the newspaper editor to stop printing the cartoons. The requests were ignored. Muslims called the cartoons blasphemous because Islam bans all ridicule of Muhammad. Newspapers in Europe felt justified in reprinting the cartoons, even though their doing so was deeply offensive to millions of Muslims. These cartoons have now been republished in almost every major European country, setting off angry demonstrations amongst Muslims from Denmark to the Far East. Several people have been killed and moderate Muslims have suffered the backlash of intolerance. Boycotts of Danish goods in Muslim countries are costing Danish companies millions of pounds. One Iranian paper, *Hamshahri*, is threatening to retaliate by running Holocaust cartoons. 'The western papers printed these sacrilegious cartoons on the basis of freedom of expression,' says *Hamshahri's* graphics editor, 'so let's see if they mean what they say, and also print these Holocaust cartoons.' [Farid Mortazavi, 06.02.2006] Freedom of speech must go hand in hand with respect and consideration for the feelings of others. This applies equally to the press and everyday life. Reporting for the *Guardian*, Tabish Khair states that:

> Freedom of expression is necessary not because it is a God-given virtue, but because if you let authorities start hacking away at it you are liable to be left with nothing. But along with the right to

express comes the duty to consider the rights of others. This applies as much to *Jyllands-Posten* [the Danish paper that published the cartoons] as to the mobs in Beirut.

Reporters Without Borders has defended the media's right to make fun, but many European newspapers argue that free speech is not an excuse for unwarranted insults. The *Guardian* argues that 'newspapers are not obliged to republish offensive material merely because it's controversial' (03.02.2006). Indeed, the British government have praised their media for acting in a prudent manner by not publishing the cartoons in their own newspapers. Appropriate press regulation and censorship of European newspapers could have stopped the publication of these cartoons, a simple thing that would have prevented the volatile demonstrations, boycotts of Danish goods, loss of innocent lives and the racial conflict that followed.

Of course, free speech is important, but the fact that some journalists are so keen to write intrusively about people's private lives is also an area of concern. Writing about her time in Iraq, Kate Adie reveals that:

> I was bothered by the tabloid press ... at least one paper had sent a reporter to track my moves and get a few embarrassing snaps ... some journalists wrote ridiculous fiction ... it comes with the turf. (Adie, 2002: 386)

The press argue that it is in the public interest, but there are a number of journalists who will not support associates whose writing is too concerned with gossip and scandal:

> We are now far too sensationalistic. You can read any amount of lies in the papers every day ... I direct my reporters to tell people what is actually happening, not what they think should be happening. (Seirerstad, 2004: 65)

Such writing is said to challenge the tradition of wide-ranging journalistic public discussion, which is important in any democratic society. In October 2000, the Human Rights Act was introduced. The act contains a right to respect for a private family life. However, some journalists believe censorship and prior restraint could prove disastrous for investigative journalism. This is aptly demonstrated by the following quote:

> Was the lying politician, Jonathan Aitken, on a private holiday when he was in Paris? If he was and the Human Rights Act on

privacy had been law at the time, how could the *Guardian* legally have discovered who paid his hotel bill? (Mass Media: Press Complaints Commission, 2006)

Despite the Human Rights Act, there is still public and journalistic disquiet over the reporting of personal details regarding people's private lives. Increased press censorship could protect privacy, promote meaningful journalism and allay concern over intrusive newspaper reporting.

In the aftermath of disaster or tragedy, newspaper sales increase dramatically. People often want to know the personal angle, therefore journalists could be said to be meeting readers' demands. Conversely, there are journalists who state that such writing is used as justification for selfish, unethical behaviour, and that it is more important for them to think about what is appropriate in the circumstances. It should, however, be borne in mind that journalists working for the tabloids are under a huge amount of pressure from editors who want powerful pieces of journalism in order to increase their newspaper sales. Many journalists are not happy with such invasive journalism which makes them feel guilty about their ruthless behaviour. However, they know that their survival depends on producing the kind of material that editors demand. Appropriate regulation and censorship should prevent such invasion into private grief. Editors would no longer be able to put journalists under such tremendous pressure to produce this emotive and intrusive writing.

To summarise, increased press censorship could prevent potential problems when dealing with concerns such as religious beliefs and privacy. Appropriate censorship would have checked the publication and repeated printing of the satirical cartoons depicting the prophet Mohammed, thus averting the anger and demonstrations amongst millions of Muslims. In turn, lives would not have been lost, people would not have suffered the backlash of intolerance and millions of pounds' worth of Danish goods would not have been boycotted in Muslim countries. Press censorship should preclude journalists from writing intrusively about people's private lives. Many journalists are not happy with writing that includes too much gossip and scandal, or that intrudes into private grief, but they are under huge pressure from their editors to produce the pieces of journalism that the public seem to demand. Increased press censorship to stop this sort of writing would alleviate pressure on journalists to deliver such work, thus lessening public concern over invasive journalism.

Here is Pete's essay:

Discuss the case for having increased censorship in the media

PLAN

Introduction
democracy & the media
censorship is alien to democracy
the problem of events

	Evidence	Argument
1 Privacy rights of the individual		
anonymity of offenders	Higham 2001	• freedom to print names might discourage reform
place of the legal system		
human rights		• individuals might be at risk
		• the law is a safeguard
		• further censorship is unnecessary
2 Self-regulation		
media can self-regulate where necessary	Press Complaints Commission 2005 Ofcom 2006	
TV warnings of disturbing material		
watershed		
difficult areas – Ken Bigley – avoid aiding kidnappers	Preston 2004	
press rights	PCC 2005	• No need for censorship
3 Public opinion as regulator		
a free press is not without restrictions	Hillsborough tragedy as reported in the *Sun*	• public opinion is powerful regulator
		• many Muslims are natives of West
reaction to Danish cartoons of Muhammad	results on BBC News	• cartoons showed religious stereotyping
Jyllands-Posten's apology	Herber – 2006 *Reporters Without Borders* – 2005 *Daily Telegraph* 03.02.2006 *Guardian* 03.02.2006	• public opinion reacts quickly to ill-advised editors

Conclusion
media must be free to make mistakes
legal frameworks & self-regulation are sufficient
public opinion is the ultimate regulator

Discuss the case for having increased censorship in the media

Freedom of expression is one of the pillars of democratic societies. By definition, democracy is government of the people, by the people and, for the most part, it is through the media of broadcasting, newspapers and, more recently, the Internet, that people's views are represented and debated. For this reason, increased media censorship would be unwelcome, as clearly, this would undermine the principle of free speech. No democracy would surrender these values in favour of those prevalent in many Middle Eastern or Asian countries where media sources are tightly controlled by governments (Reporters Without Borders, 2005). However, such a polarised world view is often tested by events, which cause even those living in democratic societies to question whether sections of the media are able to equalise the tension triangle that exists between their right to free speech, its accompanying responsibilities and their commercial objectives. This essay will focus on the broadcast and printed news media in the United Kingdom and seek to show that, in such a democracy, the inherent safeguards of the legal system, self-regulation and public opinion obviate the need for increased censorship.

When child murderers Robert Thompson and Jon Venables were released from secure accommodation in 2001, many newspapers disputed the court's decision to grant them anonymity. They argued that 'in the interests of open justice and freedom of expression, all criminals should be identified' (Higham, 2001). The danger with this argument is that it burdens offenders with the 'once a criminal always a criminal' tag and may discourage those who wish to reform. Without doubt the press were frustrated by the court's decision, which prevented the media circus they needed to sell more newspapers. However, after such an emotive and high-profile case, the men's safety was at risk, should their identities be revealed. Although their crime was horrific, the responsibility for sentencing rests with the legal system. Whatever one's view on the adequacy of that sentence, once it has been served, the men are entitled to protection from the threat of harm as a basic human right (Higham, 2001). The legal system, therefore, acts as a safeguard, preventing the media from exhibiting disproportionate emphases in favour of its commercial interest and right to free speech over its responsibilities to individuals and the wider community. Ultimately, further censorship is unnecessary.

In addition, the media can avoid censorship through self-regulation. The Press Complaints Commission (PCC) is charged with 'enforcing … [a] Code of Practice … framed by the newspaper … industry …' (PCC, 2005). Similarly, while the office for Communications (Ofcom) has statutory powers to regulate the UK communications industry, it operates 'with a bias against intervention, but with a willingness to intervene promptly and effectively where required' (Ofcom, 2006). This allows broadcasters to regulate themselves on many issues. Typically, therefore, a warning that 'viewers may find some of the images upsetting' precedes potentially disturbing news items. Similarly, programmes containing colourful language or nudity are also preceded by warnings and are shown after 9 p.m. so as not to be viewed by young children. Generally this works well. However, there are difficult areas: for example, the broadcasting of the kidnappers' videos of hostage Ken Bigley. Such episodes are a relatively new development and broadcasters must weigh their responsibility to inform against the danger of handing the kidnappers their desired publicity, while having regard to the distress suffered by those close to the hostage (Preston, 2004). That said, there is no need for censorship. The press 'have a right to report on events in a robust … fashion … balanced by responsibility. In doing this [the press] can demonstrate the strength of effective self-regulation' (PCC, 2005).

In the absence of self-regulation and legal restrictions, the media would seem to have carte blanche to target any section of society, shielded by the principle of freedom of speech. However, such an attitude can have serious consequences should their target decide to fight back. In 1989, the *Sun* newspaper misreported incidents concerning the Hillsborough stadium disaster when 96 Liverpool football fans were killed. The front-page article implied that the fans' own drunken behaviour had contributed to the disaster. The story led to a boycott of the paper in Liverpool that has lasted for 16 years, costing the *Sun* tens of millions of pounds in lost sales (BBC News, 2005). Recently, a full-page apology was published, and although this came long after the event, it demonstrates that public opinion can be a powerful force in the regulation of the media.

The violent reaction to the publication, in Denmark, of cartoons depicting the prophet Muhammad is a further illustration of the sensitivity of public opinion and the potentially destructive nature of its response. Supporters of increased media censorship would point to this as evidence for their case. However, as Lord Justice Sedley declared in a High Court judgement in 1999, 'the freedom only to speak inoffensively is not worth having' (Herbert, 2006). Denmark tops the World Press Freedom Index 2005 (Reporters Without Borders, 2005). However, by exercising this freedom without the required responsibility, *Jyllands-Posten*, along with its European counterparts who reprinted the cartoons, failed to have regard for the changing cultural constituencies of their societies. Furthermore, it is misleading to argue, as the *Daily Telegraph* does, that 'Muslims who cannot tolerate the openness and robustness of intellectual debate in the West have perhaps chosen to live in the wrong culture' (leader, 03.02.2006.). A great many Muslims are natives of the West; the depiction of the prophet of Islam as a bomb owes little to intellectualism and more to religious stereotyping, misrepresenting most Muslims' attitude to violence and increasing their sense of persecution. As the *Guardian* editorial points out, 'the right to publish does not imply any obligation to do so' (03.02.2006.). Nor does this impact only on Muslims in the West. Geographical borders are no longer a barrier to the flow of information. A weakness of the public opinion safeguard is that, almost inevitably, offence has already been caused before it can have an effect. However, if such incidents illustrate an editor's lack of understanding of the issues prior to publication, that understanding is rapidly enhanced by the subsequent public reaction, hence *Jyllands-Posten's* hurried apology.

In summary, in a democracy, the media must be allowed to make their own mistakes as society strives for tolerance and understanding. Increased censorship is both unwelcome and unnecessary where the safeguards of legal frameworks and self-regulation stand sentry. Furthermore, those editors and journalists who insist on living by the mantra 'publish and be damned' learn quickly that public opinion will not allow them to flaunt their precious freedoms irresponsibly, nor to use them as a conceit in the quest for commercial gain.

▶ Feedback

Both essays contain useful evidence, clear links and relevant quotes. Above all, they both argue their points forcibly. Both could omit phrases such as 'In summary' or 'To summarise' at the start of their conclusions because the last paragraph in an essay is obviously the conclusion. In her *Introduction*, Sadie might have explained that her essay would be limited to a discussion of print journalism.

SUMMARY

Steps for essay-writing
- analyse the question
- make a mind map
- gather information
- write a plan
- write your first draft
- take a break
- proofread and edit
- rewrite as necessary
- write final draft

Issues to keep in mind
- the question
- theories
- analysis
- your argument
- evidence and quotes
- paragraphing
- linking
- clarity and language

3 Quoting and Referencing

INTRODUCTION

This chapter will first cover setting out quotations as there are specific ways of doing this that you need to know. In the section 'References and Bibliography' you will find an explanation of how to record page numbers and other details. Quoting and referencing are very much nuts-and-bolts procedures. There's no room for manoeuvre or creativity here, and most people find these jobs a bit of a pain. Getting everything right, however, will give your assignments a professional appearance and demonstrate that you are applying academic rigour to your work.

You'll also find a section on plagiarism (using other people's work without acknowledgement). Colleges and universities are very much alive to this now – especially in relation to work found on the Internet. Getting clued up on how to avoid problems over this could save you a lot of heartache.

HOW TO QUOTE

When you quote from a book, you might copy a whole sentence (sometimes more) or just a word or two. You might use only a small proportion of the quotes you've made from your reading, but that's fine. If you have plenty of material to choose from, your work will not lack depth.

Let's assume I'm having to write an essay on A. C. Grayling's article, 'Why a high society is a free society' (see chapter 1). I might want to quote his comment on the similarities between legal and illegal substances. So I might have a sentence that runs something like this:

> Grayling feels that both legal and illegal drugs '... are used for pleasure, relief from stress or anxiety, and "holidaying" from

normal life, and both are, in different degrees, dangerous to health.'

You will see that I've used single quotation marks and that I've started with three dots to show that I've missed out the beginning of Grayling's sentence. I've introduced the quote with my own words in such a way that it flows smoothly from them. I've also carefully copied all Grayling's punctuation. You'll notice that he has put a word in quote marks himself – 'holidaying' – to show that he's giving it a slightly different meaning from the usual one. It was crucial that I copied this accurately too. If he had used any names or unusual words, I would have needed to check that I'd copied the spellings correctly.

It's quite acceptable to start and stop a quote whenever you like in order to suit the purpose of your own writing. Although you must show any punctuation that appears *within* the quote, you may terminate your quote *before* a punctuation mark if it makes sense to do that. So it would be perfectly OK to write this:

Grayling states that both legal and illegal drugs 'are, in different degrees, dangerous to health' and should therefore have equal status under the law.

I've terminated my quote *before* Grayling's full stop after 'health' because I wanted to continue my own sentence.

If you want, you can miss out a few words from the middle of a sentence that you quote. The missing words are shown by dots, like this (see Grayling, paragraph 11):

Grayling states that 'A good society should be able to accommodate practices which are not destructive of social bonds ... but mainly have to do with private behaviour.'

It's also acceptable to add or change a word to make things make sense within your own sentence, provided that you put any additions in square brackets to show that they are your own (see Grayling, paragraph 1):

Grayling believes that heroin should be freely available because 'a good society' is one in which 'the autonomy of those who wish to use [drugs] is respected.'

By the way, although the lines or single words that you copy from a book are called a **quote**, they only turn into a quote when you have copied them – or when you repeat them aloud to someone else. In their printed form in the text, they are not quotes. People sometimes get confused over this.

▶ Indenting

When quoting more than a line or two, it's best to indent. This means having a wider margin than usual on the left (sometimes on each side) of the page and leaving a line both before and after each quote. For this method, you use single-line spacing and you won't need to use quote marks as each quote will show up clearly on your page, like this:

> Grayling argues that there is no logical difference between legal and illegal drugs:
>
> > Both are used for pleasure, relief from stress or anxiety, and 'holidaying' from normal life, and both are, in different degrees, dangerous to health.

His stance on this is, perhaps, unusual, but his meaning is clear: there is no valid reason for splitting drugs into different categories.

You need to be careful not to overdo quotes as you may be accused of padding or of failing to explain things in your own words. Your tutors want to be sure that you have understood what you have read, and to do this they need to see your own explanations of topics. It's almost impossible to generalise, but a reasonable rule of thumb is not to have more than two quotes on any page, and, in general, not to quote more than two or three lines at a time. Check with your tutors, however, for local variations to this. Making as many references as are needed to the work of other writers, however, is a different activity. It's essential to acknowledge the sources for your ideas (see 'Plagiarism' and 'References' below).

▶ The problem of the half-way house

It's very important to make a clear difference between putting something in your own words and quoting directly from what you've read.

Sometimes, students get muddled and seem to try to do both at once, and this can make an essay confusing and difficult to read. The following sentence suffers from this problem (see Grayling, paragraph 6):

> Grayling says 'people who want to try drugs do so irrespective of their legal status.'

The final five words in the quote above are an accurate quote from Grayling, but the first eight were not written by him but by me and so must not be put in quotes. I didn't copy accurately and I didn't show a clear difference between Grayling's words and my own representation of them. Sorted out, that sentence above might become:

> Grayling explains that people intent on trying or using drugs do so 'irrespective of their legal status'.

Now I've quoted just a few words from Grayling, so it made sense to terminate my quote before Grayling's full stop and to use my own – after the quote.

If at first you find it difficult to fit quotes neatly into your own sentences, don't worry. The simplest way to do it is to precede your quote with a simple introductory statement such as

> Brown states that:

Then you can give the quote, indented, without any alterations. This is not a very sophisticated practice, but it usually avoids serious mistakes. Be sure to put a colon after your introductory words.

▶ Mentioning a writer's idea

When you refer to someone's idea or to the results of an experiment or survey that someone has conducted, you need to show clearly that the idea is not your own. You need to give the author credit for it just as you do when quoting someone's exact words. If I were writing an essay on drug use in Britain, for example, I might want to refer to Grayling's ideas. So I might write the following:

> A. C. Grayling has stated that some police chiefs are in favour of

legalising hard drugs in order to reduce the crime rate for other offences.

By giving Grayling's name, I've shown clearly that I've taken the ideas that follow from the work of this writer. It would also be important to get my references and bibliography correct. (See below.)

▶ Quoting from literature

If you are an English literature student, you are going to have to quote very frequently from the texts you are studying. There are specific rules on how this is done and it varies according to the kind of text you quote from.

Novels
Quoting from novels or from commentary on these by critics presents no difficulties because they are written in prose (that is, the sentences follow straight on from each other along each line). Use the procedure outlined above, with quotation marks for short quotes within your paragraphs and indentation for longer ones.

Poems
When you quote from a poem, a rough guide is that quotations of up to a line and a half can be incorporated into your own paragraphs, while those of two or more lines look better indented (see 'Indenting', above). Aim to limit your quotes to about three lines – never quote great chunks of a poem. The reason for this is that you need to analyse small sections at a time, showing exactly what it is in the poem that causes you to say what you do. When indenting, keep to the same lines as the original. The titles of poems should be put in single quote marks when you refer to them in the body of your essay.

Take special care when quoting more than one line but not indenting. You will need to use a slash (/) to show where a line ends. Here's an example taken from an undergraduate essay on William Blake's poem 'The Chimney Sweeper' from his book *Songs of Innocence*:

> Tom dreams that an angel sets the child sweeps free so that 'leaping laughing they run/And wash in a river and shine in the Sun!'

The original lines in the poem look like this:

> Then down a green plain leaping laughing they run
> And wash in a river and shine in the Sun!

Drama

It can be easier to quote from drama than from poetry, as you don't need to stick to the same line layout as shown in the text, unless, as with much of Shakespeare's work, the play is written in verse form (for which you follow the rules for quoting from poetry). You need to make clear to your reader who it is that is speaking, but you don't need to put the character's name at the side of the page in addition. Here's an extract from David's essay on Ibsen's play *A Doll's House*:

> Ibsen shocked Scandinavia with his character Nora. At first shown as a small-time housewife, she finally throws off her repressive marriage with the bald statement:
>
> > Well, that's the end of that.
>
> He undercuts the tradition of melodrama at the same time as analysing the role of women.

PLAGIARISM

Plagiarism is the act of using someone else's words or ideas as if they were your own. There are three possible offences:

- quoting directly without acknowledgement of your source
- changing parts of a quote or putting it in your own words and omitting acknowledgement
- summing up someone's ideas without acknowledgement

Every time you quote, or mention ideas you have gleaned from a writer or speaker (whether from a book, magazine, tape, disk, radio, TV, film or the Internet) you must make acknowledgement and use quotation marks where relevant. This is crucial.

You will also need to give accurate referencing for the following:

- statistics

- particular theories
- examples
- anything said or structured in a special or individual way

An essay containing plagiarised material might result in a grade of 0 being given. Clearly, that's not something worth risking. A tutor will frequently either know the book that has been used or will be able to spot the difference in writing style between your essay itself and unmarked quotes from another writer. So make sure that you have all your references in place. Forgetting to do that could get you in as much trouble as doing it on purpose.

► **Changing parts of a quote**

Let's suppose I'm writing an essay on drugs and I say the following:

> There is no justification in a decent society for using the police to monitor people's behaviour unless they are suspected of things like rape and murder.

This is plagiarism because I'm merely rephrasing what Grayling wrote (see paragraph 4 in the article in Chapter 1). Here are his original words (with an addition in square brackets, showing that the words are mine, to help the sense):

> On civil liberties grounds the latter policy [legalising currently illegal drugs] is preferable because there is no justification in a good society for policing behaviour unless, in the form of rape, murder, theft, riot or fraud, it is intrinsically damaging to the social fabric, and involves harm to unwilling third parties.

My quote is accurate now and it's essential that I give a reference (see below). Once a reference is in place, it will be clear that I'm not trying to pass off another person's writing as my own.

► **Summing-up someone's ideas without acknowledgement**

Using someone's ideas without acknowledgement is also seen as an underhand practice. Let's suppose I include the following in an essay on drugs:

> Freedom of the individual is essential in a fair society. It has been shown that use of the law to ban mind-altering substances does not protect children, or reduce crime or the number of users. Monitoring supplies to addicts, however, would result in a measurable reduction in both serious and petty crime.

Here, my offence is to sum up Grayling's ideas without admitting that they are his, not mine. As before, I *must* give an acknowledgement (see below).

You will always need:

- the writer's name
- full details of the publication where the idea appeared
- the number(s) of the relevant page(s)

WORKING FROM THE INTERNET

The Internet has revolutionised our ability to research topics at speed. It is now highly unlikely that anyone would attempt to produce a serious piece of work without making use of the Net. You will, however, need to demonstrate your ability to work from books as well. And there are certain dangers in working from the Net that you need to be aware of. To begin with, it's essential to reference work from the Net as fully as if it came from a book or journal (see the information below on Internet referencing in the Harvard and British Standard systems).

There are two other issues, however, which frequently get overlooked. First of all, there is the likelihood that ideas published one week will be disproved the next, and so lack credibility. People tend to publish work in progress so that the ideas they put forward may have a very limited shelf life. The likelihood that information will be superseded also applies to current events. In addition, even serious broadsheet journalists are apt to make mistakes in the fast-moving media world. So you can't necessarily rely on what they write.

The other problem is that theories and experiments you find on the Net might not have been reviewed by the originator's peers. That is to say, the information given might not have been scrutinised by other experts who are in a position to show whether or not it is valid. So you will need to be on your guard against using material that doesn't have a sound academic basis.

REFERENCES AND BIBLIOGRAPHY

A **reference** is a note that you make of where you found a particular idea or a sentence or two that you have quoted. A **bibliography** is a full list of the books you've consulted in the process of preparing an assignment.

There are several different methods of recording the books you've consulted for a particular essay and your direct references and quotations from any of them. Here, you will find Harvard referencing and British Standard (numeric) referencing. They are set out separately below. They are quite similar in some ways, so you need to take care not to get them mixed up. I've used the same examples in each, so if you want to compare them it will be easy to do so. I'd suggest, however, that you read only the one you need and avoid getting confused. A third system – MLA – combines aspects of these two. There's a section on it at the end of this chapter.

It's possible you will find that if your subject is English, you will need to use the British Standard system, and if it is sociology or a science subject you will be using the Harvard system. It's just not possible, however, to be categorical on this. Different departments within a college – and frequently even individual tutors – will have their own preferences. So do check what is wanted before familiarising yourself with one of the systems. Occasionally, you will be told that any system is acceptable. You'll find below the basics for each system. There are many further refinements to each, but if and when you do need to know more, your tutor should be able to help. Once you are accustomed to using a system, you can easily learn extra tricks. It's crucial, however, that you work through the whole section on the system you need in order to understand it.

The bad news is that, whichever method you use, you will need to get it *exactly* right. Every name must be correct, the order of items must be correct, and every comma and full stop has to be in the right place. You'll need to spend a little time getting to grips with the system you use, but once you've got into the referencing habit, things will be much more straightforward. Do check with your tutors, however, that the punctuation and layout shown here is exactly what you need.

For both methods, whenever you refer to the **title** of a book, journal, newspaper or magazine (at any point in your assignments), either underline it or, if you have a word processor, put it in italics. Put the title of an **article** – or **chapter** from a book – in quotation marks. It can be useful to use single quotation marks to differentiate straight quotes from speech (for which you can use double).

As you'll see below, you will need to give a lot of references. It's essential to give a reference for:

- someone's particular ideas
- their special way of writing or explaining them
- facts, statistics, tables and diagrams
- facts that are relatively unknown

There are one or two exceptions, however. You don't reference basic definitions from dictionaries; nor do you need to give proof for your belief that, for example, the earth goes round the sun or other basic facts which are common knowledge.

To make things easier for you to spot and to learn, you'll find punctuation marks in references are shown here in colour. Do *not* do this in your own work, however. Your tutors would not take kindly to it.

▶ The Harvard referencing system

Quoting from a writer
Suppose you want to quote from A. A. Gill's book, *The Angry Island*. You'll need to have a brief reference in the body of your essay, like this:

> 'The English are not so much a cocktail of mongrel blood … they are a state of self-belief, an idea of bombastic arrogance that begins in the last half of the fifteenth century' (Gill 2005, p. 30).

You give the author's surname, the date of publication of the book followed by a comma, and the relevant page number, all in brackets immediately after the quote. The dots show that part of Gill's sentence has been omitted.

If you use the author's name, you will not need to include it in the brackets:

> Gill writes: 'The English are not so much a cocktail of mongrel blood ... they are a state of self-belief, an idea of bombastic arrogance that begins in the last half of the fifteenth century' (2005, p. 30).

Mentioning a writer's ideas

Use of a writer's ideas, theories, experiments and so on, together with any statistical material you cite, must also be referenced. If you use the work by Gill (see above), but you don't actually want to quote his words, you can make reference to it like this:

> Gill states that the idea the English have of themselves grows not just from the mix of races that has formed the nation, but from confidence and conceit that has been growing for six hundred years (2005, p. 30).

Here you give almost the same information, but since you've already mentioned the author's name, it doesn't need to be put in the brackets. If you don't mention his name, it must go in the brackets:

> The idea the English have of themselves grows not just from the mix of races that has formed the nation, but from confidence and conceit that has been growing for six hundred years (Gill 2005, p. 30).

If you quote from a journal or from a chapter in a book by different authors, you give exactly the same information – writer, date and page number. For more than one book published by an author in the same year, you need to refer to the books as 2004a, 2004b, 2004c and so on.

Quoting from or mentioning audio-visual materials

Aim to give the same information as above as far as you can. If there is no author's name, you will have to give just the title of the work.

Quoting from or mentioning work found on the Internet

The same applies here as with audio-visual materials (see above).

Quoting from literature

If you are writing an essay on a particular novel, each quotation from the text itself should be followed by just the page number in square brackets. When quoting from a play, you will need to give act, scene and (whenever possible) line number. Here's a quote from Shakespeare's *Hamlet.* The number of the act is in upper-case roman numerals, the scene number is in lower case, and the line is in ordinary arabic figures:

To be, or not to be, that is the question … [III.i.56]

Your list of references

At the end of your assignment, you will need a list of the authors whose ideas you've mentioned and/or from whom you've quoted. The list must be in alphabetical order by authors' surnames, with book and journal titles in italics. Use an author's first name rather than an initial if that is what appears on the cover of the book. If publishers use '&' rather than 'and' in their names, do the same yourself. Your reference for Gill would look like this:

Gill, A. A. 2005, *The Angry Island,* Weidenfeld & Nicolson, London.

You can see from this that the order of items is as follows:

surname, first name or initial date, title, publisher, place.

It may help to be aware that there is only one full stop in a Harvard reference – at the end.

For a chapter in a book that is a collection of work by different writers, your reference would be set out like this:

Wood, Liz 1998, 'Participation and Learning in Early Childhood' in Cathie Holden & Nick Clough (eds), *Children as Citizens,* Jessica Kingsley Publishers Ltd, London, pp. 31–45.

Note the indentation after the first line to make the author's name stand out clearly. The title of the chapter is put in quotation marks. The first and last page numbers of the entire chapter appear at the end of the reference.

For an article in a magazine, journal or newspaper, your reference would look like this:

> Holmes, Bob 2006, 'Turning Back the Years', *New Scientist*, vol. 189, no. 2534, pp. 42–45.

This reference contains exact details of the issue in which the article appeared. As with the chapter from a book, the first and last page numbers of the entire article appear at the end of the reference.

For audio-visual materials, aim to give the same details as far as possible as for written sources. If an author or speaker is not mentioned, just use the title of the production. Use italics for the title of the production as you would with a book.

For work found on the Internet (as with audio-visual materials), aim to give the same information as for other written sources. What you record will vary according to the source – there will be more information on some than on others - but many references will look very much like this:

> Grayling, A. C. 2002, 'Why a high society is a free society', *Observer* 19.5.02. Retrieved 3 June 2005, from http://observer.guardian.co.uk/comment/story/0,,718108,00.html.

Notice that it's essential to show the date you found the information on the Net. Your reference will include: author (surname first), the title of the article, the publication where it originated, the date you found it and the website address. There are two full stops – one just before the word 'Retrieved' and another at the end of the reference. (That's apart from those in a date.) Wherever possible, show page numbers.

Your list of references, put in alphabetical order by authors' surnames, would look like this:

> Gill, A. A. 2005, *The Angry Island*, Weidenfeld & Nicolson, London.
> Grayling, A. C. 2002, 'Why a high society is a free society', *Observer* 19.5.02, retrieved 3 June 2005, from http://observer.guardian.co.uk/comment/story/0,,718108,00.html.
> Holmes, Bob 2006, 'Turning Back the Years', *New Scientist*, vol. 189, no. 2534, pp. 42–45.

Wood, Liz 1998, 'Participation and Learning in Early Childhood' in Cathie Holden & Nick Clough (eds), *Children as Citizens*, Jessica Kingsley Publishers Ltd, London, pp. 31–45.

Notice that the second line of any reference is indented so that authors' names show up clearly on the left-hand side.

Your bibliography

In your bibliography, you will list books you've consulted but that don't appear in your list of references as well as those that do. Like the list of references, they will be in alphabetical order by the surnames of authors. This is where the Harvard system scores: you will use exactly the same method of setting out each item in the *bibliography* as that shown for *references*.

Reminder: Do check with your tutors for local variations. In particular, in the case of Harvard referencing, you will find that some tutors will not want a bibliography – just a list of references.

▶ The British Standard referencing system (numeric)

In this system, each quote or mention of a writer's ideas, theories and so on is followed by a number. This number will correspond to the full reference (either at the bottom of the relevant page or, more usually, in a list at the end of your assignment). You need to use a number for each reference and to number chronologically through your essay, whether you are quoting directly or just mentioning someone's ideas. Numbering is shown here in colour. Do *not* do this in your own work.

Quoting from a writer

If you want to quote part of what A. A. Gill wrote in *The Angry Island*, you do it like this:

'The English are not so much a cocktail of mongrel blood ... they are a state of self-belief, an idea of bombastic arrogance that begins in the last half of the fifteenth century.'[1]

Here, you just put a number after your quote. This will refer a reader to your list of references. The dots show that part of Gill's sentence has been omitted.

If you want to mention Gill's name, you use the same method:

> Gill writes: 'The English are not so much a cocktail of mongrel blood ... they are a state of self-belief, an idea of bombastic arrogance that begins in the last half of the fifteenth century.' **1**

Mentioning a writer's idea
Use of a writer's ideas, theories, experiments and so on, together with any statistical material you cite, must also be referenced. If you use the book by A. A. Gill (mentioned above), you might write the following:

> Gill states that the idea the English have of themselves grows not just from the mix of races that has formed the nation, but from confidence and conceit that has been growing for six hundred years. **1**

Here, you have stated the writer's name and his idea.

You might decide to write slightly differently, omitting mention of Gill's name:

> The idea the English have of themselves grows not just from the mix of races that has formed the nation, but from confidence and conceit that has been growing for six hundred years. **1**

You deal with this item in exactly the same way as when the writer was mentioned by name - that is, just put a number immediately after your sentence. Your next reference would be numbered **2**.

Quoting from the Internet and audio-visual sources
Just as with quotes from writers and critics and the mention of a writer's ideas (see above), quotes from and references to audio-visual sources and the Internet are followed only by a number (1, 2, 3 and so on), so this would be the case if you were to quote from the article by A. C. Grayling (see the list of references, below).

Quoting from literature
If you are writing an essay on a particular novel, each quotation from the text itself can be followed by just the page number in square brackets. Quotes from a text that forms the subject of your essay are generally not followed by referencing numbers. When quoting from a play, you will need to give act, scene and (whenever possible) line number.

Here's a quote from Shakespeare's *Hamlet*. The number of the act is in upper-case roman numerals, the scene number is in lower case, and the line is in ordinary arabic figures:

> To be, or not to be, that is the question. [III.i.56]

Your list of references

At the end of your assignment, you will need a list of the authors whose ideas you've mentioned and/or from whom you've quoted. The list will be in numerical order, starting at 1, and each item on it will link to the numbers you've given in your assignment. So your references in this section will be in *exactly the same order* as the statements, acknowledgements and quotes that appear in the body of your work. Book and journal titles will be in italics. The reference for Gill would look like this:

> 1 A. A. Gill, *The Angry Island*, p. 30.

Use a writer's first name rather than initials if that is what appears on the cover of the book.

The order of items in the reference is as follows:

> initials. surname, title, page number.

It may help to be aware that there are two commas and one full stop in every *simple* British Standard reference. All the details, therefore, are given in one sentence.

For a chapter in a book that is a collection of work by different writers, your reference would appear like this:

> 2 Liz Wood, 'Participation and Learning in Early Childhood', in Cathie Holden and Nick Clough (eds), *Children as Citizens*, p. 35.

The details here are all given within one sentence (as in the shorter reference, above), but there are more commas.

For an article in a magazine, journal or newspaper, your reference would look like this:

3 Bob Holmes, 'Turning Back the Years', *New Scientist*, vol. 189, no. 2534, 14 January 2006, p. 44.

This reference contains exact details of the issue in which the article appeared.

For audio-visual materials, aim to give the same details as far as possible as for written sources. If an author or speaker is not mentioned, just use the title of the production. Use italics for the title of the production as you would with a book.

For work found on the Internet (as with audio-visual materials), aim to give the same information as for other written sources. What you record will vary according to the source – there will be more information on some than on others – but many references will look very much like this:

4 A. C. Grayling, 'Why a high society is a free society', *Observer* 19.5.02., accessed online 3 June 2005, from http:// observer.guardian.co.uk/comment/story/0,,718108,00.html.

Notice that it's essential to show the date you found the information on the Net. Your reference will include: the name of the author, the title of the article, the publication where it originated, the date published, the date you found it and the website address. There's just one full stop – at the end of the reference. (That's apart from those following initials, abbreviations and those in a date.) Wherever possible, show page numbers.

Your list of references would look like this:

1 A. A. Gill, *The Angry Island*, p. 30.
2 Liz Wood, 'Participation and Learning in Early Childhood', in Cathie Holden and Nick Clough (eds), *Children as Citizens*, p. 35.
3 Bob Holmes, 'Turning Back the Years', *New Scientist*, vol. 189, no. 2534, 14 January 2006, p. 44.
4 A. C. Grayling, 'Why a high society is a free society', *Observer* 19.5.02, accessed online 3 June 2005, from http://observer. guardian.co.uk/comment/story/0,,718108,00.html.

Your bibliography

In your bibliography, you will list all the books you've consulted, *including* the ones that appear in your list of references. Unlike the references, they will be in alphabetical order by the surnames of authors. Gill's book would appear like this:

> Gill, A. A. *The Angry Island.* London: Weidenfeld & Nicolson, 2005.

You can see from this that the order of items is as follows:

> surname, first name or initial. title. place: publisher, date.

It may help to be aware that there are three full stops (apart from those following initials, abbreviations, and those in a date) in every item that appears in a British Standard bibliography. These separate name, title, and publishing details. There are always commas after the surname and the publisher, and a colon after the place.

For a chapter in a book that is a collection of work by different writers, the first and last page numbers of the chapter would be included, and the entry in your bibliography would look like this:

> Wood, Liz. 'Participation and Learning in Early Childhood' in Cathie Holden and Nick Clough (eds), *Children as Citizens.* London: Jessica Kingsley Publishers Ltd, 1998, pp. 31–45.

For an article in a magazine or journal, the entry in your bibliography would look like this:

> Holmes, Bob. 'Turning Back the Years'. *New Scientist,* Vol. 14 no. 22534, 14 January 2006, pp. 42–45.

Note that the first and last page numbers of the entire article would be included.

Despite the extra information needed for entries relating to chapters or journal articles, there are still just three full stops in each entry in a British Standard bibliography (apart from any stops after initials and abbreviations).

For audio-visual materials, aim to give the same details as far as possible and in the same order as for written sources. If an author or speaker is not mentioned, just use the title of the production.

For work found on the Internet, as with audio-visual materials, aim to give full details of author, publication and date together with the date on which you found it. A. C. Grayling's article would show like this:

> Grayling, A. C. 'Why a high society is a free society'. *Observer*, 19.5.02, accessed online 3 June 2005, from http://observer. guardian.co.uk/comment/story/0,,718108,00.html.

Your full bibliography

This will include any books, magazines or journals that you might have looked at but have not mentioned or quoted from as well as those that you have (there are two extra ones in the list below). It will be in alphabetical order of surnames, like this:

> Finch, Geoffrey. *Linguistic Terms and Concepts*. Basingstoke: Macmillan Press Ltd, 2000.
>
> Gill, A. A. *The Angry Island*. London: Weidenfeld & Nicolson, 2005.
>
> Grayling, A. C. 'Why a high society is a free society'. *Observer*, 19.5.02, accessed online 3 June 2005, from http://observer. guardian.co.uk/comment/story/0,,718108,00.html.
>
> Hamilton, C. I. 'British Naval Policy, Policy-Makers and Financial Control 1860–1945'. *War in History*, Vol. 4, November 2005, pp. 371–395.
>
> Holmes, Bob. 'Turning Back the Years'. *New Scientist*, Vol. 14 no. 22534, 14 January 2006, pp. 42–45.
>
> Wood, Liz. 'Participation and Learning in Early Childhood' in Cathie Holden and Nick Clough (eds), *Children as Citizens*. London: Jessica Kingsley Publishers Ltd, 1998, pp. 31–45.

Reminder: Do check with your tutors for local variations.

▶ The MLA system

MLA stands for Modern Language Association of America. This system is now becoming quite widely used in Britain. In a nutshell, it has taken the best of both worlds and combined practices from the other two systems. In the body of an essay, when you quote or refer to a writer's idea, you can follow the Harvard system. In your bibliography, you can follow British Standard rules. You will not need a separate list of references. As with the other systems, however, do check with your tutors for local variations.

SUMMARY

This chapter has covered:

- quoting:
    direct quotes
    indenting
    mentioning people's ideas
    quoting from literature
- plagiarism
- the Harvard referencing system
- the British Standard (numeric) referencing system
- the MLA system

Part Two

Writing for Different Purposes

4 Style

INTRODUCTION

As a student, you will not be writing merely essays. You may be asked to write summaries, reports, articles, letters, and even to do some creative writing. This section of the book covers various types of assignment that you may be given, and this chapter forms a basis for each of the others. It is concerned with showing you how to make improvements to the general *texture* of your writing and demonstrating how you can write in very different ways to suit the purpose of a particular piece of work. As with other chapters in this book, just skip bits that you feel you know and concentrate on whatever is new to you.

It's often worth glancing through more simple items, however, even if you feel reasonably confident of understanding them because you can still pick up a tip or two that might be useful. The chapter begins with some fairly straightforward issues and moves to more complex ones.

The word *style* has different uses. It can refer to a person's particular way of writing, to the type of writing needed for a particular piece of work, or to writing well. Some very effective ways of making improvements to your style are to check out punctuation (see chapter 14), paragraphing (see chapter 2) and sentence construction (see chapter 13). Accurate punctuation will make your work easier to read, and helpful paragraphing will make the structure of any piece of your writing easier to follow. A clear understanding of some of the different ways in which sentences function will be invaluable.

When a writer specialises in one form of writing – for example, poetry, novels or even newspaper articles – he or she will inevitably develop a very individual style which others can often spot without being given the writer's name. This kind of thing grows slowly, but the more writing you do, the more your own style will emerge. Reading well-written material will also have a beneficial effect on your style. If you haven't been much of a reader up till now, aim to try novels, travel writing, histories, biographies, broadsheet newspapers and academic journals. All these can be useful. Follow your own particular interests, and, from time to time, challenge yourself with some difficult reading material. Wider reading will gradually have a spin-off effect on your own work. You will begin to imitate good writers without even realising that you're doing it.

SENTENCE LENGTH

If you're having real difficulties with your writing, you might like to start by sticking to a rule of having no more than ten words in any sentence. This will help keep you on the straight and narrow, preventing you from writing sentences in which various constructions become confused. It's a really good ploy to get you out of immediate trouble.

As time goes on, however, you will want to progress from this, and varying the length of your sentences will enhance your style. The section on clauses in chapter 13 will show you some ways in which sentences can be extended easily and accurately. The occasional very short sentence that follows a long one can, however, give impact. For example,

> Problems over the Norwark virus (that has killed a number of hospital patients) have highlighted the need to return to basic standards of cleanliness as advocated as far back as the nineteenth century by Florence Nightingale. Hand-washing saves lives.

SIMPLICITY AND CLARITY

One of the most important ways to improve your style is to aim constantly for simplicity and clarity. The best writing is easy to read and uses contemporary (rather than out-of-date) vocabulary. Sometimes, students feel that they are expected to aim for language that sounds important or very formal. This really is not the case. Of course, the writing in some textbooks can seem really dense and difficult, but that doesn't mean that it's written in a style that's worth copying. Don't call a spade 'an implement for turning earth'.

The best writing states its case in the simplest possible terms. This doesn't mean leaving things out or omitting to use technical words when they are essential. It means that we need to avoid all unnecessary jargon and to give sufficient explanation in order to be clearly understood. It also means that we must use punctuation and paragraphing to help the reader along.

▶ **Checklist for simplicity**

- *use a short word* rather than a long one
- *be yourself*: don't copy style from another writer
- *write the truth* as you see it
- *check your logic*: have you said what you mean, and does your writing make sense?
- *be as brief as possible* without omitting essential points
- *omit clichés* (e.g. 'in this day and age', 'the bottom line')
- *use helpful paragraphing and punctuation* (see chapters 2 and 14)
- *use active verbs* rather than passive ones (see chapter 12)
- *use concrete nouns* rather than abstract ones whenever possible (see chapter 12)

Look at this example of long-winded writing:

Many of the somewhat extended psychoanalytic case notes written and published by Sigmund Freud have become the subject of castigation by feminist writers.

There's absolutely no need to say that Freud's work was *psychoanalytic* because everyone knows that. There's certainly no need to say that it was *written and published.* That's obvious. The phrase *the subject of castigation* can be reduced considerably, and we only need one word for *feminist writers.* The piece would be much more readable like this:

Freud's work has been attacked by feminists.

This new sentence gets straight to the point and won't send a reader to sleep. The original sentence makes a really good sedative.

FINDING THE RIGHT WORD

While you are writing your first draft, it's best not to spend time worrying about individual words or phrases. Concentrate on getting the whole thing on paper first and don't spend time labouring over careful explanations. My own method is to put brackets round anything that I feel doesn't sound right. Then I can attend to it later when I'm not struggling with a whole draft. You can develop your own marker system to flag up things you know will need attention.

Finding the right word for what you want to say can be a bit time-consuming, but it's rewarding to be able to express exactly what you mean rather than approximately. If you have a *good dictionary* and a *thesaurus* you will have the right tools for the job. Get the best dictionary you can afford (Oxford or Collins). A pocket dictionary won't do as it won't contain all the information you'll need. Getting a larger version will pay dividends in the long run. A thesaurus – which will give you a choice of words for non-technical items and save you repeating yourself – can be very handy for searching out a word that says *exactly* what you mean. *Roget's Thesaurus* is the one most people use.

The dictionary will help you not just with spelling but with accuracy. People often use a word that means more or less what they intend, but not quite. Every now and then, you might try checking the definition of a word you think you are quite sure of. This can be quite an eye-opener. It's surprising how many times a dictionary definition turns out to be not quite what we expect. A good deal of your checking, however, can be done by just thinking carefully. Look at the example below from Susan's essay for her Access course – 'Discuss the proposition that education is wasted on the young':

> A reason why this proposition may be feasible is the way in
> which attending school is enforced.

The word *feasible* relates to possibility. It is perfectly possible to make *any* proposition. A word that would fit much better here is *valid*. What Susan meant was that the proposition could be shown to be in some ways convincing.

In this example from an essay on Shakespeare's *Hamlet,* Christine is clearly trying to sound formal:

> Hamlet shows his love for Ophelia on many occasions and it appears more obvious than the ways in which Ophelia's love towards Hamlet is discerned.

The word *discerned* – that is, perceived – must relate to the responses of the audience. It is they who perceive what is going on. But that sentence actually focuses on the behaviour of the characters themselves. It can't easily change focus to the behaviour of the audience. Maybe Christine actually meant *displayed,* which relates to what Ophelia was doing and would fit much better. Perhaps the problem came about because Christine didn't want to use the word *shown* as she'd already used *shows,* and she got a bit confused. You can often spot this kind of thing when you are proofreading your work (see chapter 2).

You can see from this that finding the right word can sometimes take a little time; but it's time well spent because your work will have greater strength and your command of the language will be constantly improving.

WRITING INSTRUCTIONS

If you are given an assignment in which you have to write any kind of instructions, check carefully whether what is wanted is a set of bullet points (like my list below) or writing done in full sentences and paragraphs. A list of bullet points gives just the bare bones of a piece of information. When writing instructions in full sentences, the key is to be sure to put everything in.

I'd guess that there have been countless times when you've been baffled by instructions and have muttered dire things about the person who wrote them. The problem usually relates to one or more of the following:

- information missed out
- information not clearly explained
- language for the initiated only – i.e. jargon or abbreviations
- confusion caused by incorrect grammar and/or punctuation

Some of us complain bitterly about the instructions in computer manuals. It can be particularly galling to find that somebody who herself understands computers has absolutely no trouble with the manuals. This can happen in any field, however. When we understand a subject, we tend to forget that people without inside knowledge will need to have things spelt out for them. Here's an example of an instruction that often baffles me:

> Take three a day with a main meal.

Now how many times a day would I be taking those tablets? Three times? Or can I take them all in one go? It does tell me to take them with *a* main meal. And should I take them during the meal, or can they be swallowed before or after it?

Let's improve the instruction:

> Take one tablet before a main meal three times a day.

That's a bit better. I've seen this one scores of times. But I eat only one main meal a day. I wouldn't call my breakfast toast or my lunchtime sandwich a main meal. Does this mean that I must increase my food intake while I'm on those pills? Writing clear instructions is not necessarily a straightforward business.

There's a really good exercise for practising writing clear instructions which you may already have been asked to do in one form or another:

> Write two or three paragraphs explaining how to go on foot from one destination to another a short distance away – say, five or ten minutes' walk – in a place you know well. You might choose to start at a point in your local town or village and finish at a particular room in your college. Do this as if for someone who knows absolutely nothing of the area.

You will find that you have to focus very clearly on getting your instructions just right. If you are studying with a friend, see if he or she thinks it would be possible to follow your instructions without having any prior knowledge of the area.

DESCRIBING A PROCESS

This is very similar to writing instructions, except that it often relates to something that has already taken place – like a scientific experiment.

As with instructions on a bottle of pills, accuracy is essential. Whatever your subject, aim to make your descriptions so clear that they could be understood by someone who knows practically nothing about the topic. This will mean being careful not to assume that an item is so simple that everyone will understand it. Here's an example – putting oil in my car:

> Before I begin, I must make sure that the car is on level ground and that it has been stationary for a little while. First, I unhook the catch on the car's bonnet. Then I raise the bonnet, pull out the attached rod that will support it while I work, and clip the end of the rod in place. Next, I take the dipstick out of its socket. The dipstick is a long rod that can usually be spotted by its curved handle. I then wipe the oily end of the dipstick with a rag or tissue and replace it in its socket.
>
> Then I remove the dipstick again and check the level of oil on the lower end of it. There are maximum and minimum marks. If the oil level is below maximum, I replace the stick, remove the oil-filler cap which is situated on the top of the engine, close to the dipstick socket, and pour in a little oil. I wait a couple of minutes for the oil to settle, and then recheck the level using the dipstick again. I now add more oil if the level is still below maximum.
>
> Finally, I replace the filler cap and make sure that it is fully tightened. Then I release the bonnet rod from its catch, clip it back into place, and carefully close the bonnet, making sure (with a final push) that it is securely fixed.

The first thing to notice here is the amount of detail included that will appear superfluous to anyone who is used to changing oil. The second thing you might look at is how often I reuse a noun (the name of a thing – see chapter 12) in places where we might normally use a pronoun – in this case, *it*. For example, in the third sentence, I used the word *rod* twice instead of using the word *it* on the second occasion. The reason for this is that this sentence already contains the word *it* which refers to *bonnet*. If I'd used *it* again, the unsuspecting reader might assume that this, too, referred to *bonnet*.

When doing this kind of writing, it can help considerably if you can *visualise* the process. This will help you to incorporate minor items that might be overlooked.

PERSUASIVE WRITING

The object of persuasive writing is to get readers on your side. You need to stress your main points, but it's important not to overdo things or to appear belligerent. If you want to see some examples of persuasive writing, you have only to look at advertisements. The reason for thinking about it here is that you will need to be able to write persuasively in your essays as you will have seen if you've read the section on *argument* in chapter 2.

Persuasive writing is really very simple. If you want to get someone to agree with your point of view or to take a particular action, you need to:

- show the positive features of your idea
- play down any negative aspects
- push your points strongly
- show that you are committed to your views
- take care not to offend

All this is in addition, of course, to writing simply and clearly. What follows is some work by Joan, a student on an Access to Higher Education course. Joan's assignment was to write a 750-word paper for the governors of her local community college with the title 'The need for an Access building on the main college site'. The students on Joan's course were having to spend a great deal of time travelling between two sites. Joan comes across as someone who has thought carefully about the issues and is prepared to stand up for what she believes. Here she accentuates the positive aspects of her suggestions:

> With thorough planning, costs can be kept to a minimum – but it's not all about spending money. The local area abounds with different groups that need space in order to function, so the building can be made to pay for its own upkeep by being hired out for local activities: evening classes, day classes, local drama and music groups.

Joan's final paragraph pushes hard to get her points across:

> None of this can happen with the present arrangement. With only three subjects on offer, and basic facilities too far away, the current Access course is undermined and disadvantaged. It

cannot become fully effective for the community it serves, or for the college.

Joan leaves the reader in no doubt of her views, but she makes a compelling case by sticking to the facts and presenting her ideas in a level-headed manner.

TONE

Using an appropriate tone is important for all types of writing. Tone is easiest to spot in spoken language. We know at once if someone sounds friendly, upset, impatient, formal, serious or humorous. We often react strongly to tone. You may at one time or another have said to someone, "I don't like your tone." We constantly vary our tone of voice, but tone can be a bit harder to spot in written language. Understanding how it functions, however, will make you more able to control tone in your own work.

Tone can give you a clue as to where a writer is coming from. It relates in part to how a writer feels towards the subject-matter of a piece of writing, but especially to the way in which he or she 'speaks' to the reader. An ironic tone, for example, is often used to poke fun in a sarcastic way at the topic or person being written about. It can signal to the reader that the writer's words mean the opposite of what they appear to state. An ironic tone can also be used to point up something that is irrational or incongruous. Political journalists frequently use irony.

Tone generally comes from a fusion of the items mentioned with the kind of words used (see *diction* below). Notice how the sensuous tone in the following restaurant review helps to 'sell' the restaurant to readers and make them want to eat there:

> "Ooh, that's good!" This was from my friend, Anne, as she took her first bite of oak-smoked salmon with a dill crème fraîche and pink peppercorns. From that moment on, a happy smile occupied her face for the entire evening.

If you've been asked to write an article (see chapter 9) or produce a piece of creative writing (see chapter 7), you will need to be able to vary the tone of what you write. But for essays and reports, your tone will generally need to be formal and serious, and you won't want to show any emotion.

DICTION

You may have noticed that each example of tone (above) relies very much on the kind of words used – that is, the diction. In the example above, the words 'oak-smoked salmon', 'crème fraîche' and 'pink peppercorns' work together to suggest a luxurious eating experience. With the word 'smile' added, the effect is strengthened further.

The section on simplicity (above) showed that it's a good idea to use a short word rather than a long one whenever appropriate. This can sometimes come down to preferring to use words derived from the Anglo-Saxon rather than from Latin. In English, longer and more formal words frequently have Latin (or sometimes, Greek) roots, whereas shorter words are more likely to have Anglo-Saxon (or Old English) roots. Any good dictionary will show the derivation of each word as well as its definition.

The offer of employment (see below, section C) contains no fewer than 12 words that are derived either directly or indirectly from Latin: *offer, employment, subject, receipt, references, entirely, satisfactory, medical, include, require, provision, circular.* These help to give the job offer its highly formal tone.

REGISTER

When we talk to someone, we generally adjust our language automatically for the needs of the particular listener. This is called changing **register**. When talking to a baby, we will use short, simple words with frequent repetition. When we speak to a priest or other religious person, we might use semi-formal language and would probably take care not to use words that might offend. At a cricket ground, the talk will be full of cricket terminology. There are many situations where traditional language is used. In wedding services, for instance, many of the words spoken have remained unchanged for hundreds of years.

If I turn from talking to a baby to making a phone call about my gas bill, you can be pretty certain that I will have changed register. When we write, we need to adjust our language to the particular task in hand.

Look at the four extracts below and then at the discussion of each that follows.

A Testing the installation (for a washing machine)

Refer to the programme guide for details of how to select programmes.

1 Turn on the water supply and check for leaks from fill hoses.
2 Switch on the electricity supply.
3 Select a spin programme and then press the on/off button to start the machine.

Allow the programme to continue for one minute and then switch off the machine via the on/off button. This will remove any water remaining in the machine from factory testing.

B Congratulations to you both –
And warmest wishes, too,
For nothing less than happiness
That lasts a lifetime through;
For surely both of you deserve
The very finest things,
And all the deep contentment
That a happy marriage brings.

C This offer of employment is subject to one or all of the following:

(a) The receipt of references which we find entirely satisfactory;
(b) The LEA's* Occupational Health Physician being satisfied as to your medical fitness for the post;
(c) Satisfactory LEA checks including those required under the Provisions of the Home Office Circular 47/93 (Protection of Children).

D David Cameron last night launched his groovy new non-alcoholic cocktail at Vinopolis, a wine-tasting emporium under some railway arches in south London.

---

* LEA: Local Education Authority.

Mr Cameron's team of Old Etonian chemists, who have been working 24 hours a day round a kitchen table in Notting Hill to develop the drink, say they left alcohol out of the mix in order to make it more 'compassionate'.

But right-wing drinkers are bound to question whether without the strong drink of tax cuts, the cocktail will do anything to cheer people up.

They fear the Cameron, as the new drink is to be known, could turn out to be a pale imitation of the Blair, middle Britain's tipple of choice since 1997.

The Old Etonian chemists yesterday dismissed these fears. They pointed out that unlike the Iron Lady – the last Conservative cocktail that achieved market leadership – the Cameron will leave drinkers with no hangover, and will also stop people thinking the Tories are a hangover from Thatcherism.

▶ Feedback

1 *Instructions*   The language used in the instructions for my washing machine is rather stark. There are no adjectives or descriptions of any kind. This is the language of instructions everywhere. It is simple, clear and gets straight to the point. You might have called it technical. Notice that there are a number of commands: *Refer*, *Turn on, Switch on*, *Select*, *Allow*. There is also a brief explanation of the final point. Most of the sentences are short and simple. The manufacturers don't want users to be in any doubt as to how to proceed.

2 *Greetings cards*   The wedding card doesn't say a great deal either, but the language it uses is very different. If the card hadn't mentioned marriage, you'd still instantly recognise the language of greetings cards. In contrast to the language of instructions, it focuses on feelings, and it does this very simply and in a positive tone.

As a poem, this piece makes use of rhythm and rhyme which are very powerful devices for getting feelings across. Individual words have been chosen very carefully with the purpose of the card in mind. The aim is to send to the couple a kind of blessing on their marriage. So it focuses solely on the best possibilities: *happiness* and *contentment*; and it uses superlatives*: *warmest* and *finest*. There are no such extravagant messages in the job offer that follows.

3 *Formal appointments*   The language of this job offer from a local authority is so formal and carefully worded that you might mistake it for a legal document. In fact, it is a document that could be used in a court of law if (once it has been signed and accepted) either the authority or the employee fails to stick to the agreement made between them.

Here the language is very restricted. There must be no possibility of anyone being able to find more than one meaning in these statements. If it comes to a showdown, the employer will not want to have a lawyer claiming that the words could mean anything other than what they were originally intended to mean. Notice the careful wording of the introductory statement, saying that the 'offer of employment is subject to *one or all*' (my italics) of three conditions. This allows the authority scope to demand that the employee fulfil all three criteria. This is the language of bureaucratic organisations: it is used for particular types of written evidence and for making sure that points will be understood and followed in a prescribed manner.

4 *Journalism*   It is not just the reference to a recent event – 'last night' – that tells us that this is a piece of journalism. This highly skilled writing satirises David Cameron's embryonic Conservative party policy by suggesting it's a new non-alcoholic drink. (Note that it goes on to take a sideways swipe at Labour too.) This extract from a broadsheet sketch is typical of drily witty broadsheet satirical writing. It's characterised by conciseness and by bite-sized paragraphs designed for readers with little time for reading humour. Its diction mixes contemporary words such as 'groovy' with the almost extinct 'emporium'. This seems to break the rules of register and is in itself typical of broadsheet writing. Notice that nowhere does the writer wholly divert from broadsheet journalism's semi-formal style or descend merely to cracking jokes.

---

* *superlative*: the highest form of a quality – e.g. warm, warmer, *warmest*; fine, finer, *finest*.

GENDER ISSUES (SEXISM)

Not only can sexism be annoying – even if displayed unconsciously – but it can imply things that are incorrect. For example, the statement

A carer needs all the support she can get

suggests that no men are carers, which is not true. We need to say:

A carer needs all the support he or she can get.

or

Carers need all the support they can get.

There's also the problem of words like *manageress* and *poetess* which both seem to imply that the work done in each case is not quite as valuable as that done by a man. *Manager* and *poet* are the job titles, and nowadays we can use these for anyone, male or female. The ending *-ess* has been consigned to the bin.

There have been particular problems over the word *he*. In the past, it used to be used in a general sense, to stand for, we were told, persons of either sex. The problems that were eventually spotted here were that:

- whatever we say about it, the word *he* actually implies maleness
- women were screened out of many issues
- children grew up seeing maleness foregrounded in many areas of life

Consequently, we can no longer reasonably use the word he to imply people of either or both sexes. Unfortunately, ways of coping with the problem often seem clumsy. When speaking in general terms (rather than of a male individual), we need to use phrases like:

he or she

or

persons of either sex

Sometimes, people write *s/he*, as in :

> Anyone who buys a car must tax it as soon as s/he takes it on the road.

In conversation, of course, we generally use the word *they*:

> Anyone who buys a car must tax it as soon as they take it on the road.

The trouble with that construction, however, is that it is ungrammatical. The word *they* is plural, implying that there is more than one person involved. But the sentence began with the word *Anyone*, which is singular.

Unless your main subject is English, your tutors might not worry about you using *they* to refer to one person, but it's important to understand the issue. When writing informally – as in a letter to a friend – there's no problem in using *they* to refer to one person, just as we do in everyday speech. But in academic writing, accuracy is best.

SUMMARY

This chapter has covered:

- sentence length
- simplicity and clarity
- finding the right word
- writing instructions
- describing a process
- persuasive writing
- tone
- diction
- register
- gender issues

5 Summaries

INTRODUCTION

There are different ways of making summaries. You might be asked to write a careful summary of a short text in a hundred words or so. The aim there would be to reduce the text in length, keeping as much of the original information as possible. You might, however, be asked to summarise just the main ideas in a text. This chapter will first set out the basic method for writing a summary of a short text and then give information on how to proceed with something longer.

BASIC SUMMARY-WRITING

You might be asked to produce a summary of an article or, perhaps, a couple of pages from a textbook. A good summary of this type will include everything of any importance from the original. There are distinct stages in the process, and it's very important to stick to them:

1 A first quick read
2 Note-making
3 Writing a first draft
4 Checking your word-count and editing
5 Writing your final draft

▶ 1 A first quick read

Your first reading will familiarise you with the material and so make you a little more comfortable about the task ahead. You will begin to get a feel for the central issues. Skimming will probably be sufficient –

that is, reading just the first and last sentence of each paragraph and perhaps the whole of the concluding paragraph.

▶ 2 Note-making

Your notes will form the basis of your summary, so you need to take great care at this stage (see chapter 1). You will need to copy out any technical terms, but in general, you will need to translate the original material into *your own words* as far as possible. This is crucial. If you use the writer's words, you will not be able to demonstrate your understanding of the piece and you will have great difficulty in keeping your summary to the required length without leaving out important items. Below is a copy of my notes:

1 Soc. where all drugs legal = gd. because: freedom of individual.
2 Grayling believes: a) life shd. not depend on 'substances which . . . distort reality' b) hard drugs shd. be legal.
3 Legal/ illegal drugs used for: pleasure, stress relief, escapism. Both = 'dangerous to health'. The law shd. treat both groups the same.
4 Only practices that harm soc. or 'unwilling third parties' shd. be illegal. Allowing those who 'claim to know . . . better' than others to make law = wrong.
5 Children more at risk when drugs illegal.
6 Drug-taking not prevented by laws. Relaxation of law doesn't change no. of users.
7 Prohibition in USA caused increase in crime.
8 Organised crime = serious threat to society: money-laundering, terrorism, vice rings, buying political influence. Ans. = controlled sale of drugs in chemists.
9 If addicts got safe supplies, petty crime would lessen.
10 Dangers of overdose = small.
11 If a practice isn't dangerous to soc. it shd. not be illegal. A 'good society' restricts 'interfere[nce] in private behaviour'.
12 Some people will suffer from misuse, but hist. shows little damage to society as a whole from drug use.
13 The freedom of individuals to choose lifestyles = essential in 'good society'.

▶ 3 Writing a first draft

Your first draft should be written from your notes. Try not to look back at the original while you are writing it. If you have managed to use your own words throughout your notes, this draft really will have your stamp on it. You will not sound as though you are merely parroting the original text. Aim to keep this draft short, but don't worry too much about the word-count at this stage. The mind can't cope with two complex processes at the same time. Here's mine:

> Grayling feels that people shouldn't need to 'distort reality' for plea-sure. He says that all drugs have health risks and wants consistency in the law. He sees the only justification for law as protection of third parties, and feels that those laws that coerce on moral grounds are 'bad'. They give no protection to children since all who want to try or use drugs will do so anyway. Relaxation of drug laws brings no change in user statistics, but organised crime is a threat. The danger of overdose is small and addicts could be treated on prescription. A 'good society' is not prescriptive. Legal availability would reduce both serious and petty crime, and has been seen in the past to have no adverse effect on society. It is essential that individuals have the right to choose their lifestyles. (138 words)

▶ 4 Checking your word-count and editing

Editing will depend partly on the instructions you've been given. If you have been given a word limit, you'll probably have to spend some time cutting out words and phrases that are not wholly necessary. If your summary is well over the word limit you've been given, look first at cutting specific facts and opinions that may be secondary to the text's central issues. Then, think about saying things in different ways to reduce your word count.

Your writing may just need tidying up a little; but if, by any chance, your summary is *much shorter* than the word limit, it's probable that you have omitted too much. Check your notes against the original, look for the next most important points after the ones you've already noted, and add these to your draft. You may find that you need to write your summary out more than once at this stage if it gets too messy to follow clearly.

▶ 5 Writing your final draft

Just copy out your edited version. When it's done, it's a good idea to make a final check on the word-count. If you faithfully follow the five steps, you can't go far wrong. Problems with summary-writing are nearly always the result of rushing stage 2 – the note-making. It really is essential to get down *all the key points* and to get them down in *your own words* as far as possible.

Here's the final dfraft of my summary of the Grayling article:

> People shouldn't need reality 'distort[ion]' for pleasure. All drugs have health risks and the law is inconsistent. The only justification for prevention is protection of society and 'unwilling third parties'. Laws that coerce on moral grounds are 'bad'. They give no protection to children, since all who want to use do so, and relaxation of drug law brings no increase in use. Legal availability would reduce organised and petty crime and has been seen historically to have no adverse effect on society. Addicts, under this system, could be treated on prescription. A 'good society' promotes individual freedom. (97 words)

The trick with summary-writing is to disentangle the key points from explanations, examples, jokes and blatant diversions. Note that I've specifically omitted the following items that appeared in the original article:

- explanations
- the statement on the writer's own lack of drug-taking
- the example of Prohibition in the USA
- the example of paracetamol

You can see in my first line that I wanted to quote a word from Grayling but that I needed to change it slightly to fit my sentence. So I've had to show the letters I've added by putting square brackets round them.

▶ Another example

You'll find another example below – an extract from a course-work article by Mark on sustainable rural development (approximately 560 words). After the extract, you'll find my notes on it, my first draft and my final hundred-word summary.

Sustainable rural development

What is urgently needed now are new policies that not only conserve nature but also integrate care of the Earth with care for human beings. There should be incentives to reverse the flow of people from the land to towns and cities. These people should be encouraged to do something not only worthwhile for themselves but even more worthwhile for their environments. They should be encouraged to establish communities, and build efficient and environmentally friendly homes. They should be given land to grow organic vegetables on, and they should be able to generate their own power so as to reduce their dependence on fossil fuels. These small hamlet dwellers would be able to take advantage of community farming and biomass projects. If they are well located then they could take advantage of wind, water or solar power schemes, and have little or no dependence on nationally operated utility systems. Even human waste could either be composted or put through a water reed-bed purification system. Thus we would alleviate the need to be connected to the present archaic disposal system in place today.

All that would be required to implement these ideas is a new category of land use – perhaps called Self-Sufficiency Land (SS Land). There would have to be some form of contractual agreement between the owner and the local and national authorities which would contain basic statements such as, 'I will buy and live on this piece of land and will not let it out or speculate. I will conserve nature, plant over twenty trees per acre and be a co-steward in maintaining common lands. I will co-operate with my neighbours over transport, infrastructure, power generation, waste disposal, and use of available water supplies. In return for this opportunity to experience a meaningful life I will have the freedom to build my own house to a design suited to its surroundings and will also incorporate the highest energy efficient standards possible.'

The consequences of implementing even small changes to current planning law to create areas of self-sufficient land would be enormous. Farmers would be able to apply for SS Land designation and if they succeeded then their land would sell for £10,000 per acre (price-capping would be necessary) instead of £1,000 per acre.

Communities would then be able to set up all over the country, precipitating a marked expansion in small allied industries. Another huge benefit to the new landowners would be to receive EC grants for re-creating the woodlands and hedgerows which are at present disappearing at an alarming rate. At the same time a subsidiary income would be incurred. Apart from the cash received for planting in the first place, appropriate harvesting from the renewable resource they have planted would be materially and economically beneficial.

The boom in alternative technologies related to energy-efficient architecture and renewable energy supplies would hopefully see the beginning of the end of the Industrial Revolution and its descendants in the form of over-engineering: the kinds of engineering and tech-nology which produce things that nobody really needs and use up vast amounts of valuable natural resources in a very unsustainable way. Even alternative technology, as a term, is starting to have an anti-quated ring about it. Perhaps a real shift in people's consciousness and sense of responsibility would be prompted by a new brand of innovators of the future: the engineers of the Environmental Revolution.

Notes

1 Need policies on conservation & humans
2 Incentives needed for rural living – new communities
3 Community farming/use of natural energy/environmentally friendly sewage disposal
4 New type of land use with specific agreements between owners/local authorities/government – Self-Sufficiency
5 Agreement: no speculative enterprises/tree planting & conser-vation/co-operation with neighbours on mains services. Owners able to design & build own dwellings suited to local environ-ment
6 Results:
   (a) farmers who applied to have their land SS-designated would find it rose tenfold in value
   (b) explosion of new communities = expansion of small indus-tries
   (c) landowners would get EC grants for re-creating woods & hedgerows & get profit from managing woods & selling

7 Energy-efficient building & renewable energy supplies – end of wasteful engineering & technology. All these changes cd. bring change from Industrial to Environmental Rev.

First draft

Policies are needed to protect both our land and people. Incentives are needed to establish community farming and the use of natural energy. There should be a newly designated land use – Self-Sufficiency, based on agreements between the owners and local authorities. The government would ban land speculation and encourage conservation and co-operation. The individual could design and build appropriate to his/her surroundings. Farmers who apply for SS designation would find their land values rose considerably in value. There would be an explosion of small industries. EC grants for creating woodlands and profit from sustainable harvesting would also benefit landowners. Wasteful engineering would end. The Industrial Revolution would give way to an Environmental Revolution. (112 words)

Final draft

Policies are essential to protect both land and people. Incentives are needed to establish community farming and use natural energy. A newly designated land use – Self-Sufficiency, based on agreements between owners, local authorities and government – would ban land speculation and promote conservation and co-operation. People could design and build appropriate to their surroundings. Farmers applying for SS designation would find their land values rose. There would be an explosion of small industries. EC grants for creating woodlands and then profiting from sustainable harvesting would benefit landowners. Wasteful engineering would end. The Industrial Revolution would give way to an 'Environmental Revolution'. (100 words)

SUMMARISING A TEXT'S MAIN IDEAS

You might be asked to summarise just the main ideas in a longer text. You can take a slightly more relaxed approach here and the method is different. You'll probably be given an overall length – perhaps one side of A4 paper. So the exact word count isn't important. It would be a good idea to make brief notes on each chapter immediately after reading it. When you've finished reading the book, you can then list the main issues. This can look like a very time-consuming task, so be aware that you may well not need to read the whole book. You might decide to omit less important chapters and to skim-read some parts. In summarising a book, you would probably find that chapter headings would alert you to the topics you'd need to mention. If there's a blurb on the back cover, that might help too; but beware of believing everything the publisher says. In general, you will need to be more critical and more detailed.

Before writing your summary, check the chapter headings and scan any sub-headings throughout as a further reminder and pointer to crucial areas. You are likely to need just a general grasp of what is contained. Detail won't be wanted in a summary of a long work.

SUMMARY

This chapter has covered:

writing a summary:
1 a first quick read
2 note-making
3 writing a first draft
4 checking your word-count and editing
5 writing your final draft

summarising a book:
- work on a chapter at a time
- skim-read where possible

6 Letters

INTRODUCTION

This chapter will look at the differences between formal and informal letters, at the accepted ways for setting these out in Britain, and at some of the different types of letter that you might be required to write. As well as being able to cope with an assignment that includes writing a letter, it will be important for you to know the generally accepted method of setting out a letter, especially when you apply for jobs (see chapter 16).

There's a big difference between letters and e-mails. When you send messages via computer, you omit your address and generally get straight to the main points you want to convey. Letters take things at a slower pace and have particular conventions. Phone texts, of course, are different again, keeping to the minimum number of words and even shortening the words themselves.

According to what country you live in, the school you went to, or even your age or where you've worked, there may be certain variations in how you've learnt to set out a letter. If you've worked in a business capacity, you may have been using an in-house system. There is, however, a specific layout in Britain that is generally accepted in relation to letters from private individuals, so it makes sense to follow it here.

INFORMAL LETTERS

Informal letters are often thought to be just those written to friends. It's sometimes the case, however, that letters addressed to anyone by name (rather than *Dear Sir/Madam*) are said to be informal. Both types will be looked at here. You'll find a section on *Differences* and another on *Formal letters* below. When we write to close friends, we can do exactly as we like. We can break all the rules of grammar, draw pictures and even write letters of only one or two words if we want to:

Dear Alex
Yes!
Luv,
Chris xxx

These two people clearly know each other well, so Alex will be in no doubt over what this letter means. In fact, the shortness of the letter gives impact. So with letters to friends, just continue to be yourself and don't worry about doing things right or wrong. You may find, however, that, as your skills develop, some of your letters to friends become increasingly complex. Letters can be a literary form in their own right, as is clear from the number of books published containing collections of letters.

The term *informal letters* can be rather confusing. The letter to Alex is certainly informal, but it is definitely not what tutors want to see if they ask you to write informally. In terms of your course, it's best to think of informal letters as letters that are friendly and helpful but that also adhere to the rules of grammar and letter-writing.

There are four important items that you will need to include:

- your address
- the date
- the salutation (saying *Hello*)
- the valediction (saying *Goodbye*)

If you are asked to write a letter to a friend, the layout expected is this (the blocks represent paragraphs):

[Your address]
[line space]
[Date]

Dear Bob
[line space]

[line space]

[line space]

[line space]

[line space]
Best wishes
[2 or 3 line spaces]
your first name (or nickname)

Note that, when writing a letter to a friend (even if it is for course-work), your friend's address must *not* be included. If you type or word-process, always sign your name.

You might, however, want to write to someone who is not a friend but to whom you will need to write a friendly letter. For example, you might write a letter to a local celebrity, asking if he or she would agree to open a fête or give a talk. The layout of your letter would be similar to the one to a friend except for the salutation and valediction, and the inclusion of the recipient's name and address, like this:

[Your address]
[line space]
[Date]

[Addressee's title, initial and last name]
[Address]
[line space]
Dear [Addressee's title and last name]
[line space]

[line space]

```
┌─────────────────────────────────────────────────┐
│                                                 │
│                                                 │
└─────────────────────────────────────────────────┘
```

[line space]

```
┌─────────────────────────────────────────────────┐
│                                                 │
│                                                 │
└─────────────────────────────────────────────────┘
```

[line space]
Yours sincerely
[2 line spaces]
[Your signature]
[2 line spaces]
[Your full name – in capitals if you write by hand]

There can be slight variations in the salutation. If, for example, you were to write to Robbie Williams, who is always known by his full name and would almost certainly expect you to be reasonably chatty, you'd put: *Dear Robbie Williams.* If, however, you wrote to Lord Robert Winston, the doctor who appears on TV in relation to his pioneering fertility treatments, you'd write: *Dear Lord Winston.*

When you want to be friendly, you'll include your first name in your signature as well as your last name. It's vital to print your name underneath. The person reading your letter could easily make a spelling mistake when writing back to you if there is only your signature to go on. It's also very important to use a capital *Y* for *Yours* and a small s for *sincerely.* Incidentally, notice how *sincerely* is spelt. People very often get it wrong. You might find this easier to remember if you note that the word *sincerely* contains the word *ere* (i.e. *here* without the *h*) in the middle.

You might, of course, need to write to someone in their business capacity. In this case, the *shape* of your letter will be the same as the one above, but you will always use their title rather than their first name in the salutation.

It's also important to remember that for neither of these letters do you put your name above your own address. This practice is common in some countries, and business letters in Britain nearly always have the name of the business at the top of the page, but it is not deemed to be correct for letters from private individuals. In fact, it is considered to be a mistake.

Let's suppose that you need to write to a Mr J. Fleming, the manager of Fergus Electronics, to complain about a faulty computer purchased from his company. You will set out your letter like this:

14 Lucius Street
Maxford
Nutshire
A4 7RP

15 November 2006

Mr J Fleming
Manager
Fergus Electronics
Bat Lane
Wallopford
Nutshire WP14 6RF

Dear Mr Fleming

Purchase of a fault-ridden computer

Three months ago, I took the decision to buy a new computer. I run a small translating business from my home, and increased work has meant that I need a new, up-to-date, reliable PC.

I was persuaded by your advertising, both in the local press and on television, to visit your premises for an analysis of my office needs. Once I was there, a salesman was adamant that he knew the make and model best suited to my work.

If you check your records, you will find that I have already had to return twice to have minor faults on this computer corrected. Now the machine is malfunctioning yet again.

You may imagine my anger. My business is suffering and I am losing custom. Will you please arrange to have this PC replaced with a new one without delay and inform me of the delivery date.

Yours sincerely

R. Long

ROBERT LONG

Note that, as well as using the name of the person he is writing to, Robert also includes the recipient's job title between the name and address. This is usual in business letters of any kind. The subject of the letter is given here in bold type. If you write a letter by hand, the subject must be underlined. Although he is polite here, Robert hasn't wanted to be particularly friendly in this letter so he's not included his full first name in his signature.

Two other things may have struck you in general: there are no indentations – either for paragraphs or in the lines of the addresses, and there's no punctuation in the addresses. This layout has been in use for a number of years now – especially in government offices. It's the result of research to find the simplest method of setting out letters. You might like to check the layout in any official letters that you receive. If you are not used to this, you may feel it looks a little strange, but once you start to use it, you will find that it really is very convenient, and it saves a good deal of time. Just as with an essay, leave a line between paragraphs, as it makes a letter much easier to read as well as making it look smart.

▶ Titles

There tends to be a bit of disagreement nowadays on what to do about your title (*Mrs, Mr,* and so on) at the end of a letter. If you leave it out, you may find that you don't get the right one on your reply. There are not likely to be any problems for a man with a straightforward name who generally uses the title *Mr*. If you sign yourself *John Brown,* you will get addressed as *Mr Brown*. If, however, you are a man and your name is Alex Brown, the person who writes back to you will have to guess at whether you are male or female if you omit your title. If you are the Reverend John Brown, you will not get addressed as such unless you give your title or your letter itself makes your situation obvious – that is, unless it contains such things as a reference to your parish duties.

Women may have different problems. When writing a letter to a woman whose preferred title is not known, it is usual nowadays to use *Ms*. If you sign yourself *Sally Brown,* you are likely to be addressed as either *Ms Brown* or possibly *Mrs Brown*. Government offices will call you *Ms Brown,* which is fine if you don't want to let on whether you are married or not. You'll have the best chance of getting the title you want by using it yourself, like this:

Yours sincerely
Beth Parkes
BETH PARKES (Mrs)

Put your title *after* your name, and always put it in *brackets.*

Some people, however – and perhaps it started with the ones who cut out punctuation in addresses and stopped using indentations – are now cutting out titles altogether. You may or may not like this, but it's as well to be aware of what's going on. Leaving out your own title can give the impression that you are self-confident and not bothered over minor details. Sometimes, however, you will find yourself addressed in the salutation with your full name (and no title), whatever you do.

▶ Differences between informal and formal letters

A formal letter is sometimes said to be one (like Robert Long's letter to the manager of Fergus Electronics) with the name and address of the recipient at the top left-hand side. A letter set out like that is obviously not one to a friend. Sometimes, letters are divided into informal and formal according to the salutation and valediction. A letter beginning *Dear Mrs Smith* would be said to be informal, and a letter to the same person beginning *Dear Madam* would be formal.

FORMAL LETTERS

If you have not yet read the section on informal letters, have a look at it now, as it contains a good deal of essential information on setting out all letters.

The letter to J. Fleming at Fergus Electronics begins *Dear Mr Fleming* and ends *Yours sincerely.* A classic formal letter is the one that begins either *Dear Sir* or *Dear Madam* (or *Dear Sir/Madam*) and ends with *Yours faithfully.* We generally use this form of address nowadays, however, *only* when we don't know the name of the person to whom we're writing. If you know the person's name, it's essential to use it. Then you will close with *Yours sincerely* even if the tone of your letter is very serious and formal. If you don't know the recipient's name, you'll have to put *Dear Sir/Madam* and close with *Yours faithfully.* It's

OK to put *Dear Sir* by itself *only* if you happen to know for certain that the recipient of your letter is male. If you are sure it's a woman, then you can put *Dear Madam.*

As far as the valediction is concerned, all you have to do here is to remember to use a capital *Y* for *Yours* (just as you do with *Yours sincerely*) and a small *f* for faithfully. Yes, it does all seem a bit fussy, but it's rather like knowing the accepted things to do at a wedding: everything goes more smoothly for you when you get it right.

One further bugbear can be knowing exactly who to write to. When you write a letter, you *must* address it to a particular person. This can be especially difficult when, for example, you need to write to a company and you don't know anyone's name or job title. Sometimes, I phone to check, but if I'm in a hurry, I usually write to *The Manager.* So if Robert Long didn't know the name of the manager at Fergus Electronics, he would have written a formal letter, set out like this:

14 Lucius Street
Maxford
Nutshire
A4 7RP

15 February 2006

The Manager
Fergus Electronics
Bat Lane
Wallopford
Nutshire WP14 6RF

Dear Sir/Madam

Purchase of a fault-ridden computer

Three months ago, I took the decision to buy a new computer ...

Yours faithfully

R. Long

ROBERT LONG

Robert has not put his own title (Mr) after his name. With a name like Robert, it's pretty clear that he's male, so he would get addressed as such in a return letter. It is up to the recipient to reply politely. If Robert's preferred title was different – for example, *Revd* or *Dr,* he would probably use it to make things clear.

▶ Letters of complaint

Robert Long's letter is clearly a letter of complaint. If you need to write one of these, it's important to remember to control any feelings of anger. It's a good idea, however, to be forceful. Robert stated the problem very clearly and demanded a replacement, but at no point was he abusive. It's also OK to be gently humorous, but aiming for belly laughs can suggest that you are not totally in control of your feelings or that you don't view the situation very seriously. Robert has contented himself with injecting a little mild sarcasm into the letter's heading.

E-MAIL

When using e-mail, you can omit your home address because your e-mail address comes up automatically. You won't need the recipient's home or business address either because you will have used his or her e-mail address in the relevant box. There's also a box for the subject of the e-mail, so you won't need it after the salutation. Indeed, many people omit the salutation altogether in brief or informal e-mails. Otherwise, the conventions are fairly similar to those for letters. Be chatty to friends and more formal when it's necessary. You can, however, be briefer than usual.

SUMMARY

This chapter has covered:

- letters to friends   your address – on the right
  date – underneath your address
  salutation – *Dear* [Bob]
  valediction – *Best wishes*

- polite informal   your address – on the right
  letters   date – underneath your address
  recipient's name and address – on the left
  recipient's job title, if relevant – above
     his/her address
  salutation – *Dear Mrs Jones*
  the subject of the letter (in bold type or
     underlined)
  valediction – *Yours sincerely*
  your name in capitals underneath your
     signature (with your preferred title in
     brackets afterwards)

- formal letters   your address – on the right
  date – underneath your address
  recipient's name, job title and address – on
     the left
  salutation – *Dear Sir/Madam*
  the subject of the letter underlined
  valediction – *Yours faithfully*
  your name underneath your signature (with
     your preferred title in brackets afterwards)

- e-mail

7 Creative Writing

INTRODUCTION

Many courses now include assignments in which there is a creative writing component. There are a number of reasons for this. It's now widely acknowledged that developing your imagination is important for developing your intellect, and that practice in structuring a piece of creative work is valuable groundwork for structuring essays. Creative writing exercises are also sometimes used to enable students to look at topics on a syllabus from new angles and so to become more familiar with the topics themselves. So you may be asked to do some autobiographical work or to write a poem, story or letter connected with the subject you are studying.

Autobiographical work is not set because the tutors want to pry into students' past lives. It has been found that taking a serious look at certain aspects of our past gives us a very good foundation for further study. We learn to situate our own experience within a wider context, and doing this helps us to assess issues more objectively. I'd like to reassure you at once that private issues that you want to keep private can stay that way. There will be plenty left that you are quite happy to write about, and you are likely to be given a pretty free hand over what you decide to work on.

Have you ever wondered why most of us were asked to write poems at school? It's easy to think of poetry-writing as a way of keeping children quiet for half an hour, but there are more important reasons than this for having poetry on the curriculum. Writing a poem on an event, scene, or something about which we feel strongly forces our brains to perform new tricks. Just as with autobiographical work, our writing skills and imagination come into play but in slightly different ways. Poetry-writing can be especially valuable for getting practice in writing succinctly and for thinking hard about expressing meaning accurately.

One of the reasons for being asked to write a short story is that doing this gives useful practice in structuring a piece of work. You'll need to spend time thinking about how to introduce your characters and get them interacting (the beginning), you will need to keep the plot going throughout the story (the middle), and you'll have to bring everything to a believable conclusion, with the loose ends neatly tied up (the end).This is valuable practice for essay-writing and for logical thinking.

AUTOBIOGRAPHICAL WRITING

Autobiographical work is particularly useful for forcing us to consider the differences between a personal (and often emotional) response to people and events and a more logical, detached approach. You are bound to have a degree of choice over what you write and there are sure to be some items in the following list that you'd be comfortable with:

▶ Ideas for autobiographical writing

pre-school education	school trips
evening classes	clothing
Sunday School	museums and galleries
games	money
life-changing events	primary school
secondary school	hobbies
teachers	school buildings
toys	transport
grandparents	father
rules and regulations	jobs
furniture	hospital, doctors and health
religious observation	wearing uniform
birthdays and anniversaries	sports
having children	household items and gadgets
popular music	clubs and societies
politics	mother
marriage	wider family
festivals/rituals	national events
the 1970s (or other decade)	arts and crafts

For autobiographical work, you will almost certainly be asked to tell it how it was, and then to reflect on what happened and add some comment. If you have painful memories, this kind of exercise can sometimes be a way to exorcise things and to put them in perspective. It's often by revisiting the past that we can prepare for the future. If you have time to do some really serious work on your autobiography, you are likely to find that it is an extremely worthwhile and rewarding exercise.

Writing autobiography can also develop your skills with language. In order to write about the past, we need to recall scenes and events. In transferring these memories to a written account, we have to select and describe what we record. As we struggle to do this, we are getting good practice in developing our skills with language. There is one area that your tutors may be particularly keen for you to explore, and that is your educational experience. They won't want to know about failures and expulsion from school (unless you want to focus on harsh things), but they may well want you to look at:

- what you were taught (or not)
- how classes were organised
- what the buildings were like
- what types of school you attended
- what the staff were like
- what you enjoyed/hated

They'll want to know how these things affected you at the time and how you view them in retrospect and in relation to what you now know of the rest of society. So you can see that *both* emotion and logic are vital here. It can also be very illuminating to relate our own experiences to the national situation.

▶ Digging into your memory

You may now be thinking, "Well, OK, I'm not totally against doing this, but I just can't remember anything." If so, I sympathise. There are ways, however, of overcoming this kind of mental block. Try a small experiment now. Look at the lists below and, without stopping to think too hard, pick one item, take a sheet of notepaper, and, before reading any further, quickly do a mind map on it. (For an explanation of mind-mapping, see chapters 1 and 2 .)

teachers	sports	art	money
meals	lessons	music	discipline
friends	buildings	drama	assembly
prefects	prizes	poetry	uniform
books	pictures	break times	festivals

You are likely to find that one memory will lead to another. But it's often only by actually sitting down and writing that these memories flow.

A slightly different way of getting yourself started is to construct a lifeline. Many students find this particularly helpful. For this you will probably need several sheets of A4 paper laid end to end on their sides (landscape) and taped together. Part of a roll of wallpaper would also work; but if you use this, you may need to write on it with a soft crayon rather than a pen or pencil in order to avoid tearing it.

At the left-hand side, put the date you were born, and on the right put 'NOW'. Mark the whole sheet off in decades, and then begin to fill in key dates: starting school, moving house, starting work, meeting a partner, and so on. Putting in the obvious things will cause your mind to focus more clearly. You will begin to remember things you thought you'd forgotten. This method is particularly helpful for getting an overall view of your experiences.

Another useful thing to do can be to start digging out actual items that relate to your past educational experiences. You could look for:

photos	diaries	scrapbooks
school reports	cups or certificates	newspaper cuttings
badges	letters	exercise books

Then you might start talking to relatives and friends, asking them specific questions and encouraging them to dip into their own memories for you. If you live near one of your old schools, you might visit it. If it's in another part of the country, you could write to the head teacher. There are likely to be photos and pamphlets that you could get copies of. There's always material available somewhere. Even if your old school has been razed to the ground, there are still likely to be records in the local education department and reference library. Try the internet as well. Information you locate on your searches may well be useful later for your CV. Once you get going on this project, you are more likely to be swamped with material than to be short of it, and your problem will not be wondering what to write but deciding what to omit.

▶ Relevance to academic study

You may be beginning to see that autobiographical work develops more than your literary skills. It's inevitable that you will be doing work related to both sociology and history. For example, anything you write on festivals and rituals or on clubs and societies will be relevant to social studies. You'll get good practice here in giving accurate descriptions. In historical terms, all those photos, diaries and school badges from the past are called **primary sources**. These are things that originated in the period you are looking at. Any school records you can manage to get hold of are also primary sources. If you still possess a school project on your local town or village that you put together, say, in the 1980s, you have another primary source. If you're really keen, you could also go and look at education acts and other legal documents. All these are primary sources too.

A **secondary source** looks back at what happened and comments on it. This is what historians do all the time, and it's what you will be doing too. A secondary source is usually written some time *after* events take place.

Once you begin to relate your own experiences to the experiences of others and to national events, your work will become more and more interesting. What you write will, inevitably, depend on the structure or title you've been given by your tutor; but whatever you do, you are bound to end up with a valuable perspective on certain issues from the past.

▶ Structuring your autobiographical project

The important thing here is to have a plan (see chapter 2). It's very easy to get so immersed in reminiscences that you end up forgetting the reason for doing this piece of work. Your tutor will almost certainly give you very clear guidelines. If not, check on exactly what is wanted.

You might refer to events chronologically, or you might section your material by topic. If you make a good plan, you will be able to keep focused and prevent yourself from putting in information that's not related to the assignment you've been set. Your plan needs to be logical and easy for a reader to follow.

POETRY

If you were asked to write an account of a particular poem in prose, you would probably find yourself writing something quite a lot longer than the poem itself. We can say that poets nearly always *condense* what they want to tell us. So if you've been asked to write a poem, one of the things you'll be practising is the art of getting your ideas across in a few words.

You probably know the old saying that a picture is worth a thousand words. Well, poems very often contain a lot of pictures – or **images**. The poet uses his or her imagination to come up with images that will spark a reader's imagination and so help that reader to understand what the poet is thinking and feeling. Using the imagination is a very valuable activity for developing brainpower. A brain that is used only for facts and figures is likely to function less well than one that is also used for making new and unusual connections between different topics and ideas. You may have noticed that some of your best ideas for assignments seem to come to you 'out of the blue'. This is just one example of your brain working in an apparently non-logical fashion.

One of the best ways to get yourself going on writing poems is to read some poetry. You might get a couple of books out of the library. If you are not used to reading poetry, don't feel you have to read from cover to cover. Just flick through and read whatever takes your fancy. Or you might pop into a large bookshop where you can browse for ages without being pressured to buy anything.

It is sometimes thought that poetry comes wholly from the imagination, but this is rarely the case. A good poem is usually rooted firmly in facts. Notice how, in the following poem by Carol Ann Duffy, much of the emotion is evoked through the speaker's response to everyday items in their relation to the beloved:

Tea

I like pouring your tea, lifting
the heavy pot, and tipping it up,
so the fragrant liquid steams in your china cup.

Or when you're away, or at work,
I like to think of your cupped hands as you sip,
as you sip, of the faint half-smile of your lips.

I like the questions – sugar? milk? –
and the answers I don't know by heart, yet,
for I see your soul in your eyes, and I forget.

Jasmine, Gunpowder, Assam, Earl Grey, Ceylon,
I love tea's names. Which tea would you like? I say,
but it's any tea, for you, please, any time of day,

as the women harvest the slopes,
for the sweetest leaves, on Mount Wu-Yi,
and I am your lover, smitten, straining your tea.

Poems are as different as the people who write them, and they can be on any topic under the sun. So don't feel that your poems have to conform to some set format. As the writer, you can structure your poem in whatever way you feel gets the sense across best.

I'd suggest that you give yourself two rules: no rhyme and no humour. Writing good rhyme is a skill that can be hard to learn, but writing poor rhyme is relatively easy. If you go for rhyme at this stage, what is likely to happen is that you might do it at the expense of thought and emotion. It is fatally easy to focus on finding a rhyme for a word you've just written, and consequently to lose track of depth of meaning. Humour can function in a similar way. The joke becomes more important than the meaning of the poem.

It would be a good idea now to choose a scene that you'd like to use for writing a poem. It can be useful to choose somewhere that you can go and have a look at before you start to write. If you have to work from memory, however, try closing your eyes and visualising the scene. The poem by Diana, below, relied on her memories of the past.

You might want to have a broad picture: a park, a townscape, a beach, a railway station, a mountain view or a market. On the other hand, you might like to go for a smaller picture: one building, or a single flower-bed, perhaps. The only important thing is that you need to be really interested in your subject. You will write more convincingly about a junkyard than a palace if you are fascinated by junk.

When you get a moment, go to your chosen place with a notebook and spend some time jotting down notes on whatever you find there. You are going to practise clear recording of your observations; this skill is crucial whatever you are studying. You will need to focus on things like objects, shapes, colours, textures, light, sound and movement. If there are people around, you'll need to look at their clothing and body language. Maybe one or two people stand out. Your task is to provide yourself with plenty of data. When you go home and begin to write, you will need to have enough facts to choose from in order to make your poem truthful and precise.

When you come to start writing your poem, try to make sure that you won't be disturbed. The imagination doesn't take kindly to being inter-rupted, so you may need to wait until everyone has gone to bed. Alternatively, you may find that getting up early is the answer. Start by looking through your notes. You will not want to use everything you have written down. If you did that, the resulting poem would sound more like a police report of a crime scene. Pick out things that espe-cially interest you or that seem in some way to portray the atmosphere of the scene, and, at this stage, allow your feelings to be fully involved.

The next stage is a little bit magical. Just sit quietly, mull over your notes, reimagine the scene, and then see what turns up. What goes on in the brain at this point is something about which we know little and certainly have very little control. You might like to close your eyes; you might prefer to stare out of the window. You might then find that two or three quite separate phrases occur to you, or that you start to describe one particular item. Whatever comes, write it down straight away. If by any chance you are stuck, start to describe something anyway, using your notes to help you. But don't worry if your work looks very disjointed at this stage. You can tidy things up later.

It's a good idea to aim to write a poem of between twelve and twenty lines. You might like to arrange it in from three to five verses (or **stanzas**). This will give you enough space to create a strong picture while still making sure that you condense your ideas. When you have written as much as you can, put the whole thing away for a day or so. You might very well find that other ideas now start to suggest them-selves – usually at very inconvenient times. So if you can have a jotter handy wherever you go, you'll be able to record ideas that would other-wise almost certainly be lost. My first poem began unannounced while I was cleaning the bathroom. When you go back to your poem, you might find that you want to move things around a bit, take things out, or add new ideas.

The final stage is editing, and for this you need to use all your know-ledge of grammar and punctuation to make the poem sharp and easily understood. One of the myths about poetry is that you can put anything down and that you don't have to write fully functioning sentences. Only experienced poets can get away with this kind of thing, and when they do it, they do it for particular reasons. They are unlikely to do it very often. The process of editing can be tricky, but it's all part of the fun, and it will do wonders for your language skills.

Here's an example of a student poem. It's followed by the first draft (there were others too) and the background notes that were made before starting on the poem itself.

The Solitary Summer

Excitement and anxiety gripped me,
"Just five turns in the lane and we'll be there."
Nature itself appeared to herald us, the flowers
swaying in the breeze like hands waving, the summer sun
bright and the sky as enticing as the sea on a hot day.
– Only I saw clouds on the horizon.

They waited to greet us as we arrived.
Him, imposing but smiling, and her, ever ready with hugs for all.
The cottage, like a scene from a picture postcard,
was before us. Its stout wooden door was
framed by honeysuckle, whose aromatic scent,
although admired by the others, invaded my nostrils.

Then they were gone, and we three were left,
to be looked after and loved by those, not our parents.
"They're together, that's the main thing," I'd heard them say,
but the three of us weren't together, only two,
and all I saw of them were their backs,
as we biked, climbed, or picnicked, "together".

Their time was spent on exciting adventures.
While mine was spent with she who hugged.
Our place was the kitchen all homely and warm, with its big
wooden table, and shelf upon shelf of herbs, spices, pickles, and
jams, and the big miracle milk pan which changed milk to cream.
There, without the two, I was happy, contented.

Have a look back at the imagery in this poem. It focuses on the natural world and on items in the kitchen. Here, the writer seems to have given a straight list in order to create atmosphere, but we can see from her notes that she chose carefully what to include.

First draft

Summer on the Farm

Just five turns in the lane and we'll be there,
Excitement and worry gripped me.
The blue sky had a few dark clouds on the horizon,
All we saw seemed to welcome us/the bright summer sun
The flowers waved their heads as hands saying hello
– flowers waving their heads as hands saying hello
The smell of fresh bread and cooking apples
filled the air of the old farmhouse.

Simba yelped and danced around us in delight
Big smiles from him and big hugs from her
The kitchen, its big wooden table,
shelves of herbs and spices.
Its big miracle milk pan which turned milk to cream,

the clear blue sky,
– only I saw those grey clouds on the horizon.

The almost clear blue sky except for
the hint of something threatening.

And now, luxury flats and an old people's home
remain – and memories.

▶ **Background notes**

smells
bread, apples, stewing, baking
mothballs, summer
cow dung, cut grass/hedges
lily of the valley

sounds
birds, cows, horses
tractors, Simba barking
TV, bees in long grass meadow
G & Gdad talking, cockerel
P & S laughing

inside sights
big wooden table

outside sights
large trees towering over me

high beds in my room	gates, fields
large silvery milk pan	barns, animals, tractors
row upon row of jam jars full	backs of P & S in distance
of jam, pickles & marmalade	chickens

<u>feelings being there</u>
love for Gran
adventure, being on holiday
loneliness, spending much time on my own
missing home & parents
dislike for P & S for always leaving me

In this poem, the pain of the writer's isolation from her siblings is contrasted with the beauty of their surroundings at the grandparents' home. The reason for the trip is not made clear, and it hovers with some menace in the background in the words

"They're together, that's the main thing,"

We realise from this that there has been a crisis. The fact that the writer doesn't say exactly what it was actually makes the poem stronger. Notice how the omission of the word *threatening* from the final draft also seems to strengthen the sense of menace. Omission of the final two lines from the first draft helps to keep our attention focused on the childhood experience.

SHORT STORIES

Adults often respond with shock horror to the request that they write a story, saying that they've not done that since they were at school. You can view it quite differently, however, by saying, "Well, if I could do this at the age of 8, I'll be able to do it a lot better now." Your experience of life and, particularly, of people is vast compared to that of an 8-year-old.

Character work will develop your skills of understanding and analysis, and writing the story will develop your language skills and ability to structure a piece of writing. Since your imagination is crucial for each stage, you'll be developing that too, and if you've read the introduction to this chapter, you already know the value of the imagination.

So if you're feeling at all negative about this process, you might remind yourself how much can be gained from it.

▶ Choosing your theme

You might start by recalling stories you've read and considering which ones you've especially liked. Why do certain things grab you? Is it because a plot is well constructed? Or perhaps you are fascinated by certain characters and by how people act and react. Or maybe you love good, sharp descriptions. You may be drawn to a particular type (**genre**) of fiction – historical, crime, or adventure, perhaps. Think for a minute about what you've really enjoyed.

Your tutor will be looking for a good structure (beginning, middle and end), believable characters, descriptions that make the story come alive, and language that fits your particular topic and situation. You need to focus, therefore, on providing these things. That will probably mean steering clear of the following: personal hobby-horses, politics, sex and/or violence, horror, humour, science fiction and dreams (which are usually the ultimate cop-out).

Now you're probably wondering if there's anything left. In a nutshell, what you want is some fairly simple interaction between two or three people, at least one of whom is changed – at least in some small way – by the events that you recount.

The crux of a good short story is **conflict**. Readers are interested in problems and difficulties. You don't need civil strife, but you do need to show human beings struggling with some kind of difficult situation. One of the best student stories I ever read was about a tramp living rough in a local park. A teenage girl tries, briefly, to offer him some kindness, and her boyfriend turns nasty about it. That's all. But I've always remembered this story for its sensitivity and the way in which each character came alive through brief snatches of conversation.

Your theme is the general idea that your story is based around – for example,

- money is the root of all evil
- progress can entail loss
- we cannot fully know the mind of another person
- love and loss
- romance

▶ Plot

Your plot is the particular series of events that you use to develop your theme. If you think back to any good story you've read, you'll realise that there must be an awful lot left out. If a guy goes shark fishing, for example, we don't want to know that on the previous day he washed his socks, sent his aunt a birthday card and had a bit of indigestion. What you need are key incidents that will demonstrate character and advance the plot. If your man is to encounter danger, you can begin to indicate what's likely to happen by showing him preparing his boat and being meticulous – or negligent. If your theme is, for example, lost love, you might have the following plot:

> A loves B
> B meets C and falls in love
> A is desolate

If your theme is the good (or bad) marriage, your plot might look like this:

> The Smiths move to a new home
> Mrs Smith hates the area
> They argue and problems in the marriage are revealed
> They separate/are reconciled/fight/go into counselling/whatever you like

And here are about a hundred and twenty-five other plots:

A wants to	change jobs
	get married
	buy a particular home/car
	emigrate
	save/spend
	etc., etc.
A is blocked by	B
	lack of money
	health
	B and C
	age
	time
	etc., etc.

The outcome is that A   wins through
finds a new way
commits suicide
enlists the help of D
accepts the situation
cheers up
gets angry
etc., etc.

Here are some tips on how to cope with plot outlines:

1 Lost love
Here you could keep the story short by showing just one encounter between each of the couples and giving some narrative in between. You'd need to show only one key point in the relationship between B and C for readers to cotton on.

2 The good/bad marriage
It's not necessary to describe the move. You could refer to it neatly in one sentence:

> Three months after the move to Suffolk, the Smiths' hall was still blocked with boxes.

Then you need one argument followed by its result. You don't need to accompany the couple the whole way to their changed existence.

3 Other possibilities
You can take any one person and put him or her in whatever situation you like – as long as it's believable. Choose just the key points in the episode you want to cover, add some description, a snatch or two of conversation, and you've created a human drama. You can focus on two or three events that would encapsulate the whole story. Go for highlights rather than a moment-by-moment account.

▶ Writing about what you know

This is valuable advice that is given to all new writers. If you were writing about the Smiths and their marriage problems, stick to describing the kind of people and living quarters that you have personal experience of. You will be convincing on what you know about – whether it's poverty, dog-racing or the Women's Institute.

▶ Descriptions

If you've worked through the section on poetry, you know what to do here. If your story is set in the local bus station, get along there and make some notes. You might get something like this:

> yellowing paint – peeling near seats
> concrete – hard, cold
> queues/crush of people
> lines of bus stops/ buses – red & white/coaches
> wind
> café – plastic cups
> information boards – small print
> inspector – peaked cap – holding small board
> sound – voices/ brakes/engines running
> child in pushchair – asleep
> smell of diesel

You might only use two or three items from your list when you come to write, but having plenty to choose from makes things much easier, and becoming fully aware of the place will ultimately give strength to your writing. A good way of adding description to your story is to slip some in every now and then rather than adding a whole chunk in one go. Your story might be about a couple who were once lovers and who meet by chance, after many years, while changing buses on long-distance journeys. Notice which items from the above list I've used in an opening paragraph for this story:

> The wind seemed to be blowing all the way from the Russian steppes. Pete held the plastic cup close to his chest, warming his fingers on the heat from the hot coffee. Suddenly he saw her – or thought he did. He caught sight of the auburn hair and the angular stance. Then a crush of people surging forward to the London coach got in the way. He grabbed his holdall and started round the back of the queue in a rush, slopped coffee burning his skin.

You can begin to see what the bus station is like from brief details. It's cold, windy and busy. You don't need to include a whole paragraph of description. That would slow things down. Incidentally, bus and train stations are very useful places for setting stories because people are there for just short periods and their emotions are often heightened as they meet, say goodbye or have arguments in the stresses and strains of travelling. There's also plenty to describe, such as cafés, news-stands, vehicles, architecture, other travellers, and so on.

▶ Characterisation

If you need a couple of characters and you've got a mental block, try looking in the local bus station. Or go into a pub or restaurant where you can sit and watch people unobtrusively. Alternatively, just go for a walk to your local shops. People are everywhere.

You will need some descriptions of clothes, expressions, movement, and so on. Make a list, just as I did for the bus station. Then use individual items from this list at relevant points. If I want to describe a young woman begging, I might note:

> bedraggled hair
> old brown wool coat that hangs loosely – like a sack
> trousers tucked into very worn black boots
> thin dog on a blanket
> knitted hat – rainbow colours
> thin fingers
> pallid skin
> hunched sitting position

I might decide to write a story about a successful banker who is offended by the sight of beggars. The story could show how one day his viewpoint shifts. I could begin like this:

> Martin habitually rose early. He parked his car in the Home Counties, read *The Times* in First-Class peace on the train, and walked from Waterloo Station to his office in the Strand to improve his health. He was in the habit of keeping his mind on pleasant thoughts while travelling. He often smiled at the occasional beggars on Waterloo Bridge to demonstrate to them that a better world lay within reach if only they would open their eyes to it.

Why he looked more closely at Carla he was never quite sure. Maybe the bright rainbow colours of her knitted hat reminded him of his younger sister in childhood. Perhaps it was those blue eyes staring from the pallid face like a saint in a Renaissance painting. Or maybe the long, slim fingers that stroked the half-starved dog made him think of his mother. Whatever it was that had arrested him, Martin's defences had been breached.

Carla had learnt to spot indecision. Her voice was thin but her stare acted on Martin like a tap on the shoulder from the Almighty. Without shifting from her hunched position, she asked,

"Spare something for a hot meal, sir?"

You can see again that I've not given a straight description, but have started to weave items from my list into the plot as it moves along. I need only the briefest snatches of conversation to make the characters come alive.

▶ Speech

In creative writing, we can develop character through speech to build up a picture of an individual. We have to make a character sound 'real'. So we need to choose speech that is appropriate for the type of person who is speaking and for the situation in which we have put him or her.

There are two key points to writing dialogue in a short story:

- Make it real. Real people don't often speak in carefully thought-out sentences.
- Give only the important bits.

What you want is to get the *feel* of your character on the page. The following examples will explain what I mean:

(a) "I've had enough. I can't stand it. I'm going."

This is a character in some kind of difficulty. Notice how the short sentences demonstrate frustration followed by decision. The repetition of the word 'I' puts the focus on the view from one person's angle.

(b) "Puss, puss, puss. Who's a lovely pussy-cat, then?"

This language is gentle and very simple. If your story is about a lonely person, you might underline the loneliness by demonstrating love for an animal. If those were the only words your character spoke in the whole story, this could demonstrate how he or she is cut off from society.

(c) "Where's Darren?"
"He had to go early. He sees his mother Sundays."

In this story by a student, we see a girl trying to cover up the real reason her boyfriend has departed. Look carefully at the wording. If the writer had been aiming to write grammatically, that last sentence would be likely to read,

"He always sees his mother on Sundays."

In each case above, just the key points in conversation are used. You seldom need to write much speech. You just need enough to give a flavour of a character and to heighten the reader's awareness of tensions in a particular situation. Listen to people shopping, or having an argument, or talking on the phone. You'll notice that we often speak in short bursts and frequently break off quite suddenly.

Who says what

There's nothing worse than an account which keeps repeating *he said* or *she said*. In a story in which you have two speakers in dialogue, that kind of boring repetition can be avoided quite easily, as you will see in the exchange between Jim and Dick below:

"Give me the loot, Jim." Dick held out his hand.
"What for?"
"Just hand it over and I'll stash it away." It was getting late, and Dick was beginning to get angry.
"I'm not sure," said Jim slowly, "that I like the arrangements."
"You flippin' idiot! Either we stash it or we're done for!"

The words *Dick held out his hand*, in the brief exchange above, let the reader know, without using that worn-out old phrase, *he said*, that it is Dick who is speaking. It's obvious, since he spoke to Jim, that it is Jim who replies. So I didn't need to put *said Jim*. Another comment on Dick's behaviour – that he was getting *angry* – again shows clearly who is speaking. The word *said* occurs once only, and, because of the build-up, it's clear that it is Dick who loses his temper in the end.

Another useful way of steering clear of repetition and keeping your reader awake is to use words that are more specific than said. In certain circumstances, you might find something that fits just right from the following list:

replied
shouted
whispered
giggled
moaned
snorted
spat
cooed

You can find lots more. Don't overdo the variations, however. Too much change can look contrived. But the occasional new word can be wonderfully evocative of a particular character.

▶ The beginning

Don't spend a page recounting your characters' past lives. Remember, this is a short story, not a novel. There isn't time for long explanations. Get stuck into the action straight away. I had Peter rushing after his lost love in my first paragraph (above) and Carla accosting Martin in my third. Get the characters interacting and they'll start to reveal themselves. If there's something that you *must* explain, do it as the plot moves along – as I did with my descriptions of the bus station and of Carla's appearance.

▶ The end

This is merely the ending of the story – not a summing-up of the characters' whole lives. What you need here is a resolution of whatever issues you've raised. That just means that a reader needs to know what has changed for at least one of your characters. In the story of Martin and Carla, this could be a new understanding for Martin and a consequent change in some of his behaviour. It's as well, in a short story, to stick to small changes. Readers are likely to find wholesale change unbelievable.

By the way, if you feel you absolutely must put your characters on a spaceship or in some other imaginary situation, just be sure to follow the basic rules for short-story writing. Remember that you'll have been given a creative writing assignment to practise your use of structure and expression: you'll be wanting a good mark.

SUMMARY

This chapter has covered:

- **autobiography** your memory
  sources
  planning

- **poetry** using the imagination
  observation and note-making
  drafting

- **short stories** theme
  plot
  description
  characterisation
  speech
  beginnings
  endings

8 Reports

INTRODUCTION

Report-writing involves the gathering of information, often for the purpose of discussion. This discussion is often intended to lead to a change in the way something is done. You are likely to have to write reports if you are studying a science subject, business, technology or social studies. The requirements for particular areas may be quite different, and it will be very important that you check out with your tutor exactly what is required for the particular task you've been given. In the world of work, things are different again. Some employers are happy with a restricted format. Once you are clued-up on the general nature of a report, however, it will be relatively easy to adjust to whatever is wanted.

The first section, 'Preparation', shows you how to prepare to write a report. This is followed by a guide to the items you will need to include if you are required to produce a full and comprehensive report, and then by an example of a student report. This is followed by an explanation of the type of language required (which can be rather different from that used for essays).

If you have been asked to write a report on an experiment that you've already conducted, you will already have most of the data you need, so turn straight to 'Structure'. Generally, however, writing a report is likely to entail a good deal more legwork than writing an essay. Here you will be fact-finding rather than amassing critical information. You may have less to worry about in terms of understanding complex concepts, but you are likely to need to cover more ground.

Once you've got the hang of it, writing reports is not difficult, but people often find it confusing at first. So it would be a good idea to read right through this chapter before beginning any work for your report. This will ensure that you have an overall grasp of the method before you start to work out what goes where. The examples here are straightforward. With a little practice, you will be able to produce more sophisticated work.

PREPARATION

The instructions you are given for writing a report may be quite lengthy. You are also likely to be given extra instructions and explanations verbally. If you happen to miss an introductory session, it's worth tracking down your tutor to check things out. When everyone is new to report-writing, it can be risky to rely on instructions relayed from another student because there is a great deal to remember. You don't want to incorporate someone else's confusion into your work.

It's a good idea to begin any piece of work with a mind map to get your ideas flowing (see the section on mind maps in chapter 2). Let's suppose that you've been asked to write a report on the value of the Castle Centre – a new local centre for adults with learning difficulties. Your mind map might look something like this:

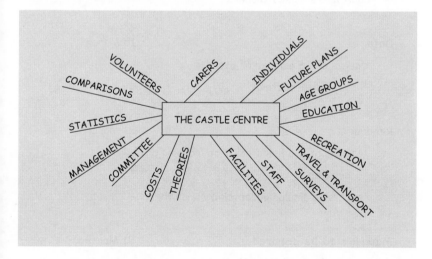

At this point, you need to work out an action plan showing all the things you need to do. If you've worked in commerce or industry, you may be thoroughly familiar with action plans. Let's suppose you need to have your report in by 20 April and it's now early February. You might decide to plan your work as in the action plan shown below.

ACTION PLAN

TASK	DATE FOR COMPLETION

Interviews   28 February

    manager

    users

    health worker

    education worker

    carers/family members

    voluntary workers

Questionnaires   15 March

    staff – views/practice

    adult users – likes/dislikes

Data   15 March

    figures on   – number of users

             – costings

Reading   31 March

    sections of academic texts on learning disability

        articles

    reports on similar undertakings elsewhere

Materials to be acquired   31 March

    copies of committee minutes

    photographs of building & site plan

    initial surveys of need in the area

    copies of newspaper reports

▶ Organising your materials

Keeping your notes and other materials well organised will be really valuable for the writing stage. Any or all of the following can be useful for recording your findings:

- loose-leaf paper
- cards (sorted alphabetically by topic)
- computer disks
- audiotapes

Devise a method of sorting at the outset, and you'll save yourself hours of trouble later. A4 sheets can be kept in separate sections in ring binders, folders or old A4 envelopes; cards need a box; and disks and tapes need to be clearly labelled. A note on each item of what else it relates to – cross-referencing – will keep you on top of things.

While you are collecting your materials, it's best to ignore all the different headings of a report. The mind can't cope with several new processes at the same time. You'll be ready to think about the structure of the report when you've completed the fact-finding.

▶ The structure of a report

What follows is an explanation of each section of a traditional report. You may find that you are given an assignment which requires only *a few* of these sections; or you may find that you are given some headings that are slightly different from what you will see below.

In essence, any report will contain the following:

- a brief note on what's in it – the *Abstract*
- an explanation of why and how it was set up and how you went about it – *Terms of reference* and *Procedure*
- a description of the things you found out – *Findings*
- an analysis of what you found out – *Conclusions*
- your suggestions for how things might be improved in the future – *Recommendations*

One of the keys to good report-writing is clear separation of those last three sections – description, analysis and suggestions.

The sections of a full-blooded report are as follows:

Title-page
Abstract (sometimes called the 'Summary')
Contents
Terms of reference
Procedure (sometimes called 'Method')
Findings
Conclusions
Recommendations
Glossary
References
Bibliography
Appendices
Illustrations
Index

Don't worry. Everyone who is new to this finds it pretty mind-boggling. The system is very logical, however; and once you've completed your first effort, you'll have little difficulty with reports in the future. The following is an explanation of each section.

▶ Title-page

This is a separate page containing just three things:

- the title or subject of the report
- the author's name
- the date the written report was completed

▶ Abstract

This is a *very brief* summary of what is contained in the report. It will usually be no longer than one paragraph. An **abstract** is crucial for giving information. It enables anyone to find out, without having to plough through the whole thing, whether or not the report is applicable to his or her field of work and therefore worth reading.

For example, imagine that you are a solicitor dealing with a client who is claiming that she was unfairly made redundant from her job with a large company. You want to find out something about that company's staffing policy, and you have managed to get hold of two reports. The titles of both are 'Staffing'. They are written by different authors on different dates. You turn to the page in the first that is labelled 'Abstract'. Here you find that this report describes a survey that catalogued numbers of employees by job title and geographical location. You look at the abstract for the second report and find that this one deals with revised staffing policy and redundancies. Clearly, this is the one you want to read.

An **abstract** is always written *after* the main body of the report has been completed. You won't be sure exactly what should go in your **abstract** until you've set out your **findings**, **conclusions** and **recommendations**.

► Contents

You will include this section only for reports that have a great many subsections. It is just a list of headings with appropriate page numbers. Its purpose is to make it easy for a reader to refer to separate items. The section on **findings**, for example, may have a number of subsections, each on a slightly different topic. The **contents** enable anyone to turn directly to what he or she needs to read. This section should also contain a list of any illustrations, photographs, tables and graphs, with relevant page numbers.

► Terms of reference

In just a few lines, you will explain here the reason why the report was undertaken, who asked for it, and any guidelines that were given for conducting it. This can all seem like stating the obvious, but remember that the person who reads a report may know absolutely nothing of how it came to be written.

It can be very useful to know whether a report was put together by an unbiased outsider or someone connected directly with the items covered. Knowing the reason why a report was written can also give readers valuable insight on the situation; and knowing the guidelines for gathering data will also help people to assess whether the report is likely to contain material relevant to their particular interests. It's sometimes helpful to pretend, when writing all these sections, that you work for the police and that every tiny piece of information must be recorded.

▶ Procedure

Here you explain how you went about gathering the information – who you interviewed and why, what types of question you asked, what you decided to include or exclude, and the places from which information was gathered. Somebody glancing at your report might decide whether to read further solely on the basis of what you say here.

▶ Findings

This is likely to be your longest section. It will contain everything you have found out – everything, that is, specifically related to the task you've been given. Your **findings** will be what you have seen, heard and read (and sometimes even what you have smelt and touched). As with an essay, however, you must leave out anything that doesn't really fit the criteria that were set for the report.

Unlike essays, however, reports benefit from being split up into sections. You do not need to worry about links here as you would in an essay; your task is just to make things crystal clear. So headings and subheadings will be valuable tools in making your work clear and easily readable.

It's crucial to remember that this section must contain *nothing* of your own ideas or opinions. Here you must act like a robot and record things exactly as you have found them. Your task is to describe very clearly what you have found out *without* commenting on any of it.

Your **findings** are likely to contain *some* of the following:

- information from any source you've consulted
- numerical data or results from questionnaires, experiments, published statistics, etc.
- details from letters and/or interviews, together with quotes

Numbering can be an important aid to organizing your information. If I were writing up my report on the Castle Centre, my **findings** might fall into four main categories:

1 views of users
2 views of staff
3 activities provided
4 other centres

Each of these sections would be likely to have subsections, and these subsections might themselves have further subdivisions. Good headings and a clear system of numbering will keep sections clearly organised and easy to read. The structure of my **findings** might be something like this:

1   <u>Views of users</u>
    1.1 results of questionnaire
    1.2 information from interviews
    1.3 information from carers

2   <u>Views of staff</u>
    2.1 salaried staff on site
        2.1.1 manager
        2.1.2 other site staff
    2.2 visiting health workers

3   <u>Activities provided</u>
    3.1 vocational & educational classes
    3.2 leisure classes
    3.3 figures on attendance

4   <u>Other centres</u>
    4.1 The Oak Tree Community Group
    4.2 The Sharp Centre
        4.2.1 mission statement
        4.2.2 summary of first annual report

▶ Conclusions

This section will, in some ways, be similar to the end of an essay. Here you look at the facts you've found and weigh up what they mean and what consequences are likely to follow from them. You must be totally ruthless with yourself here and continue to keep to yourself your own opinion on what changes should be made.

In essence, your conclusions will say something like:

The findings demonstrate that:

    a is the case
    b is the case

      c is the case
      d may occur

If it seems helpful, you can re-use here the headings you've used in your **findings**. My **conclusions** on the Castle Centre – given here briefly – might look something like this:

1 <u>Views of users</u>
The Centre is, in most respects, coming up to expectations. Responses on questionnaires to users showed an 87% satisfaction rate and responses from carers and families seem to back up this evidence of quality provision. Information from interviews was also extremely positive.

2 <u>Views of staff</u>
These are also positive in the main. The views of visiting health workers are broadly similar to those of the manager. Views of other site staff give insight into areas such as the provision of lunches and other refreshments. Certain issues here could lead to dissatisfaction if not addressed.

3 <u>Activities provided</u>
Weekly timetables demonstrate a wide variety of facilities for users. The lack of take-up on some opportunities might seem to be a result of over-provision. Figures on attendance at vocational classes, however, showed a high take-up. Sports activities achieved a lower score in most cases.

4 <u>Other centres</u>
The Castle Centre has had the benefit of both Lottery funding and the consequent design by prizewinning architects. Its facilities are of a far higher standard than those of the Oak Tree Community Group. The Sharp Centre, however, also has first-class premises and has been able to develop a particularly good system of client care.

▶ Recommendations

Ah, at last. It is here – and only here – that you can finally say something of what you think should be done about the situation. This is where you make suggestions on how you think things might be changed for the future. You will be focusing on making *improvements.* There is still one constraint, however. Your views *must* be based clearly on your **findings** themselves.

Here are my **recommendations** for the Castle Centre:

- Discuss wider choice of lunches with caterers.
- Set up a user group to provide feedback on curriculum.
- Reconsider policy on sports activities, negotiate links with local fitness centre to provide coaching and research possibility of visits from local sports personalities.
- Put on an extra maths class and a cookery workshop.
- Arrange for the manager from the Sharp Centre to give a presentation on client care to all staff at the Castle Centre.

Each of the points above begins with a verb (an action word – see chapter 12). They all state that something particular should be *done.*

▶ Glossary

You may have had to include some technical terms in your report. A **glossary** lists these, giving definitions. It will be especially useful if the report is likely to be read by people who are not experts in your particular field. They are sure to need explanations.

▶ References

These are brief notes on texts where you found particular information or from which you've quoted. References can appear either individually at the bottom of the relevant pages or in the form of a list in this section (see chapter 3).

▶ Bibliography

This is a list of books, journals, other reports and so on that you have consulted while preparing your report. The purpose of a **bibliography** is to give readers some indication of the kind of ideas *behind* your work as well as to direct them to further reading on the subject (see chapter 3).

▶ Appendices

You will place here any material which you feel is valuable for anyone reading the report but which is not absolutely essential. This is likely to include tables, graphs, illustrations, and lengthy items such as correspondence that are too long and/or detailed to be included in the **findings**. You might like to think of an **appendix** as an overspill area. You may need more than one appendix in order to accommodate different issues.

▶ Illustrations

If you have used any illustrations, the sources for them will be listed here. The format of this section will be similar to the **references** section.

▶ Index

Include an **index** only in a very detailed report. As in any book, it's an alphabetical list, with page numbers, of all topics, names and technical terms that have appeared in the piece of work.

EXAMPLE: A STUDENT'S REPORT

The report here was written by Kathleen for the Core Studies section of her Access to Higher Education course. It is very straightforward so will be easy for you to follow. Along with other students, Kathleen had completed a unit called *Practical Writing* on her English course. For this unit, each student chose a topic related to his or her main subject and then submitted the following five pieces of work on it:

- a magazine article
- a letter to a broadsheet newspaper

- a leaflet
- a brochure
- a report.

The instructions for the report were as follows:

Construct a questionnaire which will give you information on students'
views of this unit and their experiences in writing the different sections.
Then conduct a survey using your questionnaire and write up the
responses in the form of a report.

REPORT ON CORE ENGLISH
PRACTICAL WRITING UNIT
Student Experiences

Kathleen Hardy
April 2005

Abstract
This is a report into the Practical Writing unit. It shows the students' views
and opinions of the work they have been required to undertake. It also
includes views and recommendations about the overall process.

Terms of reference
This report had to be made as a part of the Practical Writing unit for Core
English. It has to show how this unit of study actually worked. The unit
comprised five pieces of work: a letter to a broadsheet, a magazine article,
a brochure, a leaflet and finally the report. All of these pieces of work had
to be related to a main theme, which in turn had to be related to each
student's main topic of study, either English Literature, Sociology, or
Environmental Science.

Procedure
After completing the work in the Practical Writing unit, a list of questions
was drawn up to gather information from the students about the work
they had done. These questions were set out as a questionnaire. Each
student then asked the questions to a number of other students individually, and by doing this, gathered data for this report.

Findings
(a) Information/Research
It was found that a lot of research, for most students, had to be done. Of

the twelve students questioned, ten felt that a lot of research was needed and two felt that they already had all the information needed.

(b) Availability of information

A number of places were used to gather information. Eight students used library services, three students had to contact organisations, which they found difficult and laborious doing, and one person needed to carry out a number of interviews for her data. Overall, most students found any information they'd needed easy to get hold of.

(c) Classwork

It was found that all students were glad that some work, especially the letter and the brochure, was able to be done in class time.

(d) Topic choice

The students were asked if they found it easy or difficult to choose a topic for this unit. Out of those questioned, seven said that they'd found it easy, and five found the choosing of the topic *very* difficult. Out of those five, three had to choose a topic relating to English Literature, and the other two had to choose a topic relating to Environmental Science.

(e) Style of writing

The data collected showed that nine students found changing their style of writing for each piece of work difficult. However, three students had found it relatively easy. Also, all twelve students noted that they had learnt a lot about changing their style of writing for different purposes in this unit.

Conclusions
(a/b) Information

It can be seen from the findings that the information collected, and research which needed to be done was quite easy for all students, although difficulty was found by some in contacting various organisations.

(c) Classwork

The most useful and helpful aid while undertaking this unit appeared to be the class time allocated to actually producing parts of the work.

(d) Topic choice

It would appear that the choosing of the main topic area was easiest for the Sociology students, and secondly for the Environmental Science students. The English Literature students had most difficulty in choosing a topic for this unit.

(e) Style of writing
From the findings it can be seen that the Practical Writing unit taught the students a lot about differing styles of writing and how it had to change and adapt to suit each piece of work. It was found that this was hard to do.

Recommendations
(a/b) Information
It would be beneficial to have a list of addresses of various national, local, and well-known organisations available to students for different topic areas.

(c) Classwork
If more class time could be made available to actually produce items of work for this unit, then this would be very useful.

(d) Topic choice
Extra advice and help would benefit those who have to choose a topic relating to English Literature and maybe Environmental Science.

(e) Style of writing
Although the importance of learning how to change styles of writing was appreciated by the students, understanding the practicalities of actually changing their own style was felt to be difficult, and therefore students would need more help in achieving these changes to a greater degree.

THE LANGUAGE OF REPORTS

Decisions we make on the language we use in a report are just as important as those we make when writing letters or articles. Reports need to be really clear and straightforward. So focus on making things easy for whoever is going to be reading your report. Keep your sentences short. It's no bad thing to make your report sound really simple. Kathleen has done that well.

You might like to look back at how I described putting oil in my car in the section *Describing a process* (see chapter 4). I concentrated there on making things easy for someone who was new to the process. I showed every single step of the job, used simple language as much as possible, and kept my sentences fairly short. That style of writing is ideal for reports.

I suggested under **findings** that you write like a robot. I wasn't joking. Your language should be:

- clear and concise
- objective
- unemotional
- jargon-free (wherever possible)
- impersonal

You will have found that in writing essays, you need to put your emotions in cold storage. When writing reports, you need to bury your feelings six feet down in solid ice. It is only in *Recommendations* that you can make any suggestions on what you've found out, and you must still aim to be unbiased.

▶ Active v. passive (see also chapter 12)

Some tutors may accept essays that include comments in the first person – that is, using the word *I*; reports, however, have traditionally been written impersonally. The reasons for this are to help prevent emotion creeping in and to enable the reader to concentrate on the facts. This means that a statement such as

I interviewed employees in three different occupations

is better if changed to:

Employees in three different occupations were interviewed

A statement in your **recommendations**, such as

I feel that further training is essential for operators of machines

is better as:

Operators of machines should be given further training

In these examples I have changed the verbs from active to passive. Educational practice is itself undergoing a great deal of change at present, however, and you might find that your tutor would prefer you to concentrate on getting your facts and structure right rather than starting to worry about passive verbs.

▶ Reported speech

If you have carried out interviews, you are likely to want to report what one or two people said. Use chapter 15 to help you here.

▶ Tense

Reports are written largely in the past simple tense (see chapter 12). Obviously, since you are describing what you found out, you are bound to use the past tense a great deal. When you talk about processes that are still taking place, however, you are going to need to use the present tense.

SUMMARY

This chapter has covered:

- your action plan
- organising your material
- the sections of a full-blown report:
  Title-page
  Abstract (sometimes called the 'Summary')
  Contents
  Terms of reference
  Procedure (sometimes called 'Method')
  Findings
  Conclusions
  Recommendations
  Glossary
  References
  Bibliography
  Illustrations
  Index

- **the key sections of a report:**
  a brief note on what's in it (the *Abstract*)
  an explanation of why and how it was set up and how you
  went about it (*Terms of Reference* and *Procedure*)
  a description of the things you found out (*Findings*)
  an analysis of what you found out (*Conclusions*)
  your suggestions for how things might be improved in the
  future (*Recommendations*)
- **the language of reports:**
  clear, concise, objective and unemotional
  jargon-free (wherever possible)
  impersonal
  reported speech
  past simple tense

9 Articles

INTRODUCTION

Some educational courses nowadays require students to write one or more articles as part of their coursework. As well as giving you practice in structuring your work, this can sometimes allow you to follow a personal interest, give you a little more freedom than you have when writing an essay, and enable you to look at a topic in a broader context than usual. It's also great for practising to communicate an aspect of your subject to a wide audience. This chapter is not, however, concerned with articles written for academic journals, which need to be as tightly constructed as a good essay and to include extensive referencing.

Article-writing can be a lot of fun. You will get the most out of it if you proceed as if you intended to submit your article to a magazine. The important thing is to make sure that you choose a topic you are interested in. Your enthusiasm will inevitably show in your finished piece. You might even produce something that you really could get published.

The way you write your article will depend on the course you are taking and the guidelines you've been given. If you want to write for children, do check this out with your tutor before beginning. In some cases, writing for children would be quite acceptable because doing this requires particular skills. For most assignments, however, it would be important to write for adults. If you have not yet looked at the sections on **Register** and **Tone** in chapter 4, it would be a good idea to do that before starting to write.

PLANNING AND RESEARCHING

▶ Starting from scratch

The first thing to do, of course, is to make a broad decision on your topic. If you've been given a general subject area, you will need to narrow this down to something quite specific. It's likely that you have been given a word limit somewhere between one and two thousand words. That will give room for you to cover one quite small area in sufficient depth.

As with all assignments, the best thing is to start with a mind map. Let's suppose that you are studying child development and that you have been asked to write a magazine article on any aspect of development of the under-fives. Your initial mind map might look like this:

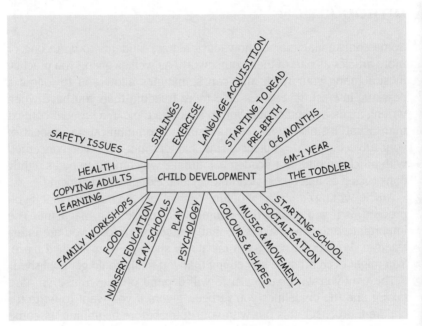

Remember that, at this stage, it's useful to throw down absolutely everything you can think of without worrying whether or not your ideas seem sensible. You might leave this map around for a day or two so that you can add any new ideas that come to you.

From this idea-finding exercise you will choose your topic area. If I were doing this assignment, I might choose 'acquisition of language' as my topic. You might feel that you don't know enough about *any* of the areas you've come up with to write on them, but we all often feel that about any assignment or essay. It's a perfectly normal initial response to the task. Look at the topics about which you already know *something* (from lectures, reading, experience, and so on) and just choose the one you are most interested in. Then you will enjoy your research.

▶ Choosing the type of article to write

Your first job will be to decide what kind of article you'd like to write. It's a good idea to base your work on a real publication as this will help to keep you focused. You might like to have a look at magazines in your college library or in large newsagents where there will be a wide selection on view. When you find a magazine that you like – and in which you think your topic would fit – you will need to look in more detail at the kind of articles printed:

- How long are the articles?
- How much detail is included?
- How long are paragraphs in the articles?

If I were to write my article on language acquisition, the facts would remain constant whatever magazine I aimed my piece at, but the number and type of facts I included and the style and language I used would be specific to the magazine I'd chosen to write for. Before going any further, it's a good idea to check with your tutor that the kind of piece you want to write will be suitable for your assignment.

▶ Researching the topic

At this stage, the work will be very similar to what you do when writing an essay: you need to find out facts, ideas and opinions. Getting the facts right for an article is just as important as in essays. If you are working on a topic covered on your course, ask your tutor to suggest books and other material that you might look at to broaden your knowledge. After all, this assignment will have been designed as a way for you to extend your knowledge and understanding. Librarians, too, are usually happy to point you in the right direction. You are likely to have more of a free hand in researching material for an article than when you are writing an essay. Here's a selection of items that might prove useful:

- books and journals
- magazines – especially those catering for your topic area
- maps

- encyclopedias
- tapes/videos/CDs
- minutes of Local Authority proceedings
- publications by societies
- journals of statistics
- autobiographies and letters

▶ **Interviewing**

Talking to someone involved in the field you are writing about can be a real eye-opener and can provide very valuable material for your article, and a quote from the horse's mouth can add strength to your own explanations. So where do you find a willing victim? There may be someone in a local college or university who works in the field you are covering. You could try the *Yellow Pages.* Failing that, someone at your local reference library might be able to suggest local societies that you could contact. Once you begin a search, one link generally leads to another.

All you have to do is ring up, explain that you have to write an article for an assignment, mention the subject matter, and ask if your intended interviewee could spare you half an hour. If the person refuses, thank them and go on to someone else. Always take a prepared question sheet to an interview. You will need to appear professional and it's hard to remember everything you want to ask when you're under pressure. Here are some suggestions for the type of questions you might ask:

- What areas of x do you cover?
- What is your specific interest?
- How often does y happen?
- What is your view on z?
- Can you explain a for me?
- Can you suggest where I might find out more about b?

Preparing a question sheet will help to get your mind in gear. It's essential preparation even if the interview takes a completely different turn. You may even be told that you will have to conduct your interview on the phone. If this happens, you'll find prepared questions especially helpful.

WRITING UP YOUR WORK

▶ Angling your topic

If I were to write that article on language acquisition, I would need to look very carefully at the level of complexity required by the magazine I had chosen. I'd do this before writing a single word. If I wanted to write for a general magazine, I'd probably need to limit the number of facts I mentioned, keep analysis quite short, and either steer clear of jargon or make quite sure that I gave explanations for any technical terms. I'd also probably need to give examples from everyday life. Many magazines use the trick of relating issues directly to individual people in order to get complex issues across.

Whatever kind of magazine you choose, facts will be crucial (as in an academic article), but any analysis needs to be especially clear. What you write also needs to be related to the expectations of your readers. If I were writing the language-acquisition article for a nursing magazine, it would be important to relate my comments directly to a nurse's experience of children within a hospital setting. So I'd probably need to talk to one or two nurses to get some inside information. When writing for members of a particular profession or for people with knowledge of a specific subject area, you need to think about what might be new to them or what might raise useful ideas for discussion.

Once you've got your material together and decided on a magazine, it's time to make a rough plan. Planning is a vital part of the process, just as with an essay. So make a working plan just to get yourself going (see chapter 2). Now you can begin to write.

▶ Openings

As with essays, it's sometimes easier to leave the actual writing of your opening paragraph until last. This is because you may not know how to introduce your article when you're not yet sure exactly what you'll put into it. When you're ready to write your opening, aim to begin with an arresting topic or idea. Here's the opening of an article about hemp farming:

> The hemp plant grows at 6cm a day and is ready to harvest in just 20 weeks. It's GMO-free and needs no pesticides, herbicides or fertilisers. Its uses range from food to building materials, and it's a crop that can add value for the small farmer.

That gets straight to the point with statistics that will probably surprise readers.

Another way to 'hook' your readers is to focus on a real person. Here's the opening to an article on allotments:

> When Roy Southcott was 10 years old in 1929, he was set to work on his first allotment to help feed the family of twelve. His plot was on the railway embankment at Whitchurch, near Tavistock, and Roy had to shield his face from the sparks from passing trains.

If you've interviewed someone and you want to quote anything they've said, keep it brief and follow the rules for setting out direct speech in chapter 15.

And here's an extract from an article by Mark, a student who had looked very carefully at how writers begin articles with that 'hook' for a specific readership. His article is called 'Sustainable Rural Development' and is aimed at *Resurgence,* a magazine that covers environmental issues, alternative lifestyles and New Age theories and ideas. The second paragraph has been included here to show how it leads really smoothly from Mark's introduction. He hits just the right note for *Resurgence* by referring to legend:

> Vortigern the Tyrant wanted to build a Great Tower, but every time he tried the tower fell down. Even his wisest counsellors were unable to tell him what was wrong. Then Merlin was brought before him.
>
> Merlin at once saw the problem, which was not only in the fabric of the tower, but more so in its very foundation. For beneath the tower was a deep pool, and beneath the pool were two hollow stones, and within the stones lay two dragons.
>
> Now if this fable were to be applied to development today, especially rural development, then one of the two dragons would represent the relentless pursuit of a false economy which in turn is used to prove the standard of 'good' living. And the other dragon would be the increasing erosion of social life and well-being.

The allusion to a story is a very clever trick to get readers 'hooked'. Few of us can resist the urge to know what happens next. The link to the subject of rural development is then made very neatly in Mark's second paragraph. You can see how much detail he went on to give by looking at a longer section of the article in chapter 5.

▶ Paragraphs and sentences

When checking on the style suitable for a particular magazine, one of the first things to do is to look at the length of paragraphs and sentences. The more serious or academic the magazine, the more its readers want to have ideas analysed in depth. That is likely to result in longer paragraphs. If, on the other hand, you are writing in the style of a very popular magazine, both your paragraphs and your sentences will need to be kept quite short and you will need to get your ideas down in very few words. (For more information on paragraphing, see chapter 2.)

▶ Structure and links

Linking your paragraphs and topics will be especially important. You will not generally need to construct as tight an argument as you would when writing an essay, but your structure in an article will need to make your material clear and easy to follow. Group your facts in the most straightforward way possible (see the sections on *Linking* and *Planning and structuring* in Chapter 2).

▶ Language and style (see also chapter 4)

The type of words you use and the way you construct your sentences are both crucial for ensuring that your article is suitable for the magazine you've chosen. This is much easier than it sounds. You may already have a good 'feel' for the magazine you've chosen and be able to imitate the way its contributors write. Here's a checklist that may come in handy:

- verbs   How lively are they?
- nouns   Do many of them fall into any particular category?
- register   Is it formal, journalistic, technical, etc.?
- tone   Is it serious, persuasive, friendly, helpful, conversational, etc.?

▶ Endings

Like openings, these can be tricky. An ending should tie things up neatly, leaving no loose ends. You might consider how you'd like your readers to feel after reading your article. Here are some possibilities:

> fired with enthusiasm
> calm
> understanding a new angle on your topic
> aware of new facts
> keen to join a special interest group

It's a good idea to relate your closing remarks to the central ideas of your article – or perhaps to the beginning. Look at how Mark managed it in his article on rural development by referring to types of people he has discussed and linking all this back to his opening:

> These ... innovators of the future would ... be those people with special skills ... Because of their new relationship with nature and indeed their sense of belonging within nature they will bring about their own deep feelings of worthiness and trust in the future. Then the dragons of the past can be put to rest forever.

Problem solved!

SUMMARY

This chapter has covered:

- choosing a magazine to base your work on
- planning
- researching your topic
- interviews
- angling your topic to a magazine
- openings
- paragraphing and sentences
- structure and links
- language and style
- endings

10 Oral Presentations

INTRODUCTION

Having to give your first oral presentation or seminar is something that often can be feared and dreaded. If you follow a careful plan of action, however, you will be able to give a creditable performance first time. The method outlined below really does work – for everyone. It can be adapted for any circumstances, including university seminars and the world of work, where the ability to give presentations is becoming more and more important.

People who are scared by giving presentations sometimes feel that the best thing to do is just to write an essay that they can then read out. Your tutor might accept this, but it has considerable disadvantages:

- essays take longer to prepare
- they are less useful for group discussions
- they frequently bore the listeners
- you've still not learned to prepare a talk

Obviously, if you have never spoken in public before, it's going to take a bit of practice before you feel wholly at ease, but if you follow the instructions below, nerves will be kept to a minimum and your audience will probably have no idea of your fears. It is, however, essential that you follow the instructions very carefully. You'll need to think about the three aspects of giving a talk:

1 the subject matter
2 the audience
3 you – the presenter

GETTING STARTED

Despite what I've said above, you will need to begin as though you were going to write an essay (see chapter 2). You'll probably have been given – or chosen – a topic. So first of all, it's a good idea to draw a mind map so that you can be clear on what you already know and can then work out what reading and note-taking you are likely to need to do. Next, it's often useful to construct a question to fit your topic. This will focus your mind. Then you can underline the key words, just as you would if you were writing an essay, so that you will stay focused as you prepare your presentation.

If you were going to talk about early nineteenth-century social life as shown in Jane Austen's *Pride and Prejudice*, for example, you might construct the question:

> What does *Pride and Prejudice* tell us about middle-class life in the early nineteenth century?

Then you might decide to look at inheritance, housing, social etiquette and careers.

If you were to give a presentation on problems in prisons, you might construct the question:

> What changes in government policy are necessary to improve prison conditions?

or

> What are the main issues that have an adverse effect on prison inmates?

It's also a good idea at this stage to begin collecting some visual materials such as photographs, illustrations, maps, diagrams and so on. Any topic can yield visual material if it's only a painting of a writer whose work you may be discussing. Visuals are useful both in terms of raising your own level of interest and focusing the minds of your listeners when you give your talk.

As with an essay, it's easier to prepare a presentation if you have more material than you need, so include with your visual collection pamphlets, articles from newspapers and magazines, and any other written material that's available. As you progress with preparation, you may want to draw a diagram that you can refer to during your talk. This might be pinned up, copied on to a whiteboard during your talk, shown on an OHP (overhead projector) or presented via a computer. Keep all your notes and visual materials as you may be asked to submit your work in order to show that you've put your presentation together in a logical fashion.

Getting your facts right will, of course, be crucial; but, because your work will not be set in stone as it would be in an essay, you'll have more leeway for expressing your personal opinions. Any presentation is considerably enlivened by a presenter who comes across as a real human being with his or her own ideas and feelings.

STRUCTURE

The plan for your presentation is going to be vital because the format is one of the key features of any talk. Start by following the procedure for planning an essay. Most people, when listening, are not able to remember more than three or four key points. You might like to play safe and work on three. This doesn't mean that you can only say three things. It means that all your points must fit under one of three headings. Anything that won't fit must be left out – or else you will have to adjust your headings until you are able to fit in whatever you want to say. Facts and examples will be important for proof, just as they are in essays.

It can be a good idea to sort your notes and materials into three lots. By doing this at an early stage, you will have a clearer sense of where you're going. You will also need to think very carefully about links (see chapter 2). Your listeners will come to your presentation cold, so to speak, with little or no idea of what you will put before them. They need as much help as possible to understand how different aspects of your talk fit together.

Because of this, your introduction is going to be especially important. It needs to be clear and simple. Simplicity at this stage in no way precludes you from giving detailed descriptions and penetrating analysis as you progress. If I were to give a presentation on snakes, for example, I might decide to introduce my talk by remarking on the widespread fear of snakes and on their appearance in myths and stories. I could then pick up on humans' fear of snakes to let my listeners know that I'll be dealing with three types of reptile:

- harmless snakes
- poisonous snakes
- those that kill by constriction

You might begin each section with things that most of your listeners will already have heard of. It will make them feel comfortable and you can then move on to new and complex information. A little (I stress, *little*) humour in the early stages is likely to put your audience in a positive frame of mind for listening to what else you have to say.

THE AUDIENCE

Think about presentations you yourself have attended. What kind of thing has made a talk come alive for you? You'll probably have noticed that the best talks have been those where the presenter has:

- shown enthusiasm for his or her subject
- had a good knowledge of that subject
- explained the material well
- spoken clearly and not too fast
- appeared relaxed and included the occasional joke

The most important of these is almost certainly the first. Talk about something you feel passionate about. Whatever gives you a buzz is what you'll talk about best. If your own interest level is low, this will affect (or probably infect) your audience. If you've been given a topic that you're not too keen on, either change it or change your attitude to it. One way to raise your own level of interest is to find out more about the topic.

An audience almost always begins by being favourably disposed towards a speaker. People nearly always want you to do well and will often ignore small slips. Frowns may have nothing at all to do with you. So if your audience looks hostile in any way, assume it's had a bad morning and aim to cheer it up.

The success of your presentation will depend in part on pitching it at the right level. So ask yourself three questions:

1 Who am I talking to?
2 What do they already know?
3 What will interest or excite them?

Although it's important to begin with simple ideas, it's essential not to bore people and to show respect for their expertise and opinions. If you're aware that some people know more than you do on one aspect of your talk (apart, of course, from your tutor) you can acknowledge that. It's easy enough to say something like, "Of course, I'm aware that some of you know a good deal about x." Be careful, however, over encouraging contributions from the audience. It's very easy to lose control of a presentation. You don't want the group taking over or chatting among themselves. Because of this, it's usually safest to wait until the end of your talk before opening up a discussion.

Acknowledging the skills of others, however, will enhance your reputation rather than diminishing it. It will show that you are aware and fair-minded. There's absolutely no need to appear to know everything. Indeed, it can be useful to point people in the right direction for further reading. Those who want to take your topic further will be glad of that kind of information. If you can suggest where someone is likely to find the answer to an awkward question, you will have covered yourself.

YOUR ROUTE MAP

When you have done your research and note-making and drawn up a plan, you're ready for writing up. Constructing a good 'route map' is your key to navigating your way through the presentation and arriving successfully at the finishing point. Instead of writing sentences, you are going to write down only key topics and phrases. This is so that you will be able to glance down to find out what comes next and then look at your audience and talk directly to them. They'll be much more receptive than if you have everything on paper and spend the talk peering at your notes.

▶ Cards

In making your route map, you will need to do everything possible to make it right for the job – that means it must be *easily readable when you are under stress*. There are various things you can do to achieve this. Many professionals use plain white cards, size 8 × 5 inches (203 mm × 127 mm), writing on one side only. This is a tried-and-tested method and will give you the best chance of success. Smaller cards force you to squash up your writing, so when you're under pressure, it's very hard to pick out the information you need.

Everything must be done to make things easy on yourself. Your cards are going to carry all the essential notes you will need to speak from. People who have never done this kind of thing before generally assume that they will never remember what they want to say without a full script in front of them. I promise you that this is not the case. With a careful layout and a little practice (see below) this will work like magic. Through the preparation of your material, you are beginning to commit it to memory, and remember that all day long you are recounting things to those you meet without even having notes on cards, let alone a full script.

Cards are much easier to handle than sheets of paper and they don't rustle. The fact that there is much less space on them than on a page of A4 is an advantage. When you are in the hot spot, the less writing you have to look at in one go the better. As long as your layout is clear and simple (see below) you're eyes won't get lost wandering around looking for a vital piece of information. Losing your place in a talk is one of the main hazards for speakers. Number your cards so that if the worst should happen and you drop the lot, you'll quickly get them back into sequence.

Roughly speaking, your cards will contain a detailed version of your plan. The most important words on each card need to be in capitals, and it can be a good idea to vary the size of your writing according to the importance of each point. Organise your material into lists wherever you can, and leave lots and lots of white space on each card. It's not possible to stress this too highly. When you are giving your presentation, you need to be able to glance down and pick out just the topic word you're looking for. If there's a lot on a card, you won't be able to do this, and you'll be embarrassed by not being able to find your place.

As with an essay plan, you might put key points on the left and evidence on the right. Use clear headings, but beware of highlighting, as in some lights this can make what's written difficult to read. Your layout can be helped by most of the following:

sections	colour-coding
headings	underlining
key words	boxes
columns	symbols
numbering	brackets
capitals	

It's also possible to add instructions to yourself on the cards –
perhaps in a different colour. For example:

- pause
- point to diagram
- emphasise

Speaking from notes on cards rather than from a script allows you to
look at the audience and to speak naturally. If you have sentences in
front of you, there is no way forward other than to read them, and that
can be very boring for your listeners. You'll see below a copy of the
cards Judith used for her first presentation. It went very well.

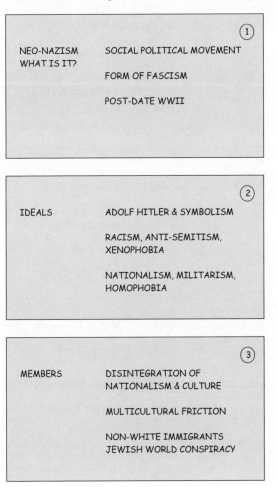

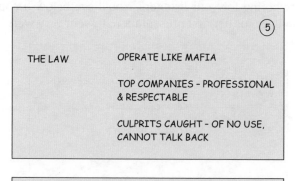

④

HOLOCAUST   DENIAL - EXAGGERATED?
REVISIONISM   (STIGMA, MASS GENOCIDE)

IMMORAL EQUIVALENCIES →
DRESDEN, ETHNIC CLEANSING

JUSIFICATIONS →
TERRORISTS, SABOTAGE,
SUBVERSION

⑤

THE LAW   OPERATE LIKE MAFIA

TOP COMPANIES - PROFESSIONAL
& RESPECTABLE

CULPRITS CAUGHT - OF NO USE,
CANNOT TALK BACK

⑥

HOW MANY?   PUBLIC OPINION - ALD, SPLC

UNDERGROUND - FUNDRAISE,
ORGANISE, RECRUIT

GLOBAL PHENOMENON

⑦

STRENGTH   GLOBAL NETWORK

STRONGEST SINCE FALL

STRONGER THAN WHEN CAME
INTO POWER

⑧

NOVEMBER 9TH SOCIETY	1977 – TERRY FLYNN INACTIVE
	KEVIN QUINN – ONLY ONE, LEAFLETS, STICKERS
	PRESSURE GROUP 2004 POLITICAL PARTY

⑨

IDEALS	AGAINST IMMIGRATION, ABORTION, COMMUNISM
	AGAINST HOMOSEXUALITY
	SUPPORTS HIERARCHICAL SYSTEM, REPATRIATION, BRITISH OWNERSHIP OF INDUSTRY, CENTRAL GOVMT. BANK

⑩

NAME	DATE IN 1923, 16 MARTYRS BEER HALL PUTSCH
	OPPONENTS – KRISTALLNACHT – ANTI-SEMITIC
	N9s OPPOSE THIS – JEWS: DEADLY ENEMY

⑪

POLICIES	CRITICISE BNP – SOFT
	'TRUTH FOR EVERYONE' – MAGAZINE ON WEBSITE
	ILLEGAL IMMIGRANTS → SWIM

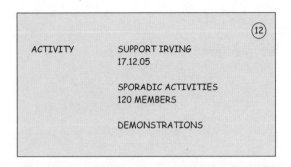

Judith's first attempt at giving a presentation and using the card system was a great success. She used a very straightforward layout with plenty of space on each card and clear print so that she was able to see her topics easily. The careful breakdown of these topics enabled her presentation to flow logically. It also meant that Judith's listeners found the presentation interesting as they felt they were in contact with a real person as she explained each point in a conversational style. This all helped to keep her stress levels to a minimum.

Judith might improve things further in future by giving a little more detail on each card. She'd clearly worked hard and had plenty of ideas in her head so that she was able to flesh out each topic for her listeners as she went along. If you want to use your material at a later date, however, or if your memory sometimes lets you down, it's best to have as much information at your fingertips as possible – without, that is, making the cards look crowded. So Judith might find the following changes useful for her next presentation:

- headings at the top (not the side)
- points on the left-hand side
- brief details on the right-hand side
- references to books, illustrations, etc., in another colour
- 'stage directions' (such as SMILE NOW) in another colour
- more cards – to allow extra space for more information

VISUAL AIDS

A presentation is always enlivened by having something to look at other than the speaker. So do include something if at all possible. A good-sized picture or diagram pinned up on a wall can set the tone for your talk. Even setting out some books on a table can lend a professional air to the proceedings. You will need to plan this carefully too. Check where illustrations can be fixed and whether they would be seen by everyone.

If, for example, you decide to use an OHP and you've never used one before, you'll need to get really familiar with how they work. You may also need to book equipment with your college's resources centre. Finding at the last minute that you can't get hold of what you need could scupper your whole performance. You will also need to check the electrics. Where are sockets located? Will the flex reach to where you will be standing? Does the equipment actually work? Think also about the size of any print you use. It must be clearly visible to everyone in the room. Visual items that can't be seen properly are worse than useless.

If you are going to provide handouts, they should be given out at the end of the proceedings. If you give your audience something to hold, they will look at it at once and will stop listening to you. Some people think that this might take the pressure off them, but it actually makes things a good deal harder, because you are likely to lose control as your audience embarks on this new activity. There's also the problem that everyone reads at different rates and people will ask you to repeat what else you've said while they were busy reading. They'll also start asking questions just when you don't want them to.

PRACTISING

You will need to have at least two practice sessions in complete privacy. You will either have been given a time-limit for your presentation or you will already know from attending seminars how long you are expected to speak. But without practice, it's almost impossible to know how long a piece will last. When a piece is too short, everyone's embarrassed, when it's too long, people get bored – or worse still, begin to leave in twos and threes. You don't want this happening to you.

So practise performing your presentation exactly as if you had an audience in front of you. This means speaking aloud, pausing where necessary, adding any jokes in full, speaking clearly and slowly, and including gestures and any movements you'll need to make towards or away from your visual aids. You also need to add time for using visual aids such as a flip chart or an OHP. If you need to cut, just keep the best bits and your talk will sparkle. If you find you've not prepared enough material, go back to your collection of notes, articles, etc., to see what else might fit. Or it might be the case that you need to slow down your delivery. If you speak fast, no one gets a chance to take in what you are saying. Or you might decide to include a personal experience. If your piece is seriously short on what you need, go on a voyage of discovery for new material. There's no knowing what nuggets you might unearth at the last minute.

PERFORMANCE

In a written text, meaning comes across via sentence construction, punctuation and paragraphing. There's a study that shows that 38 per cent of what an audience remembers from a talk, however, depends on the sound of your voice. That means you have to think about tone, about how loudly you speak, about how you project your voice, and about pauses and speed. A dramatic pause before an important point can be invaluable. But 55 per cent of the message is delivered by what the audience actually sees, and your enthusiasm and your attitude to your material will come across largely through your facial expressions and body language. A convincing speaker shows that he or she is totally involved with the material. The remaining 7 per cent is for the words themselves.

As far as your language is concerned, don't be too formal. Use the appropriate language code for the people you are speaking to. If you are in an academic situation, this will mean using appropriate technical terms wherever necessary, but otherwise being fairly chatty. Aim to create an informal atmosphere.

Obviously, if you are giving a presentation for a job interview, you will need to look especially smart and speak with a fair amount of formality. On a college or university course, however, you won't need to dress up. But either way, there are a few useful tips. Don't wear anything that you feel uncomfortable in, that is revealing, makes a noise or keeps slipping. Make sure your hair won't get in your eyes, and check buttons and other fastenings are secure before you get to the presentation room. When you speak, try to remain in one place, and don't fiddle with pens or investigate problem areas on your person.

Do, however, allow the audience to know that there's a real human being out there. Audiences usually love it when speakers reveal something about themselves. Don't overdo this, but a brief anecdote can relax people and lighten the atmosphere. Use gesture occasionally to reinforce what you are saying, and smile when it's appropriate. Look around and aim to make a connection with everyone in the room. Allow your tone of voice and your facial expression to fit your words and make sure that you show enthusiasm. If you feel nervous, pretend that you don't, and your listeners will probably have no idea of how you feel. Speak clearly and go a little more slowly than seems necessary. This is how to be sure your message gets across.

If you have an accent, far from being a problem, this will add to the sense of you as an individual. You might consider what you think are your best qualities. If you don't know, ask a friend. A practised speaker accentuates his or her good points. This might be your gift for explaining things clearly, your kindliness, your skill at making people feel at ease, or your sharp mind. Be the best you can possibly be, prepare your cards carefully, and you can't fail.

SUMMARY

Think about	subject matter audience yourself
Prepare	mind map information structure cards visual aids
Practise	alone
Time	yourself carefully
Perform with	enthusiasm appropriate language code useful body language, etc.

11 Exam Essays

INTRODUCTION

The best time to read this chapter is when you are within two or three months of your exams – possibly less. It is unlikely to be of much use to you a year before you sit them. You will only depress yourself if you start worrying about exams too early. The main reason for this is that there will still be a lot of new material to cover, so you really are in no position either to have an overall grasp of a year's work or to focus your mind on what is, in fact, a totally different undertaking from writing coursework essays. Even when you are at the end of your course, you may feel incapable of tackling an exam. It is only when you've completed the revision process that you are likely to begin to feel confident.

Ignoring exams at an early stage in the course is not to be confused with finding out what the course itself will cover. You really do need to know that. It's also a good idea to find out what general areas you will be tested on in the exam. You can then make sure that you cover these thoroughly during the year.

By the way, some people get worried about what seems to be the highly formal language in which exam questions are often written. There's actually nothing to fear here. Just as with most coursework essays, the questions are very carefully constructed so that, hopefully, they cannot be misunderstood. This can make them sound very formal – rather like legal jargon. It can tend to make the questions *appear* more difficult than they actually are. As with term-time essays, however, the questions that look difficult are often easier to answer than those that seem simple. This is because a question that gives you a very tight structure to work to can actually help you to bring out all the things you know in a highly organised manner.

Writing an exam essay is a totally different task from writing assignments – which are designed to enable you to practise writing and to *learn*. Term-time essays cannot be written without doing research, reading relevant material, and spending a good deal of time thinking. These assignments test your coverage of a particular area of work and your ability to construct a meaningful discussion of it. The fact that you probably have two or three weeks in which to think about this is taken into account by whoever marks your work. Exams are quite different. It's a good idea to give yourself some practice in writing exam answers so that you can get a feel for how much data you can get down in the time available.

The purpose of an exam is to give you the opportunity to show some of the things you've learnt during the year and to enable you to demonstrate that you can select relevant points from what you know in order to answer specific questions *in a short space of time.* Nobody can possibly remember everything that has been covered on a course, and nobody can write all there is to know on a topic in under an hour.

This chapter will first look briefly at how to revise for exam essays. It will then give an example of a student's exam answer, showing how the student has gone about tackling the essay. What it won't do is prepare you for writing short answers or coping with multiple-choice questions. For these, you'll need explanation and help from your tutor.

THE REVISION PROCESS

Taking bite-sized chunks is the name of the game here. You will need to go through all your lecture notes, class notes, handouts and any photocopied material you possess. Take these items one at a time. Your task is to read each through once, pencil or highlighter in hand. Each time you come to a key point, either circle or highlight it. Sometimes a tutor will have written one or two useful points on your essay, so highlight these too. Cover topics you will be tested on.

After *one* reading, **list** the points you've ringed or highlighted on a fresh sheet of paper in as few words as possible. Do this with everything, and read nothing twice. Fit in a short session of this work whenever you have a spare 15 minutes and work as fast as you can.

All you have to do after that (as they say on children's TV) is to condense all your lists into as few sheets of paper as possible and to colour-code the topic areas. Stick to key points and key words. If you need to remember formulae, include these on the lists. Aim to note ideas and trends where possible rather than overloading yourself with too many facts. Draw mind maps or diagrams whenever you can because these are easier to remember than lists. If you are able to add drawings, these will be even better memory aids. When you have done all this, you'll have revisited all the main areas of your course, and so you'll be getting well prepared for your exams. Keep going over your master lists, and practise trying to write them out from memory. If you have any spare time now, have a go at writing answers to past papers – or make up questions of your own to answer.

BUDGETING YOUR TIME IN AN EXAM

If your exam lasts three hours and consists of three essay questions, expect to write approximately three to four sides of A4 for each answer. Your tutors will almost certainly have explained that you need to budget your time *very* carefully in an exam. It's only common sense to expect to spend longest on questions that carry the most marks. For questions carrying the same marks, however, the following is a well-known fact:

> The combined marks for one really good answer and one poor answer are generally less than the combined marks for two average answers.

So don't make the mistake of spending extra time on your best topic. It really is essential to manage your time carefully and to give each question your best attention if you are to maximise your chance of success.

A STUDENT'S EXAM ANSWER

Here is one of Sandy's essays on a sociology paper. It's followed by some explanation of how the essay has approached various essential features of an exam answer. If sociology is not your subject, don't be put off by terms that may at first seem a little confusing. Everything will become clear as you read through the essay. The introduction and conclusion are marked separately and the paragraphs in between are numbered so that you'll be able to refer to them easily when you read my comments.

'Our bondage to society is not so much established by conquest as by collusion.' Explore this statement in the light of the relationship between culture and identity.

Introduction   Culture is all things that affect man in the society he lives in. It is the way he lives and works, and all the things he achieves. Culture only exists in our heads and only concerns our relationships and interactions with other people. It is a changing, adapting mechanism which governs our behaviour patterns. Society is the organism that displays the behaviour. So culture and society are not the same thing, although they are intrinsically linked.

1   Culture can be seen as made up of three layers. Tradition is made up of values and beliefs passed from one generation to the next, and commonly held within a society. Subcultures are commonly held beliefs, values and behaviours among like people in a society – for example, there could be people from one culture who live in another culture but still keep the characteristics of their common primary culture, and identify with each other because of the primary culture. Cultural universals are characteristics which are common to all known culture. They include systems of meaning (communication), hierarchy and leadership, a form of family, privacy and rules governing good and bad behaviour and sexual behaviour. Universal qualities may be practised differently within different cultures, but they are still a part of all culture. So every individual is exposed to these 'cultural rules' in some form or another.

2   Culture (as evident within the universals) ensures the survival of society, and its rules ensure a level of conformity and control amongst the individuals within it. For example, the rearing and nurturing of children are accepted amongst all cultures, whereas generally (except in war situations) killing others is not.

3   All cultures change, but their change is normally slow and gradual. Individuals within society get stability from the culture they identify as their own. This stability arises from the reinforcement of culture through repetition. Individuals collude with culture as they can enjoy the boundaries it provides (not wanting to be killed, and wanting children raised safely within a family).

4   Forces that affect culture are natural forces and human forces. Human forces include technological advancement, economic and political dominance, war and victory over others (conquest).

5   Culture itself can affect the inquisitiveness of society. This can affect the rates of change and willingness to change of individuals and

societies as a whole. Our bondage to society and evidence of our collusion is displayed in ethnocentricity. Ethnocentrism is the means by which we seek to protect our own culture and feel superior to others. It can be viewed as promotion of racism and yet it is also an individual's and society's attempt to prevent the infusion of values and beliefs from one culture to another, thus preserving culture and minimising change.

6   Technological advancement and media are the largest influences on cultural change. The rate of change is different between cultures and yet we often adapt readily to change and collude with advancement over which, as individuals, there is little control.

7   Often, culture and its relationship with individuals can only be explained through history. People do not have an instinct for a predetermined culture when they are born. Babies are only born with an instinct to eat and drink. A baby born in one culture and placed in another would accept it as its own (McDonald Mason 1999). America has traditions which can be dated back to 1782. They are still practised today which, as America is a country made up of immigrants since that time, also shows clearly that culture is learned by individuals.

8   Different individuals within the same culture may hold different beliefs and values. Things that can affect different individuals within the same society are age, generation and *Zeitgeist*. Age can affect values held by individuals as youths and children are more likely to absorb modernity and changes in culture, and the older people become the less receptive they are to change. It may also be that a particular generation has absorbed certain beliefs and values in youth which have stayed for life. *Zeitgeist* is when something so profound, large, different or impacting happens to a society it affects the culture of society and the beliefs and values of everyone in that society, regardless of age, generation or socio-economic background.

9   However, study conducted over a period of time showed the most impact upon culture came from individuals (H. E. Hofstede) and individualism which can be viewed in two ways: as the disintegration of existing culture which makes the concepts of social class, gender roles and status fragile, or as the breakdown of state-sanctioned normality, role models and traditions (as sanctioned by religion, the state and tradition). It can be seen as a fight against cultural norms.

10   In the past, individuals had little opportunity to express their identity either in work or social situations. Now, people are expected to make choices and be responsible for their own lives. Individuals may see this as control by themselves, only taking from culture what they choose.

11 If an individual does not like the cultural norms of a situation they are in, they can seek to make a change – e.g. from one social class to another or from poverty to wealth. Yet they are merely swapping the cultural norms of one situation for the cultural norms of another. Individuals do not have 'free will' to break away from culture per se. They just move to different parts of a culture. They may be making changes to culture or it's possible they are merely adapting to new culture as it arrives.

12 Individuals get much of their identity from the views of others within their culture. There are trends amongst individuals to better each other and seek progression while shaking off old culture. They 'plunge into modernity' and enjoy 'precarious freedom' (U. Beck 2002) and yet modern culture places an abundance of constraints and provisos on people, ranging from the rules on pension entitlement to a need to MOT the car. All individuals must plan for and take into account all constraints and provisos of modern culture as they live their lives. They cannot merely live subjectively: 'Under the surface of modern society is a highly efficient, densely woven institutional culture' (U. Beck, 2002).

Conclusion   In the past, culture's control over societies, and the individuals within those societies, was obvious. Evidence now suggests that although we believe we have the choice to opt out of a culture, it is in fact the case that culture is as controlling as ever, but less obvious. Hence rather than individuals controlling culture, culture has adapted to control, maintain and ensure the survival of modern society. It seems in modern society we accept the overarching values of our culture and even its constraints.

PLANNING AND WRITING AN EXAM ANSWER

▶ Analysing the question

The best way to start is to:

> underline the *key words* and phrases in the question

This is essential. In an exam, most of us are under stress. If ever we are going to misread something, it will be during an exam. Underlining key words forces us to focus on what is necessary and breaks the question down into its separate parts. As with term-time essays, it will be important to underline a large percentage of the words or phrases in the question. Here are my underlinings for the question Sandy answered:

> 'Our bondage to society is not so much established by conquest as by collusion.' Explore this statement in the light of the relationship between culture and identity.

▶ Planning

It's essential to make a quick plan. If you launch into writing without a plan, you have less chance of working to a clear structure and you may well forget things that occur to you as you write. If you have a plan, you can add any new ideas as they strike you. There's a further advantage: if, by any chance, you don't have time to finish your answer, whatever is in your plan might get you another mark or two. It might just make the difference between passing and failing the entire paper.

Aim to:

- write a quick *list or mind map* of the main areas or issues you will need to cover
- note any comments you might make (i.e. the argument – see below and chapter 2)
- number the issues in the order in which you'll deal with them

Selection is crucial. You're not likely to gain many marks by just writing down everything you know on a topic. Choose just those issues that relate specifically to the question. Argument will be essential, so concentrate on what you've learned of the possible angles on each issue. If the question asks for your views, it will want your carefully considered opinion after taking into account the relevant facts and the responses of experts in the field.

Once you've got a rough plan, you can begin to write. It's a good idea to tick off the points on your list (or put a line through them) as you cover them. This will give you a feeling of being in control and can cheer you up as you complete each section. If you write fast and feel comfortable with a detailed plan, note down everything you want to touch on; if you can work easily from a brief outline, that's fine too.

Here's Sandy's plan:

Culture & identity
Intro: Explain terms – culture/society
1   3 layers of culture
2   Cultural universals are 'control'
3   Change is slow. Stability from repetition
4   Forces affecting culture
5   Culture affects inquisitiveness – ethnocentricity
6   Technology & media – rate of change/collusion
7   Cultural change from history. Culture learned (McDonald Mason)
8   Individuals – diff. values & beliefs – age, generation, *Zeitgeist*
9   Biggest change (Hofstede) individualism – disintegration of
     culture or breakdown of state
10   In past, no opportunity for individualism. Now, individuals think
     they control their lives
11   Individuals' moves within a culture = swap. No free will
12   Identity from views of others. Modern constraints, institutional
     base (U. Beck)
Conc: In past – culture controlled. Now less obvious, but controlling
as ever

Sandy addressed the concept of identity (from the question) by
looking at the situation of the individual, and planned this essay paragraph by paragraph. The same essay could have been planned in
sections. If you look closely, you can see that the paragraphs fit roughly
into the following structure:

Culture & identity
Intro: explain terms – culture/society

A The role of culture
     3 layers
     universals are control
     change = slow/stability from repetition
     [paras. 1, 2, 3]

B Change
     forces affecting culture
     inquisitiveness/ethnocentrism
     technology & media – rate of change
     [paras 4, 5, 6]

C The situation of the individual
  culture is learned (McDonald Mason)
  values & beliefs – age, etc.
  [paras. 7, 8]

D Freedom & the individual
  biggest change = individualism (Hofstede)
  people now think they control their lives
  moves within a culture – no free will
  identity, constraints, institutions (U. Beck)
  [paras. 9, 10, 11, 12]

Conc: personal freedom is a mirage. Culture controls.

It really doesn't matter what form your plan takes as long as you get something that you can work with down on paper.

▶ Introduction

In an exam, there is no time for carefully thought-out introductions. If you can set the scene with a *little* explanation of the main topic or some background information, that's good. But if nothing occurs to you, just leave a few lines and launch into your first issue. If there's time, you can come back after you've written the rest of the essay and fill in some introductory material.

Sandy has begun by defining the word 'culture', showing that there are clear differences in sociological terms between this and the word 'society', so demonstrating an awareness of this.

▶ The main body of the essay

Facts, theories and examples

By the time you reach your first exams, you'll be well aware that whatever you say in any piece of academic work needs to be firmly rooted in facts. These are what give credibility to your work. You might find it helps to note briefly in your plan (or mind map) specific items and examples that you want to include in your answer.

The kind of data you use will vary according to your subject, of course. In history, acts, treaties and events will be crucial, as well as the theories of historians. In philosophy, ideas put forward by various philosophers can be treated as some of your key material. In English literature, the structure, plot and language of a text you've studied will form the basis of your essays. In sociology, theories are often key to your discussion, together with results of surveys.

Sandy's essay includes plenty of factual material, starting with a breakdown of the three layers of culture (paragraph 1). Almost every paragraph mentions theories that have become accepted tenets of sociology. There are also specific examples of recent studies and writings – the statement on a baby's relationship to culture by McDonald Mason (7) and the study on change noted by Hofstede (9). You will not need to give full referencing in an exam, but it helps if you can remember the date and title of any publication you refer to.

Quotes

Long quotes are never needed in an exam and would, in any case, be seen as padding. But if you can memorise an important phrase or sentence relating to each of the main areas you have studied, these can give further strength to your answers. Sandy has given two quotes from U. Beck that underline points on the institutional base of contemporary culture (12).

The argument

As in a term-time essay, it's important to explain *how* what you say relates to the question you've been given. In fact, a good clear argument can be the key to getting a high mark, just as in term-time essays, so show how the relevant facts that you know affect the particular situation you've been asked to write on, and give what seems to you to be the most sensible view of it all. It's fatally easy to assume that because you've written down the relevant facts, an argument is implicit. It isn't. You *must* spell out the implications and what you think about them. Different students often take very different angles on the same set of facts. Make sure you explain the situation as *you* see it, and, as you write, look back at the question every now and then in order to check that you're still on track.

First of all, it's interesting to note how many times Sandy has used terms from the first half of the question in her essay (the numbers relate to paragraphs):

collude [3]
bondage to society [5]
collude [5]

Including terms from the question demonstrates forcibly to whoever is marking that you are addressing the question. It also helps to ensure that you keep on track. Sandy also uses the terms *individuals* and *individualism* (to relate to the question's term *identity*) and *culture* throughout the essay, showing that it is focused clearly on the question's key topics.

Sandy's argument makes it very clear throughout why the essay includes particular facts and theories. The following statement concludes the explanation of the three layers of culture:

> So every individual is exposed to these 'cultural rules' in some form or another. [1]

And here's a point on cultural stability (using terms from the question):

> Individuals collude with culture as they can enjoy the boundaries it provides . . . [3]

Here's a summing-up of change brought about by individualism:

> It can be seen as a fight against cultural norms. [9]

And here's how the essay argues for contemporary culture's institutional base, supported by quotes from another sociologist:

> All individuals must plan for and take into account all constraints and provisos of modern culture as they live their lives. They cannot merely live subjectively: 'Under the surface of modern society is a highly efficient, densely woven institutional culture' (U. Beck, 2002). [12]

Every time you use facts and theories, make a clear statement on how you want them to be viewed.

▶ Conclusion

It's important to sum up what you've said on the various issues and to underline the crux of your argument. It's also very important to show clearly how your conclusion(s) demonstrate(s) that you've addressed the question. As with term-time essays, there must be no new facts and no quotes or references to other writers in your conclusion.

Sandy's conclusion sums up the essay's points, relating them closely to the question, which had asked candidates to look at how far we collude with (or suffer) our place in society by relating this to culture and identity. After commenting on the historical situation, Sandy's essay ties up its position on the contemporary situation. Its final sentence underlines the writer's position neatly:

> It seems in modern society we accept the overarching values of our culture and even its constraints.

▶ Language and paragraphing

Generally speaking, you will not need to worry about writing wonderful sentences. Getting your answers on paper is quite enough to think about. Indeed, time spent in careful crafting of your language in an exam is likely to be time wasted. The tutor who marks your script will be working fast. He or she will be looking for facts and for sensible comment on them.

The best language is clear and simple. If you've been working on improving the way you write, this will certainly pay dividends in the exam. If you've not had a chance to do this, and your exams are due soon, aim to keep your sentences fairly short so that there's less chance of getting into difficulties. Be sure to split your answers into paragraphs and, as with any piece of work, leaving a line between paragraphs will help make your answers look clear and well organised.

Sandy has made points clearly and succinctly. (There were one or two errors in the script which I've edited out for the purposes of this book.) Unless your subject is English, no one's going to worry about a few spelling mistakes or grammatical errors. Some of Sandy's paragraphs are rather short, but again this kind of thing will generally be forgiven in an exam if the essay includes plenty of facts and a strong argument.

SUMMARY

This chapter has covered:
- **revision**
  - work in **bite-sized chunks**
  - **highlight key points** from your notes, essays, handouts, etc.
  - **make master lists/mind maps**
- **planning your exam essay**
  - highlight or underline **key words**
  - make a **list** or **mind map**
  - **plan the order** of your main points
  - **budget your time**
- **writing your exam essay**
  - write a *very brief* **introduction**
  - give *at least* **one paragraph for each issue**
  - include: **facts, theories and examples**
    argument (i.e. show what seems to you the most sensible line to take)
    quotes where possible
  - tie things up in a brief **conclusion**

Part Three

The Nuts and Bolts of Good Writing

12 Verbs and Other Parts of Speech

INTRODUCTION

This chapter contains a good deal of information that you will need to understand in order to work though chapter 13 (although you won't need to learn it off by heart). In traditional grammar, all the words we ever use (well, very nearly all) fall into one of eight groups. These groups are called parts of speech – or, sometimes, word classes. Some grammarians now define extra categories, but you need not worry about those in order to have a good basic understanding of how parts of speech function.

The most important parts of speech for your purposes are verbs. Of the other seven, four are important and worth learning about, but unless you are really keen or you plan to study linguistics you can probably ignore the other three. After the section on verbs, this chapter will look at nouns, pronouns, adjectives and adverbs, and then briefly at conjunctions, prepositions and interjections.

VERBS

If you are having trouble writing grammatical sentences, it's ten to one that the key to the problem is your use of verbs. For example, unless you are studying languages, you certainly won't need to be able to set out any verbs (see below). However, once you have an understanding of how they work, you will be able to write well-formed sentences without too much trouble. If you are completely new to verbs, it will be important to read the whole section, and do at least the first three activities, but if you know something about them already, you'll probably find that you want to skip bits.

You may have terrible memories of having been unable to learn verbs at school, or you may never have been taught anything about them at all, but fear not. Like all other aspects of written English, there's no mystique to verbs. We all use them expertly when we speak. You might like to think of a verb as being the spark that gets the engine going. A verb is the central key to every well-formed sentence.

▶ **Doing words**

If your school used to teach verbs, you may remember that verbs are often called 'doing' words. Most verbs tell us something about some kind of *action.* Here are some examples:

run	drink
swim	breathe
blink	work
walk	drive
eat	talk

It's easy to imagine somebody (or perhaps some animal) doing most of those things, isn't it? They are all actions. Let's put some of them into sentences. We may have to alter some of them very slightly to make them sound right:

Jenny **runs** for her school in league fixtures.
We usually **blink** several times a minute.
Both my children **walk** to school.
Most of the time, we **breathe** very quietly.
Carl **works** on the shop floor.
Many people **drive** to work.
Politicians **talk** a lot.

There are other things we do that may not show up quite so clearly as actions, but which still count as verbs. Here are some examples of these:

like	remember
love	plan
hate	want
wonder	think
calculate	imagine

And here are some of them in sentences:

> Jamie **loves** curry.
> Cindy **hates** the dentist.
> My grandfather **remembers** the First World War.
> I **want** lots of money.
> Ben **likes** jazz and **loves** the blues.

You have probably noticed that there are actually *two* verbs in the last sentence. If we wanted, we could put more in:

> Ben **likes** jazz, **loves** the blues, **buys** CDs, and **goes** to concerts every month.

ACTIVITY 1

See if you can pick out the verbs in the following sentences. There is just one in each. Remember that you are looking for words which tell you what somebody or something *does*.

1 I wash the car on Saturdays.
2 Horoscopes foretell the future.
3 The farmers long for rain.
4 Before winter, many birds migrate to warmer lands.
5 Marco sends faxes to America.
6 We all desire happiness.

▶ The verb *to be*

The verb *to be* has nothing at all to do with 'doing'. You might have heard of this verb because it's in a very famous speech from William Shakespeare's *Hamlet*:

> To be or not to be. That is the question ...

In the play, Hamlet's father, the old king, has been murdered, and his ghost appears to Hamlet asking him to take revenge and kill the murderer. The old king has actually been murdered by his brother, who has seized the throne and married the old king's wife.

Killing does not come easily to Hamlet, who is a scholar, not a fighter, and he spends a great deal of the play just trying to decide what to do. He even considers the possibility of suicide, and when he says, "To be or not to be" he is thinking about life and death – existence or non-existence.

If you are interested in New Age therapies and ideas, you may have heard of the idea of just 'being'. Some people, exhausted with what they see as the 'rat race' of modern life, have decided that they no longer want to rush around 'doing' things but that they prefer just quietly existing. The verb *to be* may look rather insignificant, but it does some very important work. It's the one we use when we want to describe things. It probably gets more use than any other verb.

Describing people, animals and things

The following words are all parts of the verb *to be*: **am**, **is**, **are**, **was**, **were**, and **will be**. We use one or another of them whenever we describe anything, or when we give a brief explanation about it. Here they are in some sentences:

> I **am** busy.
> You **are** wonderful.
> Alan **is** Australian.

> We **were** the winners.
> Hamlet **was** miserable.
> The footballers **were** muddy after the match.

> The train **will be** late.
> The carnival **will be** exciting.
> The runners **will be** exhausted.

You may have noticed that each of those three groups of sentences is written in a different time-scale – present, past and future (see below), and that some of them have two parts. A verb can have up to four parts.

The verb *to be* as an auxiliary (i.e. helping) verb

Look at the following three sentences:

> Darren *was swimming* strongly.
> My son *is swimming* in the shallow end of the pool.
> Charlie Blunt *will be swimming* in the championships.

The words *was, is* and *will be* each help to put the verb *to swim* into different time bands (see below).

► Having

Verbs are about three things – doing, being and having. We've looked at the first two of these, so all we have left now is a *very* small group of words that tell us about owning things – such as *have, own* and *possess.* Here are some examples of them in use:

Joe **has** a cupboard full of cricket gear.
Chris **owns** a pub.
Aladdin **possessed** a magic lamp.

The verb *to have* as an auxiliary verb
Parts of the verb *to have*, like parts of the verb *to be*, are often used to help another verb, like this:

I **have lived** in Britain for three years.
Sue **has finished** her essay.
Michelle **has given** Lucy some chocolates.

ACTIVITY 2

Underline the verbs in the following sentences and note down whether each is a 'doing', 'being' or 'having' verb. There is only one verb in each sentence, but it may have more than one part.

1 Mary ate a pomegranate.
2 Max has six fossils.
3 We will be crossing the border at six tonight.
4 The earth goes round the sun.
5 The lions were very hungry.
6 The view from the mountain is beautiful.
7 The dog had fleas.
8 Terry will have £300 by next month.
9 The flies were buzzing round the meat.
10 The calculation will be difficult.

► Time

When we speak, we all use verbs expertly to show *when* something happens. Let's imagine that the mother of a teenager called Jenny is speaking to a friend. She might say:

"Jenny **runs** for her school in league fixtures."

Her mother means that whenever there's a league race, Jenny is in it. This is the current state of affairs – it tells us about what is happening in the **present**.

Let's suppose that Jenny has now grown up, and that her mother is recalling her schooldays in a letter to a friend. She might write:

Jenny **ran** for her school in league fixtures.

She's now talking about what Jenny did in the **past**.

Now let's suppose that Jenny has only just been picked to run for the school, and that her mother is explaining what this means in a letter to Jenny's grandmother:

Jenny **will run** for the school in league fixtures.

Now Jenny's mother is talking about the **future**.

The verbs in those three sentences are written to show whether something happens in the **present** (*runs*), the **past** (*ran*) or the **future** (*will run*). There's a word for this: **tense**. We can say that those three sentences are written in different **tenses**: the **present tense**, the **past tense** and the **future tense**. You will find full examples of all the tenses at the end of this chapter.

ACTIVITY 3

Look at the following sentences, and write down **past**, **present** or **future** for each one:

1 Margaret Thatcher led Britain's Conservative party for many years.
2 America's President lives at the White House.
3 Napoleon won many battles.
4 Denise will sit her final exams in June.
5 I go to my guitar lesson once a week.
6 At 10 p.m., the supermarket will close.

7 Some animals hibernate in winter.
8 Mark will get redundancy pay from his employer.

Perfect tenses

Let's suppose that Jenny's mother is talking to a neighbour. We've seen that if she says:

"Jenny **runs** for her school in league fixtures"

she is obviously talking about what is going on now. She's talking in the **present tense**. But she might put this slightly differently. She might say:

"Jenny **has run** for her school in league fixtures."

Here she means that *up until this point* Jenny has run in the school's league fixtures. If she puts it this way, she's probably implying that the situation might not continue – Jenny might not get picked next time. When we want to show that something has happened up till now or that the action is now finished, it's done in the **present perfect** tense – in this case, *has run*.

There's also a **past perfect** tense. We often use this when we want to show that two things happened at different times in the past. If Jenny's mother says:

"Before she **won** the cup, Jenny **had run** in league fixtures for five years"

we can see that running in league fixtures had *preceded* winning the cup (which itself is in the past). This is what had happened up to the point when Jenny won the cup. The clue to the past perfect tense is in the use of the word *had* along with a verb in the past tense. It implies that something happened a long way back or prior to something else.

And if Jenny's mother says:

"By the time she's eighteen, Jenny **will have run** for her school for six years"

she'll be explaining *what will have happened* up to a particular point in the future. She'll be using the **future perfect** tense.

ACTIVITY 4

See if you can say which of the following are in the **present perfect**, which are in the **past perfect** and which are in the **future perfect**.

1 All the members of the club had attended the previous meeting.
2 Cindy has been to the theatre three times this week.
3 We had worked on the boat all morning.
4 Palab will have played in every match this season.
5 The children have put away their football things.
6 The dog had eaten his dinner.
7 By this evening, Tracy will have finished painting her bedroom.
8 I have found the map.
9 It will have stopped raining by the afternoon.
10 Sean has given his mother a watch for her birthday.

Continuous action (sometimes called progressive)
We show when an action is continuing to happen by adding '-ing' to a verb and preceding it with a part of the verb *to be*. This is called **continuous** action:

Last week, Martin **was thinking** about a holiday.   **past continuous**

John **is thinking** about a holiday.   **present continuous**

Soon, Cherie **will be thinking** about a holiday.   **future continuous**

In each sentence, the person doing the thinking is spending quite a bit of time at it – the action is *continuing* over a period.
We can also show that a continuous action is finished and done with, has been happening up till now or will still be happening at a date in the future by combining the continuous with the perfect in each tense, like this:

Martin had been thinking about a holiday all last week.
John has been thinking about a holiday all day today.
Cherie will have been thinking about a holiday for a whole year next month.

Below is a table that you can use as a checklist for all the different tenses.

Checklist for tenses

I wash the car every week.	**present simple**
I am washing the car now.	**present continuous**
I have washed the car this morning.	**present perfect**
I have been washing the car all morning.	**present perfect continuous**
I washed the car last week.	**past simple**
I was washing the car with a new shampoo.	**past continuous**
I had washed the car by six o'clock.	**past perfect**
I had been washing the car on Thursday.	**past perfect continuous**
I will wash the car this afternoon.	**future simple**
I will be washing the car this afternoon.	**future continuous**
I will have washed the car by six o'clock	**future perfect**
I will have been washing the car for two hours soon.	**future perfect continuous**

ACTIVITY 5

Write down the tense for each verb in the following sentences:

1 I want a drink.
2 Jane broke her coffee mug.
3 Mark will laugh at the photo.
4 After the exams, the students will be celebrating.
5 Marie had been eating her breakfast.
6 Stan had considered the problem.
7 Kirsty will have been cooking all evening.
8 We were enjoying Disneyland this time last year.
9 We're having a wonderful time.
10 Stan will have considered the problem.
11 The cat has washed itself.
12 The cat has been washing itself for half an hour.

▶ Conjugating (i.e. setting out) verbs

Setting out a verb is a bit of a bother, and you won't ever be asked to do it (unless you are a student of languages), but it can be very useful just to see how it's done. Once you've understood the pattern, you will find that it works for all verbs. It shows how a verb is used for different people.

Remember, you almost certainly do the whole thing accurately when you speak. The diagram just shows what you actually say. I'll use the verb *to talk*. This is a regular verb – which means that *-s* is added for he, she and it (3rd person singular) in the present simple tense and *-ed* for the past tense.

The verb *to talk*
SIMPLE TENSES

Singular   *Plural*

Present Simple

I	talk		we	talk
you	talk		you	talk
he/she/it	talks		they	talk

Past Simple

I	talked		we	talked
you	talked		you	talked
he/she/it	talked		they	talked

Future Simple

I	will talk		we	will talk
you	will talk		you	will talk
he/she/it	will talk		they	will talk

CONTINUOUS TENSES
Present Continuous

I	am talking		we	are talking
you	are talking		you	are talking
he/she/it	is talking		they	are talking

Past Continuous

I	was talking		we	were talking
you	were talking		you	were talking
he/she/it	was talking		they	were talking

Future Continuous

I	will be talking	we	will be talking
you	will be talking	you	will be talking
he/she/it	will be talking	they	will be talking

PERFECT TENSES
Present Perfect

I	have talked	we	have talked
you	have talked	you	have talked
he/she/it	has talked	they	have talked

Past Perfect

I	had talked	we	had talked
you	had talked	you	had talked
he/she/it	had talked	they	had talked

Future Perfect

I	will have talked	we	will have talked
you	will have talked	you	will have talked
he/she/it	will have talked	they	will have talked

PERFECT CONTINUOUS TENSES
Present Perfect Continuous

I	have been talking	we	have been talking
you	have been talking	you	have been talking
he/she/it	has been talking	they	have been talking

Past perfect continuous

I	had been talking	we	had been talking
you	had been talking	you	had been talking
he/she/it	had been talking	they	had been talking

Future Perfect Continuous

I	will have been talking	we	will have been talking
you	will have been talking	you	will have been talking
he/she/it	will have been talking	they	will have been talking

You can see that regular verbs have very few changes, and that any changes are made mainly for the third-person singular – sometimes also for the first-person singular.

Some verbs are **irregular**, which means that they do not follow this pattern. For example, the past tense of the verb *to think* uses the form *thought* (not 'thinked'). You might have noticed that when small children are learning to talk, they often start by using the *-ed* construction for the past tense of irregular verbs. A toddler is likely to say, "I thinked" because that's the construction he or she expects.

The verb *to be*

As you've seen above, the verb *to be* is rather a special verb and can be used as an auxiliary. It's conjugated (set out) like this:

Singular			*Plural*	
		Present		
I	am		we	are
you	are		you	are
he/she/it	is		they	are
		Past		
I	was		we	were
you	were		you	were
he/she/it	was		they	were
		Past perfect		
I	had been		we	had been
you	had been		you	had been
he/she/it	had been		they	had been
		Future		
I	will be		we	will be
you	will be		you	will be
he/she/it	will be		they	will be

Note: People vary as to whether they say *you were* or *you was* for the second-person singular in the past simple tense. In what is generally known as standard English (that used by people such as writers and journalists, newsreaders, lawyers and lecturers) the accepted form is *you were* (as above).

▶ Actives and passives

In a simple sentence, the person at the beginning can usually be seen to be *doing* the verb, so to speak. We call this type of verb **active**. But sometimes, the verb is being done *to* him or her. The verb in this case is called a **passive** verb. The difference between **active** and **passive** verbs shows up in the following two sentences:

> I was bitten by the dog.　**passive**
> I bit the dog.　**active**

In the first sentence, the biting was done *to* me. In the second, I did it myself. In both sentences, the focus is on 'I'.

If I really had been bitten by a dog, as in the first sentence, I'd be more likely to say:

> The dog bit me.

You can see that the focus is now on what the *dog* did. It has become the most important item in the sentence. Now that I've changed the verb in that first sentence from passive to active, the sentence has also become much more lively. It's simpler and more informal too. In passive verbs, as explained above, the person *preceding* the verb (whom you'd normally expect to be 'doing' it) is having it done *to* him or her. These days, we don't use the passive much because it often seems rather cold and dead.

Below are some active and passive verbs. You can see that sentences that use active verbs are generally sharper and punchier.

ACTIVE	PASSIVE
Present	
Maisie **is watching** the parrot.	The parrot **is being watched** by Maisie.
Hazel **likes** everyone.	Everyone **is liked** by Hazel.
Past	
I **bit** the dog.	The dog **was bitten** by me.
Sue **phoned** the TV company.	The TV company **was phoned** by Sue.
Future	
Tim **will give** a vote of thanks.	A vote of thanks **will be given** by Tim.
The President of the United States **will meet** the Russian envoy.	The Russian envoy **will be met** by the President of the United States.

Don't worry about how to write passives – you'll do it automatically when necessary. I'm showing you here how to *spot* them. Unless you are an English language student, however, the only time you are likely to need to know much about passive verbs is if a tutor comments that you are using too many of them. A piece of writing filled with passives can sound rather lifeless. That said, you will find that you will need to use them for the following jobs:

- focusing on the *receiver* of an action
- writing up *reports* and scientific *experiments*
- showing that the *doer* of the action is *unknown*

Here's an example of that last item:

The baby was abandoned in the church.

Because we don't know who did the abandoning, the only way we could make that sentence active would be to say:

Someone abandoned the baby in the church.

You can read a little more on passives in the section **The subject of a passive verb** in chapter 13.

ACTIVITY 6

Note down A or P (active or passive) for each of the following sentences:

1. The priest tripped over the bridesmaid's foot.
2. Food was provided by the bride's sister and her husband.
3. The couple's friends were greeted by the bride's parents.
4. The bride wore a beautiful dress.
5. All the speeches were brief.
6. The bride was given a kiss by the groom.
7. The little bridesmaid was looked after by her mother.
8. The wedding guests were served by catering students.
9. A journalist reported on the wedding in the local paper.
10. The day will be remembered for a long time.

MORE PARTS OF SPEECH

▶ Nouns

In a nutshell, nouns are **words for people, places and things**:

People	Places	Things
boy	New York	table
girl	Adelaide	car
Mrs Thatcher	Japan	clock
Buddha	Niagara Falls	milk
Mick Jagger	St Paul's Cathedral	computer
Bill Gates	the French Riviera	grass
Susie	South West England	newspaper

The **names of animals, birds, insects and sea creatures** are also nouns:

dog	eagle	beetle	whale
cat	sparrow	bee	seal
lion	duck	moth	octopus

The **names of government departments, companies, corporations and shops** are nouns too; and so are **brand names**:

Berkshire County Council	Marks and Spencer	Coca-Cola
United States of America	the Catholic Church	Nescafé
Microsoft	McDonald's	Ford
Toshiba	Debenhams	Porsche
Barclays Bank	Macy's	Persil
Live Aid	The Foreign Office	Tesco

Seasons, periods of time and **words relating to weather** are also nouns:

spring	hour	snow
summer	minute	sunshine
autumn	month	wind
winter	century	rain

Here are some sentences with the nouns highlighted in bold:

Joan threw the **ball** across the **garden**.
Toshiba are building a new **factory** in **Wales**.
The **French** are known for good **food**.
The **moon** and **stars** shine brightly on a clear **night**.

One way of understanding nouns is to remember that *it is usually possible to see and/or touch them.* You can put some nouns in your pocket, eat some for breakfast, meet some for a drink, read about them in the paper, or look at pictures of them.

ACTIVITY 7

Underline the nouns in the following sentences:

1 Mrs Steele sent a letter to the Queen.
2 Bees make honey.
3 Carlos has been living in France for six years.
4 Mary wanted a bike.
5 Julius Caesar ruled in Rome.

The whole category of nouns can also be divided into two groups – into what are known as **concrete** and **abstract nouns**. Concrete nouns are the ones we have already been looking at. These are the ones that can be seen, touched, or found in some form. Abstract nouns, as the name suggests, are things that it is not possible to find. Below are some examples of the two types. Notice that each concrete noun is related to a corresponding abstract noun on its left:

Abstract	*Concrete*
beauty	flower
education	book
war	gun
kindness	gift
love	ring
crime	thief
sadness	tears
religion	church

Abstract nouns are things that we often talk about but we wouldn't be able to see. They are usually generalised ideas or emotions. Concrete nouns, on the other hand, can be found somewhere – even if it takes some searching.

So things like the heart and lungs are concrete rather than abstract nouns because, in an operation, they are visible. Ghosts, too, surprisingly, are concrete. If they exist, they are visible and very specific. On the day that I see one, I shall be able to describe it in detail. Air and other gases are concrete too, because they can be measured. We could obtain a jar of hydrogen, so it's not abstract.

Abstract nouns can only be talked about – never found. We can see a beautiful painting or person, but we can't find a piece of beauty; we can find students, lecturers, books and universities, but we can't get hold of a piece of education.

ACTIVITY 8

Underline the concrete nouns and put a ring round the abstract nouns in the following:

1 Water is essential for life.
2 Exercise is important for health.
3 The atmosphere in the bar was dense with smoke.
4 The monk had great understanding.
5 The members talked endlessly about strategy.
6 Paul was studying philosophy.

▶ Pronouns

Pronouns save an awful lot of time. They are used *in place of nouns*. It would be both boring and time-consuming to have to write the following:

> Jack was born in Toronto, but soon Jack's parents moved to Britain. Jack went to school in Huddersfield. Jack has now started Jack's own business, making greetings cards.

Obviously, we all use pronouns a great deal. If you look back to the section on conjugating verbs, you will see that they follow the same pattern as the list of *personal pronouns* below – from first-person singular to third-person plural:

I/me	we/us
you	you
he/him/she/her/it	they/them

There are also some other types of pronoun, but it is not necessary for most people to worry about these. They are *relative, possessive* and *demonstrative pronouns*:

relative pronouns
who, whom, that, which

possessive pronouns
my/mine, your/yours, his, her/hers, its, our/ours, their/theirs

demonstrative pronouns
this, these, that, those

▶ Adjectives

Adjectives are words that describe something. Look at the following sentence:

The old lady owned a beautiful red necklace.

There are three describing words in that sentence: *old, beautiful* and *red*. The first one tells us something about the lady. The other two tell us what the necklace looked like. You might start to wonder what it was made of – coral, perhaps, or rubies.

Did you spot that *lady* and *necklace* are nouns? The rule is: **adjectives describe nouns**. In the following sentences, I've underlined the adjectives:

There was an <u>enormous</u> dog in the office.
John's <u>crazy</u> mother brought a <u>large, fat</u> hen to church.
Pat Patch owned a <u>noisy</u> parrot.

Adjectives are also used to describe pronouns:

He was <u>hot</u>.
They are <u>happy</u>.

You can see from the last two examples that adjectives can be used in a simple way with parts of the verb *to be*. Here are some more examples:

> The children are <u>hungry</u>.
> The dress was <u>expensive</u>.
> The sun is <u>hot</u>.

▶ Adverbs

Since adjectives describe nouns, you may have guessed that **adverbs are used to describe verbs**. They show us how things are done. The good news here is that the vast majority of adverbs end in *-ly* so they are usually very easy to spot. They are formed by putting *-ly* on the end of an adjective. Look at the following sentence:

> Sarah walked home <u>slowly</u>.

You'll remember that most verbs are action words. The verb here is *walked*. The word *slowly* tells us *how* Sarah walked, and gives us the beginning of a visual picture. While you are practising spotting the difference between adjectives and adverbs, it's a good idea to ask yourself: Which word is being described and what part of speech is it?

You might say, "Which word does *slowly* describe? Is it *Sarah?* Well, she is going *slowly*. But that doesn't quite seem quite right. I can't say that Sarah is *slowly*. Let's try *walked*. Ah yes, that fits." If I ask myself the question, "How did Sarah walk?", I'm bound to come up with the answer *slowly*.

You can see the difference between adjectives and adverbs in these two sentences:

> My room is tidy.
> I have arranged my room tidily.

In the first sentence, the word *tidy* describes the word *room,* which is a noun. So *tidy* must be an adjective. In the second sentence, the word *tidily* tells you how I *arranged* the place. The word *arranged* is a verb. It tells us about an action. So *tidily* must be an adverb because it describes a verb.

There are a few adverbs that are not quite so easy to spot, but they work in just the same way as the *-ly* adverbs, for example:

The boy ran <u>fast</u>.
We worked <u>hard</u>.

The word *fast* tells us how the boy *ran.* The word *hard* tells how we *worked.* The words *ran* and *worked* are both verbs, of course.

If we want to be a bit more academic about this, we can use the term *modify* instead of *describe.* It's a little more precise because, rather than confining the job solely to describing, it implies that the effect of a particular word is *changed* slightly.

As well as modifying verbs, adverbs can also modify adjectives and other adverbs – though it's less important for you to remember this. If you want to pursue this one, take a few minutes to see if you can work out how adjectives and adverbs function in the following sentence:

The soldier will probably easily outrun his very heavily loaded colleague.

If we start at the end of the sentence, we can see that *colleague* is a noun. The word *loaded* describes it, and so is an adjective. That word is modified by the word *heavily*, which must therefore be an adverb. This, in turn, is modified by *very,* which must then be another adverb. The verb is *will outrun* and it is modified by *easily,* which is therefore yet another adverb. Finally, the word *probably* modifies *easily* so that, too, is an adverb. Here's the list:

Nouns	*Verb*	*Adjective*	*Adverbs*
soldier	will outrun	loaded	probably
colleague			easily
			very
			heavily

There are also a few words which are adverbs although you might not, at first glance, expect them to be, for example:

how, where, when, why

In the following sentences, each of the above words modifies a verb. The verbs are in bold type.

How **is** John?
Where **is** Joan's coat?
When **did** you **buy** your car?
Why **was** Roy **laughing**?

Notice that, in the last two sentences, the verbs (which, in those sentences, have two parts) are split apart.

The words *here* and *there* are also adverbs. Again, the verbs are in bold type:

Please **put** your boots here.
I've **left** my rucksack there.

ACTIVITY 9

Underline the adverbs in the following:

1 I felt I'd managed the first essay beautifully.
2 Slowly and silently, the cat crept through the grass.
3 I finished my lunch quickly.
4 Cheetahs can run fast.
5 Jason has worked harder and harder throughout the year.
6 The athlete jumped high.
7 Josh had a green jacket that he loved dearly.
8 Dan answered the question rather rashly.

▶ Conjunctions

A conjunction is a word that connects either two other words or whole constructions such as phrases or clauses (see chapter 13):

and	because
but	if
or	although

Here are a couple of examples used in sentences:

I'll come down the pub **if** John gets home early.
I'll come down the pub, **although** I'm short of cash.

▶ Prepositions

Prepositions have a number of uses. The main function of a preposition is to appear before a noun or pronoun and link this word in some way to another part of the sentence. Examples of prepositions are:

> at, from, of, through, without, during, for, with

Here are some of them used in sentences:

> I left my umbrella **at** the hospital.
> I had a present **from** my aunt.
> I've come **without** my diary.
> I'll be away **during** March.

Perhaps the most common use of prepositions is to show the position of something in relation to something else. Look at the following sentence:

> I put the saucepan **on** the cooker.

Other prepositions for showing position are:

> in, beside, under, near

▶ Interjections

These are usually one-word shouts, such as:

> Hey! Oops! Bother! Ouch! Ugh!

They are also one-word greetings (or the opposite), such as:

> Hello! Hi! Cheers! Goodbye!

▶ Memory-jogger

You can use a very basic sentence as a way of remembering the four main parts of speech: nouns, verbs, adjectives and adverbs. You'll probably find it easiest to focus on one line at a time. You might like to take a ruler or a piece of paper and place it so that you can see just the first line, and then slide it down each time you are ready to look at the next one.

adjec-tive	noun	verb	adverb		adjective	noun
The	cat	sat		on the		mat.
The black	cat	sat		on the	red	mat.
The frisky	kitten	sat	slyly	on the	new	rug.
The thin	Siamese	squatted	shyly	on the	Turkish	carpet.

If you've been really keen, you might have realized that *on* is a preposition. The word 'the' is what is called a **determiner**, but it's not necessary to remember that.

SUMMARY

Verbs
- Verbs tell us about: doing
                                            being
                                            having
- The majority are *action* words – i.e. doing
- The verb *to be* helps us to *describe* people and things – e.g. *is, are, were*
- We show *when* something happens through using different *tenses*
- Many verbs have more than one part
- *Active* verbs are more lively than *passive* ones

Nouns
people, places, things, brand names, shops, companies and any other observable items
   concrete nouns: all the above
   abstract nouns: concepts and feelings (that can be spoken of but not found)

Pronouns
words that stand *instead* of nouns – e.g. *he, it, they*

Adjectives
words that **describe nouns** – e.g. *hot, happy*

Adverbs
words (often ending in *-ly*) that **describe verbs** – e.g. *quickly*

Conjunctions
link words that connect two other words, phrases or clauses – e.g. *and, but, so*

Prepositions
words that often point out place – e.g. *on, at, beside, from, for* they also link parts of a sentence – e.g. *from, through, during*

Interjections
shouts – e.g. "Bother!"
greetings – e.g. "Hello!"

13 Writing Clear Sentences

INTRODUCTION

Everybody knows roughly what a sentence is, and this works fine when we leave notes around for people we live or work with or write simple letters to friends. It's when we start to write about complex topics that difficulties can arise. This chapter will cover the basic rules for writing grammatical sentences, looking briefly at verbs, subjects and objects. It will also show a number of pitfalls and how to avoid them. You might find that you need to refer to the sections on verbs in chapter 12 as you work through.

You'll also find some information on clauses here. It's not always necessary to understand how clauses work in order to write well, and ways of analysing grammar are currently undergoing change, but a basic understanding of traditional clause analysis will help you to get a sense of how sentences are composed of a number of working parts. Understanding a little about clauses can have other benefits, too. You will begin to have greater control over what you write and your thinking will be sharpened. A further benefit is the effect on your reading. When reading difficult material, you can use your knowledge of clause analysis to help you to spot more quickly the central statement in any complex sentence. It can take a while to become familiar with clause analysis, however, so aim to get a broad understanding rather than trying to learn things off pat.

I THE BASICS

▶ Simple rules for a good sentence

It's not likely to be news to you that a sentence needs to start with a capital letter and end with a full stop. Beyond this, there are three rules for writing good sentences.

A sentence must:

- make sense by itself
- contain a working verb
- contain a subject for the verb

Making sense

Meaning is crucial for whoever reads what we write. Look at this sentence:

With all his football kit.

I'm sure you can see that there's a problem here. This 'sentence' doesn't make sense, does it? It's what is called a *sentence fragment*. I'd better improve it:

John went to school with all his football kit.

Now you know what I mean. A sentence should always tell us something clearly. It makes some kind of *statement*. In this case, I've communicated information about John going to school with his kit. You may want to know who John is, or the name of the school, and whether John was just practising or was playing in a match, but you now have a basic idea of what was going on.

A good test of whether a sentence works is to check whether someone reading it would be able to ask a sensible question about it, or whether the likely response to it would be a very puzzled "Eh?" My first example was only half a sentence, and you probably found it rather confusing. The words I used could have referred to any number of different people or places. They just seem to hang in the air, and it's hard to know what to make of them.

Look at the following extract from Susan's essay on education. She has made a very common error. Most of her sentences are well formed, but while concentrating on explaining what she means, she suddenly forgets the rules:

A majority of children and teenagers benefit greatly from the structure and compulsory nature of school attendance. For many from a background of poverty, school can mean a haven. A warm and stimulating place.

Susan's final sentence doesn't make sense by itself. It is actually part of her explanation in the previous sentence. We could improve the final sentence like this:

> It is often a warm and stimulating place in which disadvantaged children can begin to catch up with their peers.

If a tutor has written 'not a sentence' in the margin of your work, the problem may be that you have not been aware of this first crucial rule on making complete sense. You may have been writing down things as you would have said them. When we speak, we frequently break the rules of written grammar, but we still easily make ourselves understood because we also use facial expressions, gesture, and tone of voice to get our meaning across.

It's worth looking closely at the kind of thing that happens when we speak. In the following snatch of conversation, look carefully at what Sam's mother says:

> "Where are my pyjamas, Mum?" asked Sam.
> "On the floor!" replied his mother crossly. "Where you left them."

Sam's mother has spoken two 'sentences', but neither of them makes sense by itself. It's OK for her to say,

> "On the floor!"

because Sam knows (a) exactly what is on the floor, and (b) which floor she's referring to. He knows from the tone of her voice that she's cross, and he'll hear the sarcasm in

> "Where you left them."

His mother will probably put a heavy stress on the word *left*. She'll probably also use facial expressions and body language to get her meaning across. Not only does his mother give lots of extra clues to her meaning, but both Sam and his mother know a good deal about those pyjamas. So when they speak to each other, they can use a kind of shorthand. When we are writing, however, our sentences must make complete sense by themselves, because whoever reads them cannot hear us or pick up clues from our expressions or body language. Readers must not be left to guess what we mean.

If I were writing a story about Sam and his mother, I would have to explain things very carefully if I were not going to use conversation. I might do it like this:

> When Sam pestered his mother to find his pyjamas, she brushed him aside crossly, telling him to go and look for them on his bedroom floor where he had thrown them that morning.

You can see that I've had to give quite a bit of extra information to make things quite clear.

ACTIVITY 1

See if you can work out which are real sentences – that is, sentences that make complete sense by themselves:

1 about half-past nine
2 you don't often see kangaroos in Britain
3 I want a Coke
4 all by himself
5 whether you like it or not
6 wearing light blue trousers
7 I'm hot

Working verbs

The next crucial thing for a sentence is that it must contain a **working verb**. If you're not too clear on what a verb is, have a look at the verb section in chapter 12 before you read any further. By *working verb*, I mean one that is actually doing a job. The lack of a working verb is the cause of by far the greatest proportion of ungrammatical sentences that are written. The really annoying thing is that if you are leaving out verbs, you are probably doing it only occasionally, and so it's often hard to spot just the one or two instances in a piece of work where you've made the error.

The verbs that are set out in chapter 12 are shown as we use them to do a wide variety of different jobs. Each is headed by its name: *to talk* and *to be*. The name of a verb is known by the term **infinitive**. So *to talk* and *to be* are both infinitives. They are not doing any specific work, but are just hanging around doing nothing, so to speak. An infinitive on its own in a sentence won't be enough and it's easy to see why if you look at the following poorly constructed sentence:

I to walk by the sea.

This makes no sense. But if I add a working verb it will be fine:

I like to walk by the sea.

As you can see, it's OK to have an infinitive in a sentence as long as there's a working verb there as well.

By the way, be careful not to confuse the two functions of the word *to*:

I went to Paris.
I like to swim.

In the first sentence, the word *to* introduces a place; in the second, it's part of an infinitive – *to swim*.

The subject in a sentence

You are probably used to using the word *subject* to mean either *area of study* or *topic*. So if I ask you what subjects you are studying, the answer is likely to be "English and history", or "science and maths", and so on. Or if I ask what was the subject of the lecture you went to yesterday, the answer might be "the poetry of John Keats", or "the French Revolution", or "Recycling waste materials".

The word *subject* used in relation to grammar has a rather different meaning. It is closely linked to verbs, and verbs are about doing, being or having. A sentence always tells us about somebody (or something) doing, being or having something. That person or thing is the subject of the verb it fits with. Look at these two sentences:

Roy ate cheese sandwiches for his lunch.
Sarah sold her car last week.

Each of these sentences gives us information about a particular person. We know what Roy ate, and what Sarah did with her car. Roy is the **subject** of the verb *ate* and Sarah is the **subject** of the verb *sold*.

This rule functions in exactly the same way with animals, birds, insects and things, too:

Polar bears live in the Arctic.
Spiders have eight legs.

The church stands beside the river.
Water freezes at 0° centigrade.

The subject of a verb is the person or thing that is doing the doing, being or having. In the sentence about polar bears, the verb is *live*. So we can ask ourselves who or what is doing the living. The answer is polar bears. So the subject of the verb *live* is *polar bears.* In the second sentence, we can ask who or what is doing the having, and the answer is *spiders.* So we now know that the subject of the verb *have* in that particular sentence is spiders.

Remember that the word *subject* here means the *subject of the verb.* Any sentence will have a topic. It can't help being *about something.* But it must also have a grammatical subject for its verb. The *topics* of those four sentences above are:

the geographical habitat of polar bears
the physiology of spiders
the position of the church
the properties of water

But the *subjects* of the verbs are *polar bears, spiders, the church* and *water.*

The following confusing sentence, from an essay by Susan on the topic 'Discuss the proposition that education is wasted on the young', lacks a subject and working verb:

Pressures from their peer group, like keeping up with the latest fad, fashion, and pop sensations.

With a small addition, this sentence can easily be made to make much better sense:

Young people often encounter pressures from their peer group, like keeping up with the latest fad, fashion, and pop sensations.

Now the sentence has a subject – *Young people,* and a working verb – *encounter.*

This kind of error is very common. If you look at Susan's previous sentences, you can see how the problem occurred:

In secondary school, mainly, young people come into contact

with all sorts of influences as a whole new social scene emerges. These include drink and drugs which, previously, young people would have been sheltered from at primary school. Pressures from their peer group, like keeping up with the latest fad, fashion, and pop sensations.

What happened was that Susan started writing as if she were speaking. She added in another idea without considering how to construct the sentence.

ACTIVITY 2

In the following sentences, underline each working verb and then put a ring around the subject of that verb.

1 Jimi Hendrix died young.
2 Beatlemania swept Britain in the 1960s.
3 Fraser plays guitar in a folk band after work.
4 Duke Ellington is a favourite with traditional jazz musicians.
5 Perhaps surprisingly, Mick Jagger still performs to large audiences.
6 Salsa is becoming a highly popular dance.

In any sentence that contains more than one verb, there will be more than one grammatical subject. For example:

The kitchen *looks* awful since **the dog** *chewed* the curtains and **the baby** *spilt* blackcurrant juice down the wall.

Here there are three verbs so there must be three subjects: ***the kitchen***, ***the dog*** and ***the baby***.

Subjects at different places in a sentence
You can see that each of the following sentences begins with an introductory *phrase* – that is, a group of words *without* a working verb (see below). Then comes the subject and its verb:

Three hours after sunrise, **Bill** *spotted* the heron.
Despite the rain and cold, **Bill** *had waited* by the stream.
By a roundabout route, **Bill** *returned* to the town.

In the following sentences, the usual order is reversed in order to give impact. The subject of each verb, therefore, sits right at the end of the sentences:

> Out of the cave, *crawled* **Brian**.
> Beside the motorbike, *stood* **its owner**.

The subject of a passive verb *(see 'Actives and Passives' in chapter 12)* Most verbs are active. This means that the subject is the person or thing *doing* the verb. In the case of passive verbs, something is being done *to* the subject. Look at these sentences:

> **Ray** *was bitten* by the dog.
> **Ray** *bit* the dog.

It's easy to see that, in the second sentence, *Ray* is the subject of the verb *bit*. Biting is what he did. It's not so easy to see that *Ray* is also the subject of the first sentence. You might assume that, since the dog did the biting, it is he (or she) who is the subject. But the *focus* of the sentence is on *Ray,* and *was bitten* is a *passive* form of the verb *to bite.* It's in the past simple tense (see chapter 12).

Similarly, in *both* the next two sentences, the subject is *Polly* even though, in the second sentence, the alien wins:

> **Polly** *ate* a toffee apple.
> **Polly** *was eaten* by a creature from outer space.

In the next two sentences, however, the subject of the first is *Max,* and the subject of the second is *the referee:*

> **Max** *was shouted* at by the referee.
> **The referee** *shouted* at Max.

The verb in the first sentence is passive, and the one in the second sentence is active.

You could make the point that it is Max's experience that is more important than the referee's in both sentences here. In the second sentence, however, the verb is active: the referee is doing the shouting. It is the referee's action that is the focus of attention.

'Extended subjects'*

It often happens that a *group* of words (rather than a single person or item) functions as the subject of the main verb in a sentence. Here are some examples:

> **Planning a holiday** *is* fun.
> **To err** is human.
> **Worrying about exams** *is* a waste of time.
> **Collecting wood for the fire** *took* a long time.
> **Looking after the horse** *was* Sid's responsibility.
> **That Patrick was in two minds** *was* clear from the way he hesitated.
> **That nations must co-operate in order to achieve lasting peace** *is* obvious.

In each case here, we can check out the **subject** by asking ourselves a question. What was it, for example, that *took a long time?* It was *Collecting wood for the fire.* What was *Sid's responsibility?* It was *Looking after the horse,* of course.

ACTIVITY 3

Underline the subjects of all verbs in the following sentences:

1 Carl won the race.
2 After breakfast, Ron did the washing up.
3 Over the hill, rode the cowboy.
4 Pam was given a bonus by her boss.
5 Tomorrow, a belt of rain will cross the county and high winds will make driving difficult.
6 Every morning, Maxine was shown a different job in the greenhouses.
7 The children ate all the chocolate but the buns were left untouched.
8 To work at a satisfying job is a pleasure.

---

* This term is my own. I made it up for convenience. You are unlikely to find it in any other grammar books.

II OBJECTS

▶ The definition of an object

You are probably used to using the word *object* to mean something like a reason for doing something, as in *The object of reading this book is to improve my writing.* In grammatical terminology, an **object** is a person, animal or thing which is on the receiving end of the doing (see the section on verbs in chapter 12).

A very simple sentence will be composed of a subject followed by a verb. Many sentences also contain an object:

> **Jack** *hit* John.
> **I** *threw* the ball.
> **Peter** *owns* a Porsche.

Just as you can ask yourself who is doing the verb when you are looking for its subject, you can ask yourself who or what is, for example, being hit, thrown or owned when you are endeavouring to find an object. The answers to those questions here are *John*, *the ball* and *a Porsche*. These are known as **direct objects**.

ACTIVITY 4

Put a ring around the objects in the following sentences:

1. The gangsters robbed the casino.
2. The police rounded up the suspects.
3. Gamblers clutched their winnings.
4. Rudy started a fight.
5. The newspapers reported the events.
6. The mayor wanted calm.

Many, many sentences have this basic structure of subject, verb, object.

Extended objects

Extended objects function in a similar way to extended subjects (above). The objects in the following three sentences are not single items but a group of words:

Sid liked looking after the horse.
Jess wondered what the outcome of the vote would be.
The delegates agreed that nations must co-operate in order to
achieve lasting peace.

The subjects here are *Sid*, *Jess* and *The delegates*; the verbs are *liked*,
wondered and *agreed*. You can check out the object in each case by
asking yourself:

What did Sid like?
What did Jess wonder?
What did the delegates agree?

The answers, of course, are:

looking after the horse
what the outcome of the vote would be
that nations must co-operate in order to achieve lasting peace

Indirect objects

In a sentence that includes an **indirect object**, the relationship
between this and the subject is clear, but it is *not quite so close* as that
of subject and direct object. For example:

Louise *sent* <u>Father Christmas</u> a letter.
The children *gave* <u>their teacher</u> a present.
Ron *gave* <u>the dog</u> a bone.

direct objects	*indirect objects*
a letter	Father Christmas
a present	their teacher
a bone	the dog

If I write the sentences slightly differently, using the word 'to', you can
see things more clearly:

Louise sent a letter to Father Christmas.
The children gave a present to their teacher.
Ron gave a bone to the dog.

ACTIVITY 5

Underline the indirect objects in the following sentences:

1 Jim will show you the photographs.
2 The schoolteacher set Class IV an exercise.
3 The homoeopath gave her client some pills.
4 The Chancellor's Budget will save us money.
5 The reflexologist gave me a treatment.

The pronouns *I* and *me* as subject and object

When speaking, everyone automatically uses the words I and *me* correctly most of the time. The word *I* is used for a subject and the word *me* for a direct or indirect object. The trouble usually arises whenever we have a friend or colleague with us. Look at the following sentences:

subject

I	went to the cinema.
John	went to the cinema.
John and I	went to the cinema.

It's incorrect to say or write:

John and me went to the cinema

because *me* can only be used as an object, never as a subject.

More problems arise when there's a business associate involved or when we want to be sure to be polite. Many people are worried about sounding pushy and will say:

Mrs Smith and myself went to the meeting.

This is *not* what's needed, though you will frequently hear things like it. The correct way to say this is:

Mrs Smith and I went to the meeting.

Similar problems occur when the word *me* is used as an indirect object. This is how it should be done:

	direct object	*indirect object*	*direct object*
1 John gave		me	the tickets.
2 John gave		Jane and me	the tickets.
3 John gave	the tickets to	Jane and me.	

By the way, there's a very simple way to check whether you need to use *I* or *me* when two people are involved: mentally omit the other person. You'd never say *Me went to the cinema* or *John gave I the tickets.* The correct constructions, therefore, are:

> John and I went to the cinema.

and

> John gave Jane and me the tickets.

III SOME PROBLEM AREAS

▶ The infuriating *'ing'* problem

The good news is that just as the greatest proportion of errors are caused by the lack of a working verb, the greatest proportion of working-verb difficulties are the result of one specific type of problem. This means that once you are aware of this particular issue, you can quickly learn to look out for it. I call it the *ing* problem. It generally occurs when someone is struggling to get a complex idea on paper and lapses momentarily into speech patterns. Here's a simple example:

> Ken had been at the football ground all afternoon. Watching the match.

The problem occurs because this would sound OK if it were read aloud. The first sentence is fine, but the second has several problems. To start with, it doesn't make sense. It also lacks both a subject and a fully working verb. If you look at the table of **continuous verbs** in chapter 12, you'll see that these all have more than one part.

There are two ways we could sort out the example above:

1   Instead of putting a full stop after *afternoon,* we could use a comma. Then the statement about the match becomes a small piece of information added to the first sentence:

> Ken had been at the football ground all afternoon, watching the match.

Now we've got just *one* sentence. The working verb is *had been,* and the subject of that verb is *Ken.*
   In this particular sentence, we could omit the comma altogether:

> Ken had been at the football ground all afternoon watching the match.

2   We could make sure that the second sentence has a subject and that the *ing* verb has *at least two parts* to it:

> Ken had been at the football ground all afternoon. He **had been watching** the match.

The second sentence now has both a subject (someone doing the *watching – He*) and a fully working verb.

All *ing* verbs have at least two parts. Our example above has three – *had been watching* – and you'll come across instances where there are four. As long as you remember that any *ing* (continuous) verb at the start of a sentence – and whose **subject** is in the previous sentence – must have *at least two parts*, you won't go far wrong. Once you've alerted yourself to the problem, your knowledge of the language will automatically supply you with what you need.
   The classic place for the *ing* problem to occur is, as in the example above, just after a full stop. Here it is in a more complex piece of writing by Mark, a student on an environmental science course. This is from an article he wrote on sustainable rural development:

> Even human waste could either be composted or put through a water reed-bed purification system. Thus alleviating the need to be connected to the present archaic disposal system in place today.

The best way of sorting this one out would almost certainly be to change the full stop after *system* to a comma. Otherwise, I think Mark would have to change the wording slightly. He could have begun the second sentence like this:

This type of process would alleviate the need ...

The *ing* problem also occurred in Sandra's opening to her essay on *Hamlet*:

Shakespeare ensures that nothing can be taken at face value in the play *Hamlet* by showing us many different sides to the characters. One side often contradicting another.

Again, the easiest way to sort this one out is to use a comma. With a comma after *characters,* that ungrammatical final sentence would become part of the main sentence, and so the lack of a working verb in those final words is no longer a problem. If she had wanted to keep that final statement in a separate sentence so that it stands out more, Sandra could have done it in various ways:

(i) We often see one side contradicting another.

With the addition of the working verb 'see' and its subject 'we', the fact that 'contradicting' only has one part no longer matters.

(ii) One side often contradicts another.

ACTIVITY 6

See if you can sort out each of the following sentences in two ways: once as one sentence and once as two. (You'll probably find only one way of writing number 6.)

1 Lucy ran home. Crying all the way.
2 Ken's dog had been annoying the neighbours. Barking all morning.
3 Brad ran down the road with the cheque. Laughing all the way to the bank.
4 The children came home covered in mud. Looking absolutely filthy.
5 English grammar can be difficult. Causing all sorts of problems.

6 I couldn't think how to get the cork out of the bottle. Trying everything I knew.

7 The wolf set off through the forest. Looking for the cottage belonging to Little Red Riding Hood's grandmother.

ACTIVITY 7

Now see if you can sort out these longer sentences. Do each *one* way only.

1 Nursery schools are places where children learn some of the basic skills they will need for primary school. Recognising their names, making simple models, and getting along with others.

2 My local school has started a monthly newsletter. Believing this will help make local people more aware of all the activities available for children and parents.

3 This essay will look at both sides of the argument in order to show the complexity of the issues involved. Crucial issues affecting every aspect of our lives.

*A **word of warning***: An *ing* word can appear perfectly legitimately at the start of a sentence if it is part of an **extended subject** (see above) – as in *Collecting wood for the fire was Sid's responsibility.* The point at issue is generally whether the '*ing*' word looks forward or back. If it is linked to the previous sentence, it's likely to be a problem. '*Collecting*' here looks forward to '*Sid's responsibility*'.

▶ **Word order**

The order in which we arrange the words in any sentence is important for making meaning clear to a reader. Problems sometimes occur when descriptive or explanatory phrases are put beside the wrong person or thing. I sometimes think of this as the 'local wedding problem' because it often used to be seen in reports of weddings in local papers (and sometimes still is). Here's an example:

The bride was given away by her father wearing a dress of antique lace.

Obviously, it was not the father who was wearing the dress. So information on the dress needs to go with the person to whom it refers – the bride. The sentence should read:

> The bride, who was wearing a dress of antique lace, was given away by her father.

Here's another example:

> I saw the van arrive standing beside the photocopier.

This sentence actually states that when the van arrived, it was standing beside the photocopier. Corrected, it could read:

> I saw the van arrive when I was standing beside the photocopier.

or

> When I was standing beside the photocopier, I saw the van arrive.

Look out for this kind of thing when you are proofreading. Aim to check that what you say is logical.

▶ Referring to the right person

There is a particularly important thing you need to know about using pronouns (see chapter 12). Make sure that you have used the relevant noun first and that the pronoun lies fairly close to it.

Can you see what's wrong with this extract from Andy's essay?

> In the Neolithic era, many tools were already in use and archaeological remains can tell us much about the undertakings of daily life. They were able to make stone tools for their agricultural needs.

When we are reading, we need to be absolutely sure of the noun to which any pronoun refers. Otherwise, things may not make sense. The rule is that a pronoun will stand for the closest previous noun. Generally speaking, as readers, we automatically work out which noun that is without thinking. But, as writers, we need to be in the habit of making sure that we've got things correct so that there can never be any confusion.

In this extract from Andy's essay, I have to look for a plural noun because he has used the plural pronoun *They*. The closest plural noun is *undertakings*. Andy's second sentence would not make sense, however, if I were to substitute *undertakings* for *They*. What he actually meant was:

> People were able to make stone tools for their agricultural needs.

The noun *People* had not appeared anywhere, however, so the pronoun *They* couldn't refer to it and shouldn't, therefore, have been used at all. The sentence needed alteration.

The more complex the topics you write about, the more important it is to make sure that a pronoun lies close to the noun it stands for. If I write the following, it could become quite confusing:

> Education is vital for all children, and financial survival is crucial for everyone, everywhere. Governments are morally bound to provide it.

The word *it* is singular, and I had intended that it should refer to *Education*, but the closest singular noun is *survival* with its adjective *financial* (see below). Now *financial survival* is, of course, crucial for everyone. So anybody reading what I wrote is likely to assume that I meant that it is essential for governments to make sure that individuals are given the means for *financial survival*. Obviously, *financial survival* is likely to be largely dependent on education; but my intended focus on the importance of education itself is quickly becoming obscured. What's happened here is that I have not fully explained what I meant. I should have written something like this:

> Education is vital for all children and governments are morally bound to provide it. Without education, a young person has less chance of a job; without a job, he or she has little chance of financial survival.

Now the word *it* clearly refers to *Education*, which is the closest previous singular noun.

There can also be another difficulty. In the following sentence, who do you think is referred to by the word *her?*

> Ruth is Jack's fiancée. He saw Ruth and Wendy coming up the path. He ran out and gave her a hug.

We would assume that, since Jack is engaged to Ruth, it was Ruth that he hugged. But *Wendy* is the closest noun to *her*. So maybe, for reasons we're not aware of, he hugged Wendy. Maybe she had just suffered a blow to her financial survival and needed cheering up. It just isn't clear from the way I've written the two sentences. Let's rewrite them:

> Ruth is Jack's fiancée. When he saw her coming up the path with Wendy, he ran out and gave her a hug.

Now that I've clearly used the word *her* to relate to Ruth in *he saw her coming up the path*, it must relate to Ruth again when it's used a second time.

   If you are writing an essay on one person – Hitler, for example – a good rule of thumb is to use the name at or near the beginning of each new paragraph and to continue with *he* throughout the paragraph (or *she* where relevant). Of course, once you start mentioning different statesmen and other historical figures involved in situations with (or relating to) Hitler, you are back with the problem of having to check very carefully that any pronouns you use do actually stand for the person you had intended.

▶ **Sentences that fork**

Sometimes, you will want to make a statement that refers to several issues in the remainder of the sentence. For example:

> The council official suggested that I should write in with my complaint and explain exactly what happened.

You might like to think of the beginning of the sentence as the handle of a fork and of the issues related to it as prongs. In a well-written sentence, the prongs will all be similar, and it's easiest to see this in diagram form:

The council official suggested that I should <u>write</u> in with my
                                    complaint
                                    and
                                    <u>explain</u> exactly what
                                    happened

Each of the prongs begins in exactly the same way – in this example, with a doing word (a verb). Here's another example:

Ways to improve your memory include visualising what you need to remember and revising frequently.

And here it is in diagram form:

Ways to improve your memory include   <u>visualising</u> what you
                                              need to remember
                                              and
                                              <u>revising</u> frequently

Here the first word ends in *ing*, so the first word of the second prong must also end in *ing*.

You don't need to know the names of the constructions you use. All you need to do is to copy the first. Here's an example of a fork with four prongs:

Questions on the legalisation of drugs revolve around evidence of harm to users and others, views of the public, cost, and intervention by medical authorities.

Here's the diagram:

Questions on the legalisation
    of drugs revolve around   <u>evidence</u> of harm to users
                                              and others
                                              <u>views</u> of the public
                                              <u>cost</u>
                                              and
                                              <u>intervention</u> by medical
                                              authorities

Here, each prong begins with an item – a noun (see chapter 12). Look at the following sentence written by Susie:

> If euthanasia is to be legalised, it is important that a patient is of sound mind when consent is given and to be sure relatives are not bringing pressure to bear.

The first part of this sentence is *If euthanasia is to be legalised, it is important that*. So all the items that follow need to match. But here they don't. The first prong begins with an item (a noun) – *patient*. So the second must also begin with an item – not, as in this case, with a verb: *to be*. Improved, the sentence could look like this:

> If euthanasia is to be legalised,
>   it is important that   a patient is of sound mind
>   when consent is given
>   and
>   relatives do not bring
>   pressure to bear

Here's Joe's sentence on committees:

> For the committee to be viable, members need to understand procedure, they must make succinct contributions to discussions and get their facts right.

Here the first word on the first prong is a verb. So to make the prongs match, we need to make a small alteration:

> For the committee to be viable,
>   members need to   understand procedure
>   make succinct
>   contributions
>   get their facts right

A sentence with matching 'prongs' reads more easily and is clearer and more forceful. All you need to remember is that however you construct the first prong, you just copy the structure in subsequent prongs. Here's another example:

If someone has a bad
fall, it's important   to leave the patient where s/he fell
                         to cover him or her with a blanket or coat
                         to phone for an ambulance
                              and
                         to give reassurance that help is coming

▶ A note for people who like to use the correct terminology

The formal name for my term *working verb* is **finite verb**. The word *finite* means *having boundaries*. This is opposite to the *infinitive,* which is open-ended – like infinity. I also made up the term *ing* word because it is an easy way of referring to those parts of verbs ending in *ing* that can cause difficulties when writing sentences. My term also demonstrates exactly what it is referring to. The correct term is **present participle**. You will find a present participle in any example of a present continuous verb – for example, *barking* in the following sentence:

The dog **is barking**.

The present participle here – *barking* – is from the verb *to bark.* The *ing* form also appears in the **past continuous** tense. You can tell the tense of a continuous verb from the bits that precede the *ing* word. The present continuous tense uses *is* and *are*; the past continuous uses *was* and *were*; the future continuous uses *will be* (see chapter 12).

The same type of problem as the *ing* problem can occur with a **past participle**, but this happens far less often. A past participle very often ends in *ed*. The past participle of the verb *to bark* is *barked.*

If you are happy with this formal terminology, you will no doubt use it to refer to issues discussed in this chapter. If, like many people, you find jargon a bit intimidating, stick to thinking of *ing* words and *working verbs.*

▶ Breaking the rules

There are certain times when rules can be broken. When we write conversation (see chapters 7 and 15), there are likely to be lots of sentences without verbs. You will also find what might appear to be ungrammatical sentences in novels and in journalistic writing. This could be because the material is badly produced, but it is more likely to result from the writer having taken a conscious decision to write in a particular way in order to create a particular effect. Chatty writing sometimes omits verbs, and sometimes omission is used for impact.

It's a good idea, however, not to do this until you are really familiar with writing correctly. It's OK to break the rules once you know what you're doing and why, but unless you're on a creative writing course, your tutors are not likely to be very happy to see sentences that lack either verbs or subjects.

IV TRADITIONAL CLAUSE ANALYSIS

▶ Main clauses

In a nutshell, a clause is a group of words containing a working verb and its subject. Look at the following sentence:

My dog Rex fancies the cat.

The working verb is, of course, *fancies,* and the subject is *My dog Rex.* This is a simple sentence consisting of one clause.

When a sentence contains more than one working verb (and there may be several), one of them will be more important than the others. It's called the **main verb**. (There is a minor exception to this (see below).

Look at the following sentence (the verbs are in bold type):

My dog Rex **fancies** the cat who often **sleeps** in the dog basket.

Because there are two working verbs here, there are two parts to the sentence:

1 My dog Rex fancies the cat
2 who often sleeps in the dog basket

You can probably see that the first part of the sentence is more important than the second. The words *who often sleeps in the dog basket* just give us some extra information about the behaviour of the cat. The main focus here is on the dog.

The part of the sentence which contains the main verb is called the **main clause**. So the main clause in that sentence is:

My dog Rex fancies the cat

A main clause could always stand alone as a sentence, and we saw this clause functioning as a simple sentence at the beginning of this section.

▶ Subordinate clauses

The name given to any other group of words containing a working verb in a sentence is a **subordinate clause**. So *who often sleeps in the dog basket* is a subordinate clause.

The following sentence also contains two working verbs (which are in bold type). This means that there must be two clauses:

John **was** cross with his dog because it **had eaten** the pie.

The main clause – or statement – is:

John was cross with his dog

The second clause,

because it had eaten the pie

is a subordinate clause because it gives us some extra information which is less important here than the main statement. This sentence *focuses* on John's feelings towards his dog.

Now you might feel that the loss of the pie is crucial and therefore more significant than how John felt about it. That pie may well have been John's dinner. The issue here, however, is my intention as the writer of the sentence. I want to stress John's anger. The fact that the second clause begins with the word *because* shows that it contains an *explanation* rather than a straightforward statement of the situation, so it must be a subordinate clause.

This sentence could be lengthened by adding more clauses (the verbs are in bold):

John **was** cross with his dog because it **had eaten** the pie which Sarah **had made**.

Even though he **is** an easy-going man, John **was** cross with his dog because it **had eaten** the pie which Sarah **had made**.

Even though he **is** an easy-going man who **loves** animals, John **was** cross with his dog because it **had eaten** the pie which Sarah **had made**.

Even though he **is** an easy-going man who **loves** animals, John **was** cross with his dog because it **had eaten** the pie which Sarah **had made** while he **had been shopping**.

We now have a sentence with six working verbs in it. That means that there are six clauses – one main and five subordinate. Here, the main clause is still *John was cross with his dog*. All the other clauses merely help to explain the situation. The main clause could stand alone as a fully functioning sentence, just like the one about Rex. It makes sense by itself. Subordinate clauses, however, can't stand alone because they are just fragments of sentences and don't make sense by themselves:

Even though he **is** an easy-going man
who **loves** animals
because it **had eaten** the pie
which Sarah **had made**
while he **had been shopping**

Introductory words
Subordinate clauses can often be spotted by means of the words that introduce them. The following are frequently used:

although	while	since
even though	despite	unless
if	which	until
because	where	who

Here's a sentence by George, an Open University student, from his essay on architecture in the 1920s and 1930s. By using the words *who* and *which* to relate ideas, George was able to build up a lengthy sentence that functions accurately. The verbs are in bold so that you can more easily spot the separate clauses:

The architect Mies van der Rohe, who **used** the International style vocabulary of flat roofs, white walls, windows flush with walls to suggest volume, and the visible continuous steel supports which **were** part of Le Corbusier's architectural vocabulary of expressed structure, **created** a block of flats which **was** later **copied** all over Berlin.

Here's the analysis:

The architect Mies van der Rohe **created** a block of flats
> main clause

who **used** the International style vocabulary of flat roofs, white walls, windows flush with walls to suggest volume, and the visible continuous steel supports
> subordinate adjectival clause

which **were** part ... expressed structure
> subordinate adjectival clause

which **was** later **copied** all over Berlin
> subordinate adjectival clause

Note the very long clause in which the working verb is *used*. It contains the word *suggest* which is, of course, also a verb, but it comes as an infinitive – *to suggest* – so it does not have a clause to itself. Note also that the final clause does not contain two verbs but one verb split apart by the word *later*.

▶ Changing the emphasis

Can you spot the main clause in the following sentence?

I love chips, even though the fat is bad for me and I gain weight every time I eat them.

The most important thing I'm telling you here is that I'm very keen on chips. The main clause is *I love chips* and the main verb is *love.*
There are three more working verbs here: *is, gain* and *eat.* So there are three subordinate clauses:

even though the fat **is** bad for me
and I **gain** weight
every time I **eat** them

Now, just as with John and the pie, you may not agree with me here.

You might feel that gaining weight is the most important thing I've mentioned. In my sentence, however, I wanted to *foreground* the information that I'm keen on chips. I wanted the other points to appear less important – that is, subordinate.

If I wanted to stress the point on weight gain, I would need to construct the sentence slightly differently in order to put the *focus* on weight:

> I **gain** weight every time I **eat** chips, although I **tell** myself that it **does**n't matter and that a little fat **will** not **hurt** me.

Now, the main clause is

> I **gain** weight

and there are four subordinate clauses:

> every time I **eat** chips
> although I **tell** myself
> that it **does**n't matter
> and that a little fat **will** not **hurt** me

The chips are now in a subordinate clause. Notice that the word *not* isn't part of a verb so doesn't show in bold, but it has split apart the two parts of the working verb *will hurt*.

ACTIVITY 8

Try your hand at underlining the **main clause** in each of the following sentences. It might help to put a ring round all the verbs first. (The main clause will not always be at the beginning of the sentence.)

1 There are fairies at the bottom of my garden where I haven't cut the grass.
2 Although it is freezing, I refuse to wear woolly undies.
3 Place all gallstones in the bucket provided after you have sewn up the patient.
4 As I came out of the supermarket, I bumped into a small horse.
5 A problem shared is a problem halved, as long as the trouble is either legal or is not divulged to a serving police officer.
6 It's hot.

▶ Co-ordinate clauses

I suggested above that there can sometimes be more than one main clause in a sentence. It's easy to spot these because they will be linked by the words *and, but* or *or*:

> My dog Rex **fancies** the cat *and* he **hates** the hamster.
> The customer **gave** me an odd look, *but* he **said** nothing.
> You **can study** in the library *or* you **can go** home.

In each sentence, the two clauses have the same value – they are each as important as the other. So we call them **co-ordinate clauses.**
   Subordinate clauses, as well as main clauses, can be co-ordinate if they are linked by those words *and, but* or *or*:

> After you **have added** all the ingredients *and* **put** the mixture in the tin, **bake** the cake for an hour and a half.

> Main clause: **bake** the cake for an hour and a half
> Subordinate clauses: After you **have added** all the ingredients
>   and **put** the mixture in the tin

There are co-ordinate subordinate clauses in my sentence about the chips (above):

> even though the fat **is** bad for me
> and I **gain** weight

There are also co-ordinate subordinate clauses in the *revised* sentence on gaining weight:

> that it **doesn't matter**
> and that a little fat **will** not **hurt** me

▶ Nominal clauses

These are sometimes called noun clauses because the whole clause functions as an item as if it were one noun. In this way, a nominal clause can act as the subject or object of a verb (see *'Extended subjects'* and *'Extended objects'* above). For example:

It was clear that Patrick was in two minds.
That nations must co-operate in order to achieve lasting peace is
   obvious.

The nominal clauses are:

that Patrick was in two minds
That nations must co-operate in order to achieve lasting peace

In the first sentence, the nominal clause is an object; in the second, the
nominal clause is the subject.

▶ Adjectival clauses

These are sometimes known as relative clauses. Just like an adjective
(see chapter 12), an adjectival clause describes or explains (qualifies) a
noun or pronoun, like this:

The athlete *who won the race* was accused of taking steroids.
That is the girl *whose father taught her Chinese.*
Josh bought the book *which Ray had recommended.*

The nouns that each of those clauses describes are *athlete, girl* and
book.
   Adjectival clauses usually begin with one of the following words:

which, that, who, whose, whom

Sometimes, a preposition (a linking word) comes first:

This is the boat *in which* the refugees sailed.
Those are the people *with whom* Nelson Mandela had discussions.

The words *where* and *when* can also sometimes be used to begin adjectival clauses:

I saw the house *where* she used to live.
It was the day *when* the factory burnt down.

▶ Adverbial clauses

Adverbial clauses describe working verbs, infinitives and adjectives as well. They can tell us about a long list of different types of information: time, place, manner, reason, purpose, conditions, results, concessions and comparison. For example:

I'll make some coffee *when I've finished this report.*	**time**
The phone rang *while I was painting the bathroom.*	**time**
I planted the apple tree *where we can see it from the window*	**place**
Put your things down *wherever you can find a space.*	**place**

Typical words for introducing adverbial clauses are:

because, as, since, if, unless, whether, although

▶ Phrases

Phrases are much easier to understand than clauses. In traditional grammar, a phrase is a group of words that obviously fit together but do *not* include a working verb. In the sentences below, the phrases are in bold type:

Seth moored his boat **at the edge of the lake**.
Tomorrow morning, I'll start painting the dining room.
The boys were playing football, **despite the rain**.

SUMMARY

A sentence must always:
- make sense
- contain a working verb
- contain a subject for that verb

Subjects and objects
- A **subject**: the person or thing doing the doing or having
- An **object**: the person or thing on the receiving end of the doing

- An **indirect object**: the person or thing that is less close to the subject than a direct object and often prefaced by the word *to*
- I   is a subject
- me   is an object

Some problem areas

- an *ing* verb   at the beginning of a sentence must have at least *two* parts
- word order   put descriptions and explanations beside the person they describe
- referring to the right person   make sure a pronoun lies close to who/ what it refers to
- sentences that fork   use a matching construction on each prong

Clauses

- main clause   the most important statement in a sentence
- main verb   the working verb in the main clause
- subordinate clause   a clause that contains less important information
- co-ordinate clause   a clause (either main or subordinate) that has the same value as its partner clause
- nominal, adjectival and adverbial clauses   these do the job of nouns, adjectives or adverbs
- Phrase   a group of words *without* a working verb

14 Punctuation

INTRODUCTION

At school, most of us were told that punctuation is used to show a reader where to take a breath. Well, there's some truth in that, but it's not the whole story, by any means. Punctuation is used in order to make our writing make sense. If you were to find a book that had no punctuation in it, you would find that it took much longer to read than usual and that some parts were difficult to understand.

Now you may be wondering why I say that there's a difference between having your writing make sense and showing a reader where to breathe. Well, for a start, breathing is only important if you have to read aloud. When we're reading silently, we don't say to ourselves, "Ah, here's a full stop. I'll pause here", or "I'd better take a quick breath after this comma." When reading silently, your breathing is probably almost as regular as when you are asleep.

It's also interesting to note that when people do read aloud they often add more pauses than are indicated by the punctuation marks. Reading aloud is actually closer to talking; and when we talk, we start to use all sorts of extra tricks to make ourselves understood. We vary the tone of our voices, pause on certain words for emphasis, constantly change the expressions on our faces, and may even start waving our arms around or moving about. All this will help a listener to understand what the words mean and even how we feel about what we are communicating.

FULL STOPS*

If you have read chapter 13 on sentences, you have already looked hard at how a sentence functions. Whenever I'm having to read some-

---

* In American English, a full stop is called a *period.*

thing I find difficult to understand, I find that full stops can be incredibly helpful for understanding meaning. From the beginning of a sentence, I run my eyes down the page until I come to the next full stop. Then I can go back to the beginning of the sentence, reread it, and start finding out how its parts fit together and what it means. This technique not only allows me to see how much information I need to take in one chunk, so to speak, but it also makes me feel more comfortable by showing me exactly where the next logical stopping-point is. I can be confident that, when I have understood this sentence, I will have put in place the building block for understanding the next one and, in this way, I can slowly progress through a complex text.

Full stops are used to separate one statement (and any closely related qualifications of it) from the next. For example:

> Sooner or later, people want to learn to use the Internet. They then have access to a vast range of information – ranging from courses offered by colleges in distant countries to diagrams of the combustion engine.

In the above, I have used a full stop to separate a sentence about the desire to use the Internet from one that explains the results of using it. The desire and the effect are separate items. Each needed its own sentence.

Here's another example:

> Jo has finally applied to major in modern European history. This was a tough decision for her because her hobby is going on archaeological digs and she's also fascinated by the medieval period. She eventually decided to study modern history because she wants to teach in secondary education, and she thinks she'd be more likely to get a job with a background in twentieth-century events.

The three sentences here focus separately on:

1 Jo's application to study modern history
2 the reasons why her decision was difficult
3 the reasons why she chose the modern period

Each sentence, therefore, is concerned with one small but specific area of information on Jo's application for a university place.

COMMAS

In order to get to grips with writing clear essays (and other material), you need to understand how commas function. But that's not the walkover it's often thought to be. Commas can be some of the trickiest things to get right.

When you are reading aloud, you'll be likely to pause briefly where you see a comma. Indeed, doing this will help your listeners understand what they're hearing. In fact, they have to be given quite a bit of help from your tone of voice and your emphasis, unless they have a copy of what you are reading in front of them. But when you're writing, you need to focus on putting in commas *solely in order to make your meaning clear.* As far as you are concerned, the readers can gasp, exhale, or hold their breath till they explode. All that concerns you is that there should be *no possible confusion in the meaning* of what you have written.

▶ Lists

The simplest use of commas is for separating parts of a list:

I went shopping and bought oranges, apples, pears and bananas.

You have probably been taught never to put a comma before the word *and* in this type of construction. So the punctuation in my example will look correct to you. Actually, the use of a comma before *and* is optional in a list. In a simple list like the one above, a comma is usually unnecessary, but it can be very useful in some cases in order to make it clear that the last two items in the list are quite separate.

Look at this:

Knowledge of the identity of objects and features in the environment is obviously valuable to us. Not only does the apparent stability and permanence of most of them create a feeling of security; it also enables us to react to them rapidly and appropriately. We learn by experience what are the uses of houses, shops, and other buildings.*

---

* M. D. Vernon, *The Psychology of Perception,* p. 13.

In the final sentence, the writer has put in a comma after the word *shops* – which comes before *and*. This makes it quite clear that he is talking about three categories of buildings:

> houses
> shops
> other buildings

If he had omitted the comma after *shops,* it would be possible to read his sentence as talking about two categories:

> houses
> shops and other buildings

This may not seem a crucial distinction when we're talking of things like pears and bananas, but it can be really important when we're trying to distinguish between several complicated ideas. On the other hand, it might just be crucial with the fruit. Let's suppose that you are responsible for seeing that fruit and vegetables are packaged for distribution to retailers. You have left the following note for one of your team:

> Please pack the oranges, apples, pears and bananas in boxes
> from the store.

Your team member might have ended up with three boxes of fruit when you had wanted four. A comma after *pears* would have made your meaning absolutely clear.

▶ Descriptions

Commas are also used to separate descriptive words. For example,

> Josh stared at the long, dark snake.
> A single, shrill, piercing whistle was heard in the wood.

A comma is never used between the last descriptive word and the item described.

▶ Marking off extra information at the beginning of a sentence

It is very common for a sentence to begin with some introductory words that set the scene, so to speak, but are not part of that sentence's main statement. These can be marked off with a comma. In the following example, the words *During the summer* fulfil this introductory function:

> During the summer, Malcolm laid out his new garden.

The crucial statement here is *Malcolm laid out his new garden*. It is a statement showing what Malcolm did. The fact that he did it during the summer is interesting and important, but it's not so important as the fact that he completed the job.

We all know the next example:

> Once upon a time, there lived an old king who had a lovely daughter.

Those last two examples both relate to time. Here are two that relate to place:

> Underneath the cushion, I found the scissors I'd lost.
> Beyond the town, the mud road stretched into the distance.

Commas are very useful for marking off all kinds of extra information from the main statement in a sentence:

> Stretching up on his hind legs, the dog peered over the low fence.
> Wrapped in blankets, the walking wounded shuffled to the helicopter.

▶ Marking off extra information at the end of a sentence

Here, the main statement comes first and the extra information follows it:

> Six boys were following the old man, jeering and catcalling.

Meera used to make all the family's clothes, helped by her
ancient sewing machine.

▶ Marking off extra information in the middle of a sentence

Maria, the girl who defied a brutal regime, walked to the river.

Here, the main statement is:

Maria walked to the river

but we have some very interesting extra information about this person.
When you put extra information in the middle of a sentence, always
mark it off by two commas – one before and one after.

I wonder if you agreed with me when I stated that *Maria walked to
the river* was more important than the fact that she *defied a brutal
regime*. In terms of Maria's whole life, a trip to the river seems a minor
occurrence when compared with her bravery. But in this particular
sentence, I'm *focusing* on the *walk* and I've made that the main statement in my sentence.

Now look at the following examples:

Paul, the man Josie had always loved, eventually married Kate.
I ran, stumbling and moaning, back to the hut.
My dog Bruno, who barks ferociously, wouldn't hurt a fly.

Notice that, in each case, you could leave out the extra information and
the sentence would still make perfect sense:

Paul eventually married Kate.
I ran back to the hut.
My dog Bruno wouldn't hurt a fly.

By putting commas around the extra information each time, I've
demonstrated that I want my readers to concentrate on the other material in the sentences. For example, I want people to concentrate on
Bruno's gentleness rather than his bark.

▶ Changing meaning by using a comma

Look at the following two sentences and see if you can work out why I've used a comma in the first but not in the second:

> Maria went for a long walk, taking her lunch in a small bag.
> Maria went for a long walk across the fields to the river.

This is where the fun starts. Lots of people would want to put a comma in the second sentence as well as the first, but there's a subtle difference. We're taught that a sentence always makes a statement. It would actually be more correct to say that a sentence always contains a statement. It may also contain other information as well, as we've seen in those examples above.

In the first sentence here, the statement is

> Maria went for a long walk

and the words

> taking her lunch in a small bag

give us some extra information. But in the second sentence, the statement is the whole sentence. The information on where Maria went is crucial to and part of that statement. That sentence, as it is written at present, must be taken in one go.

But we could write this story slightly differently and so change the *emphasis*. We might say:

> Maria went for a long walk, slowly crossing the fields to the river.

Now *the fields* and *the river* become slightly less important. They are now extra information. The main feature of the sentence is the *long walk* and the itinerary takes second place. The change in emphasis has been achieved partly by changing (in this case adding) punctuation.

▶ Changing the effect

As we saw above, extra information can be put in different places in a sentence. Look at the following sentences:

> Swinging her bag in her left hand, Maria walked to the river.
> Maria walked to the river, swinging her bag in her left hand.

In both those sentences, the main statement is the same:

> Maria walked to the river.

The effect of the two sentences, however, is ever so slightly different. The first seems to me to contain a little suspense; we have to wait until the end of the sentence before finding out what happened. Now the reader will want to know what happened next. The second sentence seems more gentle. The position of any extra information can subtly vary the impact of your words.

▶ A common problem with commas

There's a problem with the following sentence that many people wouldn't spot. I wonder if you can see it:

> I went into town to do some shopping last week, it took me ages.

We've said above that a sentence always contains a statement. Well, sometimes it contains more than one. The statements here are:

> I went into town to do some shopping last week
> it took me ages

The problem here arises partly because we've all been told that the reason for using punctuation is to allow the reader to take a breath. So if I read that sentence aloud, pausing at the comma, anyone listening to me would understand perfectly. This is because they would hear two separate statements *as if these had been separated by a full stop.*

If there are two statements within one sentence, we must show how the second relates to the first. In the section above, where extra information was added at the beginning, middle or end of a sentence, I used commas to mark it off and to show that, in each case, it was not the most important thing in the sentence. But here we have two statements that appear to be equally important. I can sort out this problem by adding the word *and*:

> I went into town to do some shopping last week, and it took me ages.

Now it's ten to one that you're thinking, "That's wrong. When I was at school, we were told never to put a comma before *and*." Well, if you think back to the simple use of commas to separate items in a list – for example,

> oranges, apples, pears and bananas

I think you'll see that it was in relation to lists that the rule was drummed into you. That rule about not putting a comma before *and* only applied to lists (and, as I said above, the practice is optional there anyway).

So let's look at some instances of sentences containing more than one important statement:

> Sue's grandma still rides a bike, she's 93.
> I'm going to get rid of my car, it's so old it's falling apart.
> There was a queue at the traffic lights, I took a left turn to miss them.

All these sentences need sorting out because the meaning is not quite clear. It's *not* OK to separate two *equally* important statements with only a comma. There are two possible solutions. I could either replace the comma in each sentence with a full stop, or I could add a connecting word (or words) in each case to explain how the second statement relates to the first:

> Sue's grandma still rides a bike. She's 93.

Here, the short sentences give impact to the statements.

> Sue's grandma still rides a bike, *even though* she's 93.

This gives the information in a slightly more gentle fashion. In this case, it would be OK to omit the comma altogether. Similar things can be done with the other sentences above:

I'm going to get rid of my car. It's so old it's falling apart.

or

I'm going to get rid of my car *because* it's so old it's falling apart.

and

There was a queue at the traffic lights. I took a left turn to miss them.

or

There was a queue at the traffic lights, so I took a left turn to miss them.

Can you spot the problems with commas in the following piece of student writing? Claire has written a poignant description of a time when she had to travel without her children:

It felt most strange watching my children wave me off, they looked so small standing on the vast now empty platform. As the train pulled away, they had tried to keep up by running alongside, they were aware that this was not possible but had tried anyway.

In the first two lines, Claire needed to separate the two statements with a full stop. Short sentences can have impact and would work particularly well here because both statements about the children would then be emphasised, and we would be forced to take the information more slowly and so to empathise even more with the writer.

There's also a problem with the comma after *alongside* because there is an important statement on each side of it. Because of the length of this sentence, I think that Claire could improve her piece with a full stop here too.

Commas need very careful handling. A good rule of thumb is: *never use one unless you know exactly why you are doing so.* They are better omitted than used incorrectly.

ACTIVITY 1

Add commas, where necessary, to the following sentences:

1 Marian has travelled in France Spain Australia India and the USA.
2 We were watched by a lean ageing kangaroo.
3 After two weeks on buses and trains it was a relief to smell sea air.
4 Jason our guide walked fast and spoke little.
5 Air disasters it is well known are fewer than accidents on the roads.
6 Taking a foreign holiday despite problems with accommodation currency and language can be a liberating experience.
7 Day after day the grey rocks dotted here and there with small plants formed a backdrop for our trek.
8 Taking a foreign holiday can be a liberating experience.

SEMICOLONS

A semicolon is usually thought of as indicating a longer pause than that given by a comma. Well, that's partly true, but a rather better definition would be to say that it indicates a slightly shorter pause than that given by a full stop. The reason for turning the definition around is because it now carries an implicit reminder that, when you use a semicolon, whatever you write on *each* side of it *must* function *as if it were a separate sentence.* That means that there must be a clear statement, including a subject and working verb (see chapters 12 and 13) on *each* side of the semicolon – like this:

Many Westerners **like** Eastern food; Indian restaurants and take-aways, for example, **have opened** in most British towns.

The working verb in the first statement is *like* and its subject is *many Westerners.* In the second statement, the working verb is *have opened* and its subject is *Indian restaurants and takeaways.*

The use of semicolons is generally a matter of choice. They could almost always be replaced by full stops without harming the sense of what you write. Their usefulness lies in allowing you to keep within one sentence statements that are very closely related to each other. Like all other punctuation marks, they are used to assist meaning.

Semicolons could be used as another way to sort out the problem with commas shown in the previous section. Instead of the following incorrect sentences:

> I'm going to get rid of my car, it's so old it's falling apart.
> There was a queue at the traffic lights, I took a left turn to miss them.

we could write:

> I'm going to get rid of my car; it's so old it's falling apart.
> There was a queue at the traffic lights; I took a left turn to miss them.

Semicolons can also be used in certain lists:

> I went shopping for apples, pears and bananas; flour, sugar and spaghetti; milk, cheese and yoghurt.

In this case, the semicolons separate one *group* of items from another type.

Semicolons can also be very useful for separating sections in a long sentence where

> (a) the sentence follows a pattern

and

> (b) you need to use commas within the separate sections.

For example,

> It was decided that a steering group should be formed, consisting of six members; that publicity, particularly via the local media, would be essential; and that a celebrity, preferably from TV, should be approached to be patron of the new society.

The pattern shows up clearly if I make the sentence into a table:

It was decided: that a steering group should be formed . . .
                             that publicity . . . would be essential
                             that a celebrity . . . should be approached . . .

I used semicolons (above) to separate those three areas. You need semicolons, however, *only when the individual sections themselves contain commas.* The following sentence needs none:

It was decided to form a steering group consisting of six members, to seek publicity via the media, and to approach a TV celebrity for the position of patron.

ACTIVITY 2

In the following paragraph, it would be possible to replace **two** of the full stops with semicolons. Which two? Why?

Many people have strong opinions on the use of the private car. Some feel that it has liberated the individual and brought with it a new level of personal freedom. Others feel that the threat to the environment posed by fuel emissions must be curtailed. Governments can find themselves caught between these mutually exclusive standpoints. They don't want to be seen as autocratic and reactionary. At the same time, they are aware of global warming and of the fact that they are likely to be held responsible for environmental decline.

COLONS

Colons are handy for introducing lists:

I bought various items at the hardware store: nails, paint, brushes, a screwdriver, a hammer and some string.

They are also useful for introducing quotations, like this:

When Hamlet sees his mother die and realises the poisoned drink was meant for him, his response is swift:

> O villainy! Ho! Let the door be lock'd.
> Treachery! Seek it out. [V.ii.317]

If you look through this book, you will see that I've used colons a great deal for introducing instructions and explanations. Here is another example:

> Make the sauce as follows: first melt an ounce of butter in a saucepan, then add a tablespoon of flour, and finally slowly add about half a pint of liquid.

There's a further use for colons in which they indicate a kind of balance between the two halves of a sentence and in which the second half elaborates on the first. For example,

> I'm an optimist: my glass is generally half full rather than half empty.

> Television can be seen as having both positive and negative aspects: it is an unrivalled means of communication, but it can ultimately dull the responses of viewers.

BRACKETS

Brackets can be used in order to add extra information in a rather similar way to the use of a pair of commas:

> Dale (who was always a difficult child) refused to go to school until he had been bribed with the promise of hard currency.

Brackets can also contain information that qualifies what is being said in a sentence:

> Britain's Queen Victoria was (in most respects) a strong woman.

Or they can add extra information which, while being important, does not strictly fit into the grammatical construction of the sentence as it stands:

Queen Victoria (1819–1901) ruled during a period of industrial expansion.

In my garden (I have a small plot at the side of the house) I grow vegetables and roses.

You'll notice that the first examples – on Dale and Queen Victoria – can be read straight through, including what is in the brackets, without harming the sense. The next example does not read quite so smoothly, and the section in brackets in the final sentence is grammatically quite separate from the main sentence. All of these are acceptable, but the first two are rather neater than the others.

DASHES

These can be used in a similar way to brackets to add a separate piece of information to a sentence. When this information is in brackets it can seem to be cut off from the rest of the sentence. Using dashes can keep the information in the foreground. When you use a pair of dashes in the middle of a sentence, you'll need to make sure that whatever lies between them fits into your sentence smoothly and grammatically, like this:

Britain's Queen Victoria was – in most respects – a strong woman.

A dash can sometimes be particularly handy, however, for adding a piece of information at the *end* of a sentence *without* having to fit it carefully to the grammar and sense of the sentence itself. This use of a dash can be dramatic, but if you do it too often in essays, your work may look slipshod. Keep it up your sleeve for occasional use only. It's done like this:

Joan is always on hand to help with the decorating – she's very reliable.

There were a number of pieces missing from the puzzle – sixteen, in fact.

Always leave a space before and after a dash so that it won't be confused with a hyphen.

HYPHENS

Hyphens are used in various ways to join two words. They look similar to dashes, but they are actually slightly shorter and there is no space between a hyphen and the letters on either side of it. Hyphens can be a bit tricky because of the number of different rules on how and where to use them. Their use is subject to change over time, and, in general, they are being used less and less frequently nowadays. The British tend to use more of them than the Americans. For example:

non-standard	British English
nonstandard	American English

Sometimes, two words that began life separately are then written with a hyphen and finally come to be known as just one word. For example, the word *today* was once written *to-day*. Language changes all the time – new words come into use and certain words fall out of use, sometimes becoming so old-fashioned that they don't seem relevant to our lives any more. While this is interesting, it can result in many more language changes than we feel comfortable with.

Hyphens have three uses:

1 at the end of a line where there's no space for an entire word

For example:

The British comedian Eddie Izzard has suggested
that when your cat is sitting behind your couch and
purring, the situation may not be as innocent as it
sounds. Although you may think your moggy is peacefully resting, he may actually be drilling. "Some of
them go down as much as forty feet," he said.

When splitting a word in this manner, aim to break it smoothly in relation to both the sound and the appearance of the word. It would have looked a bit strange if I had broken *peacefully* as *pea-cefully*.

2 in words that are regularly written with a hyphen

For example:

book-keeping
re-export

In both of these words, the hyphen is used to avoid awkwardness with a double letter. This is often a clue as to whether or not you need to use a hyphen. But it's not a hard and fast rule; many people now write *cooperate* rather than *co-operate.*

3 for joining two or more words to make a new one

For example:

a sky-blue dress
a half-eaten sandwich

If the hyphen is omitted in cases like this, it must be possible for both words to be *separately* applicable to the word being described. If I had written

A sky blue dress

I would have said something rather different from what I said when I used a hyphen. I would have implied that the dress was both *sky* and *blue.* The first of these is clearly nonsense. If I omit the hyphen from my description of the sandwich, I would imply that it was both *half* a sandwich *and* an *eaten* one – which also sounds pretty silly, because if it was *eaten,* it wasn't there at all.

If you say aloud to yourself the examples of the dress and the sandwich, you'll probably notice that, when we combine two words to describe something, we run them together and speak them more quickly than when we are using them separately. Thinking about the sound can be a rather useful way to help to decide whether you need to join with a hyphen words that are usually separate.

Omission of necessary hyphens can clearly cause quite serious problems of meaning. For all examples except the joining of two words to make a new and imaginative description, it is often best to check the dictionary. It's also a good idea to memorise any hyphenated words which are specific to your own subject and which you will need to use frequently.

EXCLAMATION MARKS

Probably the best advice here is: don't use exclamation marks, except when writing dialogue in stories. It is usually felt that we should demonstrate important points through our writing itself and not rely on exclamation marks to do the work. In fact, these marks are actually frowned upon when they appear in essays because they indicate strong emotion, and the best essays are generally logical and unemotional.

Exclamation marks are, however, very handy in stories for showing when someone is shouting or screaming, like this:

"Let go!" yelled Mick.

or

"Fire!" shouted the Principal.

or

"Help!" screamed Pat.

It's also fine to use exclamation marks in letters to friends where there are no rules to worry about. Most people do this from time to time. One year, all my letters to distant friends contained exclamation marks. I had been having a particularly difficult time decorating my kitchen, and I wrote about both the difficulties and the cost:

The week when I had to use the steam stripper to remove six layers of wallpaper from the wood panelling was, of course, the week of the heatwave. Now I know what a Turkish bath is like! And the cost of decorating that one wall was, would you believe, £70!

It's also very important to remember not to use a full stop as well as an exclamation mark. Only *one* punctuation mark is used at a time.

QUESTION MARKS

These are sometimes called 'interrogation marks' – particularly in American English. The main thing here is to remember to use them. It's amazing how easy it is to forget to use a question mark after a question. The lack of one is, however, horribly apparent to a reader. As with an exclamation mark, never use a full stop as well as a question mark. Don't forget, however, that a question mark always terminates a sentence, so you need to follow it with a capital letter.

Questions can be a real problem in essays and other formal documents. You will find a section on how to deal with reporting questions that others have asked in chapter 15 and another on raising questions in essays in chapter 2.

APOSTROPHES

Apostrophes have two jobs to do – and these are quite distinct. One is to show when there is a letter (or letters) missing from a word. This will usually be in conversational speech or informal writing. This is called **contraction**. The other is to show when something *belongs* to someone or something. This is called **possession**.

▶ Contraction

This is really simple. In the following sentence, I have used an apostrophe to show that the letter *o* is missing:

I didn't get where I am today by ignoring apostrophes.

If I had written this in full, I would have put *I did not get . . .*

The following table gives a selection of the kind of examples that are found in everyday speech:

You'll find this easy.	You will
We *won't* be long.	will not
I *wouldn't* do that if I were you.	would not
He'll be here next week.	He will
They'll do their best.	They will

| *Aren't* you clever! | Are not* |
| I *wasn't* at work today. | was not |

► Possession

This is where you may be having difficulties. You probably have some vague memories from school about putting an apostrophe before or after an *s* but it's ten to one that you can't remember why or when; and a lot of people have become so muddled as to think that every plural word needs an apostrophe. That is certainly not the case.

Because there has been such confusion over possession, I'd like to suggest that you ignore that old *s* rule and use a rule that is new and simpler. All you need to remember is to put an apostrophe *immediately after the owner*. Take the following sentence:

The dog's tail got caught in the door.

Whenever you write down something where possession seems to be involved, you just ask yourself one simple question: who is the owner? In this case, we need to ask: who owns the tail? The answer is the dog. So you put the apostrophe immediately after *dog*.

There may be some examples that you feel are tricky, but if you apply the new rule, you will find that it really is very simple:

1 Jacks scooter was lying on the grass.
    Q Who owns the scooter?
    A Jack
   Jack's scooter was lying on the grass.

2 From the hill, we could see hundreds of cars lights on the motorway.
    Q Who (or what) owns the lights?
    A the cars
   From the hill, we could see hundreds of cars' lights on the motorway.

---

* This is no longer used in full. The remark, "Are not you clever?" would sound odd and very old-fashioned.

3 We could see the elephants trunks waving over the wall.
   Q Who owns the trunks?
   A The elephants
We could see the elephants' trunks waving over the wall.
4 Peoples tastes differ.
   Q Who owns the tastes?
   A People
People's tastes differ.

If you try to *combine* this rule with the old s rule, you will confuse yourself. Make a clean break, apply the new rule, and, I promise you, you can't go wrong. By the way, if you have ever worried about using an apostrophe for the *Smiths* or the *Joneses,* the following may help:

> I borrowed old Mr Smith's lawnmower last week. Then I lent it to Mrs Jones' aunt. The Smiths' son was furious, but the Joneses' daughter thought it was all very funny.

Smith is a fairly easy name to cope with as it doesn't end in *s*. Where a name does end in *s*, it sounds a bit odd to add another one to indicate possession. So all we need is an apostrophe – *Mrs Jones' aunt*. It would not be wrong, however, to add another *s* if you prefer – *Mrs Jones's aunt*. The name *Jones* is changed to *Joneses* (showing that the word is plural) when we want to talk about the family. An apostrophe is added to this if, and only if, we want to indicate possession *at the same time*:

> the Joneses' daughter – i.e. the daughter of Mr and Mrs Jones

▶ It's and its

The first of these is a **contraction** and the second shows **possession**. There's just one problem here: how do we remember which is which? Well, there's a very simple solution. Each time you write *its,* you just ask yourself, "Do I mean *it is*?" (Occasionally, you might mean *it has*). If the answer is "Yes", you put in an apostrophe and move on. If "No", you just move on anyway. The important thing here is not to hesitate and start wondering if you really have got it right. That will only lead to confusion. Just ask yourself the question and act decisively on the answer.

Contraction

It's raining.	*It is* raining.
It's not often you see a gnu.	*It is* not often you see a gnu.

The word *it's* is used in conversation, in stories, and in informal writing such as letters to friends. I've used it a good deal in this book because I didn't want to sound formal. In your essays, however, stick to writing *it is* because that is the correct form for academic writing.

Possession

The word *its* (without any apostrophe) is one of a group of words that deal with possession. Some of them also end in *s*, but none of them uses an apostrophe. The others are: *my, his, her/hers, our, ours, your, yours, their, theirs.* They are called **possessive adjectives**, but it's not necessary to remember that term. Here is the word *its* used to show possession:

The cat ate *its* dinner.
The ceremony moved towards *its* ending.
The storm was at *its* height.

The words **its** and **it's** look very similar; but now that you can see that their meanings are, in fact, very different, you'll quickly learn to use them accurately.

ACTIVITY 3

Add apostrophes, where necessary, to the following sentences:

1 Its only when I laugh that it hurts.
2 Its a lovely day today.
3 Johns fathers got his brothers coat.
4 When its raining, that dog always stays in its kennel.
5 Its easy to see how the cat shut its paw in the Browns gate.
6 The hyenas eyes were visible in the bushes everywhere we looked.

Until quite recently, items like *VIPs* and *the 1990s* were always given an apostrophe (*VIP's, 1990's*). Now, however, it has become usual to omit the apostrophe. I think this is neater.

As a general rule, use an apostrophe only when you are certain you know where it goes. An apostrophe in the wrong place looks much worse than one omitted.

SUMMARY

• a **full stop** is used to	separate one statement and its closely related information from another
• a **comma** is used to	separate items in a list
	separate two or more words used descriptively
	separate any two statements that are linked by *and, so, but, because,* etc.
	mark off extra information from the main statement: at the beginning or end of a sentence in the middle of a sentence – two commas
• a **semicolon** is used to	keep two statements closer than when using a full stop
	Note: whatever is on *each* side must have its own subject and working verb
• a **colon** is used to	introduce a list, an explanation, a quotation, or some instructions
	demonstrate balance between two statements
• **brackets** are used to	incorporate extra information
• **dashes** are used to	incorporate extra information: in the middle of a sentence (two dashes) or at the end of a sentence
• a **hyphen** is used to	split a word at the end of a line show the separate parts of certain words
	join words to make a new word

- an **exclamation mark** is used to   demonstrate passion in speech

- a **question mark** is used to   indicate a question
- an **apostrophe** is used to   show contraction (a letter or letters missing) or possession
- **its** is used to   show possession
- **it's** is used to   stand instead of *it is* or *it has*

15 Getting Conversation on Paper

INTRODUCTION

This chapter will cover both the rules for writing down the exact words that a person says – **direct speech** – and writing what is called **reported speech**, which is a way of recording that is particularly useful for reports, letters and committee minutes.

The ability to write direct speech is essential for creative writing, but can come in handy for writing essays as well. You might want to quote something said on TV or radio by a politician or academic. The ability to write reported speech is essential for essays and other assignments.

SETTING OUT DIRECT SPEECH

The term **direct speech** refers to the *actual words* that somebody speaks. The rules are really very straightforward. To begin with, everything that a person says is shown *inside* speech marks:

"The garden is going to look wonderful."

There's no fixed rule on whether you use single or double quotation marks for speech. Using double, however, allows you to keep it distinct from quotes from books and articles – for which you use single marks (see chapter 3). The opening speech marks lean forwards and the closing ones lean back towards what has been said; but there is no need, when writing by hand, to put in those little blobs that sometimes show up in print. You can also see that the speech begins with a capital letter and ends with a full stop, just like any ordinary sentence. And notice, too, that the full stop is *inside* the speech marks – this is most important.

There are also hard and fast rules on how we show who is speaking:

Tom said, "The garden is going to look wonderful."

Here, I've begun with the speaker's name followed by the word *said.* Then I've added a comma, and then I've carried on just as before. We can also do this the other way around. But here, there's an extra rule to remember:

"The garden is going to look wonderful," said Tom.

This time, I had to put a comma at the end of the speech instead of a full stop, because I was going on to explain who spoke. But just like the full stop, the comma goes *inside* the speech marks.
Here are two more examples of those two ways for showing who speaks:

Tom said, "There's a lot of earth to shift."
"There's a lot of earth to shift," said Tom.

Remember that whichever way you write this, the *punctuation mark* that follows the words spoken is *always inside* the speech marks.
Imagine that Tom and his neighbours in some council flats are reclaiming a piece of waste ground where they live. It's hard work, and Tom, who's in charge, won't always be speaking calmly. We can show this in two ways: by the use of an exclamation mark to show that he's raising his voice, and by changing the word *said* to something more expressive:

Tom shouted, "Get stuck in, everybody!"
"Get stuck in everybody!" shouted Tom.

Perhaps you've spotted a further problem here. I was not able to use a comma following the word *everybody* in the second sentence because I wanted to use an exclamation mark to show that Tom shouted. (By the way, it's *never* OK to use two punctuation marks beside each other.) An exclamation mark functions just like a full stop in that it marks the end of a sentence. So you might reasonably have expected the word *shouted* to begin with a capital letter. This, however, is the one exception to the rule on capitals following full stops, question marks and exclamation marks. The word *said,* or any substitute for it, always starts with a small letter when it follows somebody's actual words.

Here are some more examples:

> "Mind your backs!" yelled Jeff.
> Jeff yelled, "Mind your backs!"
> "Where do you want these planks?" Angie called out.
> "Angie called out, "Where do you want these planks?"

You can see that a question mark, like an exclamation mark, functions similarly to a full stop by marking the end of a sentence.

There's just one more basic rule for setting out speech. Sometimes, when writing, we want to put *he said* or *she said* in the middle of what a person says, rather than at the beginning or the end. We do it like this:

> "I want to help," said Tom's 5-year-old son, "when you build the pond."

You can see that we don't use a capital letter for the second half of the sentence. You're likely to want to set out speech this way if you're writing a story. This construction allows you to vary the *he said/she said* set-up and it can usefully add a little tension because we have to wait until the end of the sentence to find out the full implication of what is being said.

The reason there is no capital for the word *when* in the example above is that it is *not* the beginning of a sentence. If we could actually hear the boy speaking, we would hear:

> "I want to help when you build the pond."

The following example is constructed in the same way:

> "This garden," said the TV reporter, "is being constructed entirely by the residents of the Brook Lane flats."

Notice that, in each of these split items of speech, there are two commas – one after the first part of the speaker's sentence and one after the small section that shows the speaker's name with the word *said* – or *shouted* or *called out.*

At this point, I suggest you have a go at the following activity to practise these rules for speech. Refer to my examples while you do part A. Then see if you can do part B without looking anything up.

ACTIVITY 1

Add speech marks and *all* necessary punctuation and capital letters to the following sentences.

Part A

1 jack said my partner is expecting a baby
2 i was born in tunis said pierre
3 where is the post office asked the tourist
4 the toddler yelled i want an ice cream
5 that dog said john always disappears when i want to bath it
6 why asked tom have you put the beer under my bed

Part B

1 mary said the eggs are in the fridge
2 high tide will be at three this afternoon said the sailor
3 come back here yelled the policeman
4 sam asked politely how much extra will I have to pay
5 I havent laughed so much said ben since the chicken coop collapsed
6 the main difficulty explained the leader will be getting the tents across the river

Now you know the punctuation rules for conversation, we can look at how to set it out on the page. The usual rule here is: *new speaker, new line.* It's also usual to indent two or three spaces when a person starts to speak. Here's an example of how a local newspaper might report on the building of the garden (but note that newspapers don't always have enough space to stick to the rules all the time):

The residents of the Brook Lane flats are working flat out. Since the beginning of the year, they've been transforming an unsightly piece of waste ground into a gorgeous garden. Angie Stevens, who works on the plot every weekend, told me,
"I never thought I'd be doing this."
Angie's partner, Tom, was voted Chief Gardener. "We've had a lot of support from the Council," he explained. "They

donated spare paving stones for the path and they're going to organise an opening ceremony."
Even the children have been getting involved:
"My twins rush home from school every day to help," said Jeff Rogers with a smile. When I asked what the residents would be doing next, Jeff grinned. "We've got our eyes on the Town Hall gardens," he laughed.

Remember that the words inside speech marks are those that were actually spoken. Of course, in newspapers, journalists sometimes give approximations of what was said, but doing that could get you into hot water in academic work.

ACTIVITY 2

The following is part of an article on Bob Crooks, a glassmaker. I have omitted all punctuation marks, capital letters and speech marks. Copy out the extract, putting in all speech marks, capitals and punctuation. Don't worry if you don't get this activity exactly right. The important thing is for you to have some practice in thinking out what to do.

I sense theres an excitement for bob crooks in work where hes in dialogue with his material mixing colours and never being 100% sure of the final outcome because of the speed of the materials reactions
I dont want to battle against the material he says so in the final heating I let the glass do what it wants to do it is by this means that bob is able to create the fluid forms hes known for hes influenced by geometry architecture and the natural world I cant make anything as beautiful as what's in nature he goes on but I like taking elements of different things and turning them into something whole

INDIRECT OR REPORTED SPEECH

Before reading any further, you might need to check over the sections on *tenses* and *pronouns* in chapter 12.

By using **reported speech**, we can do away with speech marks because we are making a statement *about* what someone said rather than using the exact words that were spoken. It's done like this:

Actual speech	Ron said, "The library is closed."
Reported speech	Ron said that the library was closed.

As you see, the words in reported speech are very similar to the original ones used. There have, however, been some very important changes:

- a word has been added: **that**
- the verb *is* has changed to *was*   **tense change**

When we write formal reported speech, we need to add the word *that* before the body of what was said. If you want a more informal effect, you can omit *that,* but it's a good idea to keep using it until you are really familiar with writing reported speech.

We also have to go back in time because we are now referring to something that happened earlier. We go back one **tense**. In the example above, the present simple tense has changed to the past simple. Look especially at the tense changes in the following examples:

Actual	The MPs said, "We won the battle for votes."	**Past simple**
Reported	The MPs said that they had won the battle for votes.	**Past perfect**
Actual	The MPs said, "We are winning the battle for votes."	**Present continuous**
Reported	The MPs said that they were winning the battle for votes.	**Past continuous**
Actual	The MPs said, "We were winning the battle for votes."	**Past continuous**
Reported	The MPs said that they had been winning the battle for votes.	**Past perfect continuous**

Don't feel that you need to learn the names of tenses. I've just put them in as a guide. just focus on getting a feel for going back in time.

Visualising what you need to do can be a very powerful reminder. When students are learning a foreign language, the tutor sometimes uses lots of gestures. To remind people to use the past tense, he or she might jerk a thumb backwards over a shoulder. You might find it helpful to imagine doing this when you need to write reported speech.

Before you get too confused over all this, it's a good idea to remember that, as with many features of grammar, you have almost certainly been getting the tenses right, as you speak, for years.

The future tense can be a little tricky, but here again, you doubtless get it right when you speak. Here *will* changes to *would:*

Actual	"We **will put forward** improved policies on housing and taxation," promised the members of the new party.
Reported	The members of the new party promised that they **would put forward** improved policies on housing and taxation.

Concentrate on remembering that *will* changes to *would*. Technically speaking, the **future indicative** has changed to the **subjunctive mood**. But here we are touching on areas that are beyond the scope of this book.

As well as the word *that*, the key issues you will need to remember are:

1 pronoun change
2 time change
3 place change
4 setting out questions
5 greetings

You will find below a selection of examples for each of these items. Many of them are fairly obvious, but some are a little tricky.

1 Pronoun change

Actual	"I'm finishing my essay," said Nick.
Reported	Nick said that he was finishing his essay.
Actual	"We went to the cinema," said the children.
Reported	The children said that they had been to the cinema.
Actual	Beverley said, "I'm exhausted."

Reported   Beverley said that <u>she</u> was exhausted.

2 Time change
Actual   "I bought a new car <u>yesterday</u>," said Ruth.
Reported   Ruth said that she had bought a new car <u>the day before</u>.

Actual   "I bought a new car <u>today</u>," said Ruth.
Reported   Ruth said that she had bought a new car <u>that day</u>.

Actual   My sister said, "It's raining <u>now</u>."
Reported   My sister said that it was raining <u>then</u>.
or
My sister said that it was raining <u>at the time</u>.

3 Place change
Actual   "I'm sure I put the money in <u>this</u> box," said Anne.
Reported   Anne said that she was sure she had put the money in <u>that</u> box.

Actual   Rob said, "The letters are all <u>here</u>."
Reported   Rob said that the letters were all <u>there</u>.

4 Setting out questions
Actual   "Where's the science block?" <u>said</u> John.
Reported   John <u>asked</u> where the science block was.
or
John <u>asked</u> for directions to the science block.

Actual   "Why is Sam going?" <u>said</u> Ben.
Reported   Ben <u>asked</u> why Sam was going.

Actual   "What's the time?" <u>said</u> Ben.
Reported   Ben <u>asked</u> what the time was.
or
Ben <u>asked</u> for the time.

In each of the above examples, the questioning word (*where, why, what*) is often repeated in reported speech, but the order of words is different. Note also that we *never* use a question mark in reported questions. A reported question isn't actually asking anything; it merely points out that a question has been asked by someone at some point.

5 Greetings
Actual "Good morning, ladies and gentlemen," said Mr Fox.
Reported Mr Fox greeted everyone.

ACTIVITY 3

See if you can now turn the following eight brief statements made by Kwame into reported speech. The first one has been done for you.

1 "I drive to work every day," said Kwame.
Kwame said that he drove to work every day.
2 "I am driving a Ford, now," said Kwame.
3 "I drove to Italy last month," said Kwame.
4 "I have driven 500 miles this week," said Kwame.
5 "I have been driving for 10 years now," said Kwame.
6 "I was driving at night when the brakes failed," said Kwame.
7 "I will drive to Spain next year," said Kwame.
8 "I will be driving a Porsche next year," said Kwame.

SUMMARY

Checklist for direct speech
- put speech marks around the *exact words spoken*
- begin with a *capital letter*
- keep punctuation *inside* speech marks
- use a lower-case letter for *he said* and *she said*
- when following the speech with *he said/she said,* add a *comma* before closing the speech marks
- when using *he said/she said* before the words spoken, add a *comma* after *said*

Checklist for reported speech
1 add the word *that*
2 go back one tense
3 check pronouns
4 check time and place

Part Four
Moving On

16 Your CV

INTRODUCTION

Maybe you're ahead of the game and you've already written up a basic CV. If not, you'll find guidelines here to get you started. Sooner or later, everyone needs a CV, and the good news is that, once you've got the basics in place, writing later CVs should be a reasonably painless process. You just build on your earlier work.

If you can find the time to do this work early on in your course, it will save you precious time in your final year when you are beginning to apply for jobs. Not only that, you can use your CV to apply for valuable part-time experience while you are still at college or university. Students who have shown early interest in their chosen field of employment are likely to be looked on especially favourably by employers.

Your first task may be the most time-consuming. You will need to gather together every scrap of information you have about your education and work experience – whether paid or voluntary. If your first thought is that you possess nothing, or that you've never done anything worth mentioning, don't worry – that's a common response. What this chapter will do is explain how to create a document that you feel happy with and that shows you in the best possible light. And that goes for everybody. There are no exceptions.

WHAT IS A CV?

The initials CV stand for *curriculum vitae*. This is a Latin phrase that just means *the course of your life*. A CV will show an employer what jobs you've done, what schools and colleges you've attended and what qualifications you've got or are studying for.

A CV is a document that:

- contains essential information about you
- presents you in the best possible light
- is essential for job applications
- is 50 per cent of the means by which you get an interview
- can be referred to by both parties during an interview

If you are planning on working in education, local government, the Civil Service or other public bodies, you are likely to have to fill in an application form rather than sending a CV. All the information for this, however, will be contained in your CV (except your statement – see chapter 17), so it's just a matter of copying from your CV what you need in the order shown on the form. It's not a good idea to omit to draw up a CV since you never know how things will pan out or how soon you will get permanent full-time employment in your chosen field. It's also the case that you can be asked to provide a CV "just for our records" after you have begun work in a job for which you applied by application form.

SELLING YOURSELF

The job of a CV is to secure you an interview. You may find the idea of selling yourself a bit strange or unpalatable, but whether you like it or not, a CV is the first stage in your sales pitch. The whole object is to persuade an employer to want to see you. To reach the interview stage, your application must demonstrate how s/he would benefit from having you on the payroll.

Imagine the scenario: you send off your application for a job on which you are really keen. Then you watch the post for a response. Meanwhile, your prospective employer is receiving twenty or thirty applications and must choose five or six applicants to call for interview. He or she will bin any CVs that are untidy, misspelt or ungrammatical. From the remainder, s/he'll be looking for:

- experience
- qualifications
- personal qualities
- a keen interest in the job

The last of these is likely to come across most strongly in your covering letter – which will underline key aspects of your CV (see chapter 16). And qualifications either exist or they don't. Experience and personal qualities, however, can be put across in such a way as to maximise your chances of being noticed.

WHAT WILL I NEED?

There's a lot involved here, so the list may look a bit daunting. But this is a one-off process. Once you've completed this initial stage, you'll never have to cover the ground again. Don't assume that you must tick off everything on this list. The first three items are essential, but beyond that, aim to find as much as you can. You may well need to make some notes on things for which you have no documentation. Don't rely on your memory at this stage. You need to work towards having everything ready for applying for jobs.

It's a good idea to use a box-file or just an ordinary cardboard box to put papers in as you go along. Getting your materials together may take a few weeks if you have to search the attic or make contacts for information. But since you'll be dealing with documents that may be vital for your future, do give them the importance they deserve. The good news is that much of the work you do here will be useful for your covering letter as well as for your CV.

▶ Materials you require

- a list of past employment, including: names and addresses of employers (with dates)
  job titles
  key tasks you performed
- the names of schools and colleges you've attended since the age of 11 (with dates)
- educational certificates
- a note of any school achievements
- sports certificates
- music, drama, art or handicraft certificates

- any other certificates (e.g. for attending courses, day schools, workshops, etc.)
- a note of any prizes you've received (for absolutely anything)
- written references or positive letters from employers
- a list of evening classes you've attended
- a note of goals you've achieved
- any letters of thanks addressed to you
- a note of any position you've held such as secretary or treasurer of a committee
- a note of any voluntary work you've done
- printed details of any charities, etc., you've worked for
- details of home care you've undertaken – looking after children or other dependants
- experiences of teamwork
- a note of any languages you can speak and whether at a basic or advanced level
- experiences of working to deadlines
- a list of your hobbies (past and current)
- a list of your interests (e.g. historic buildings, alternative therapies, wildlife conservation, etc.)
- membership of clubs and societies (past and current)
- a list of your skills and abilities (e.g. driving, playing an instrument, instructing others, making clothes, gardening, etc.)
- anything else which you feel might be relevant

Note: When you are offered a job, you may also need your birth certificate and national insurance number.

Getting all this together is likely to take some time. But if you work in bite-sized chunks, and spend some time on the process each week, your materials will soon mount up. Just as with writing an essay, you are going to need plenty of material so that you can (a) pick the best bits, (b) give a full picture of your abilities, and (c) choose relevant items for particular jobs. Once you've put together a basic CV, you can vary it according to the different positions you apply for. For example, the fact that you may have kept an allotment for growing vegetables could be useful if you apply for a marketing job in the food industry, but you'd probably leave it out if you applied to market computers.

► Lost certificates

If you've mislaid certificates, you may need to get copies. In order to do this, you will need to know the name of the awarding body – for example, City & Guilds, OCA, RSA or AQA. If you can remember the name of the body, either look it up on the Internet or get in touch with your local reference library where they'll be able to give you the address and phone number you need.

If you don't know the name of the awarding body, phone the school or college where you sat the examination. If you tell them the year that you sat a particular subject, they may well be able to answer your query. If you find that your school has been razed to the ground, phone the Local Education offices. They may well have records. Don't over-look the possibility of getting the information you need from friends and relations – or the fact that your GCSE certificates might still be in your childhood home.

► Lost addresses of employers

It's usually a good idea to show the full addresses for work you've done in the last five years. For employment further back, just the name of the town is likely to be enough. It depends partly on how many jobs you've had and partly on the level of the work. The fewer the number, the more important it is to give full addresses.

If, for example, you lived in Nottingham for three years and worked as a bar person in six pubs during that time, you could get away with listing just the town and the outside dates:

2002–2005	various employers	bar work
	Nottingham	

If, however, you'd held three jobs in Nottingham between 2002 and 2005 and each gave you valuable experience and was a step up from the previous one, it would be important to show employers' names and addresses clearly. You might need to look through the *Yellow Pages*. If you're really stuck, try your local reference library.

YOUR DUTIES AND KEY TASKS: ACTION WORDS

When you've got together lists of your past jobs, you will need to look at the main duties you performed in each. A prospective employer will want to know what you've actually done. The idea here is to list the duties you've undertaken and starting with a verb – an action word – like this:

- prepared spreadsheets
- supplied clients with product information
- liaised with outside companies

If you are coming back to work after a break or you have been bringing up children, it's easy to feel that you have little to show here. You may, however, be underestimating your experience. When faced with writing a CV, Anne, a student on an environmental science course, began by saying, "I've done nothing in my life. All I've done is watch TV." When pressed, however, she revealed the following information:

- she was bringing up 4 children
- she was secretary to her local residents' group
- she sometimes helped out at her children's playgroup
- she did the paperwork for her husband's small farm
- she helped out on the farm

On a CV, this might be shown something like this:

1998–2006	home responsibilities	cared for children
		undertook secretarial duties
		assisted with early-years education
		kept business accounts
		cared for farm animals

Whatever you've done, it can be made to look interesting by putting it into formal language.

YOUR SKILLS AND ABILITIES

People sometimes land jobs for the strangest reasons. You might have applied to teach French in secondary education and then pipped another candidate to the post because you once attended dance classes and so could help with the school's production of *West Side Story*. Your prospective boss in an insurance firm might finally choose you because your previous experience in the fishing industry means that you'll be useful in dealing with fishing claims. So it's important to make a full list of your skills so that you can dip into it when you need to. You will need this information for both your CV and your covering letter or statement. If you're stuck, you might like to start by putting things under the following headings:

- coping with data
- working with people
- developing ideas
- working with things
- the arts

Anne might compile the following list:

- childcare
- money management
- bookkeeping
- organisation
- negotiation
- word-processing
- communication
- record-keeping
- planning
- animal care

YOUR PERSONAL PROFILE

Many people, nowadays, like to put a *Personal profile* at the head of their CV. This means writing three or four lines explaining the kind of person you are, together with an outline of your skills, abilities and achievements. The *profile* reads rather like an advert and generally contains no working verbs.

Let's suppose that you have worked as a legal secretary, managed a small office and are now studying personnel management and applying for your first job in personnel work. Your *Personal profile* might read like this:

> A confident and conscientious administrator with proven office experience and the ability to work under pressure either alone or as part of a team, and having a keen interest in all aspects of personnel work.

If you have helped run a playgroup since your children were born and are studying to be a primary teacher, you might write:

> An efficient organiser who has run a playgroup while managing a home and bringing up children and is able to empathise with early-years children, helping them to learn and to practise their social skills. Adaptable, resourceful and keen to participate in all aspects of primary school work.

Or maybe your work experience was mainly bar work and cleaning and you then stayed at home to bring up your children. You might decide to construct a *Personal profile* that focuses on your college or university experience. Let's suppose you're studying interior design. You might write the following:

> An innovative and effective designer who has worked on designs for a college common room and won a student award for designs for the living room of a show house. Able to plan, budget and take full account of client needs.

You can see that each *Personal profile* showcases the writer's key abilities and achievements in the light of the job being applied for.

▶ **Career profile**

Sometimes, this piece is headed *Career profile*. This heading can be used if you already have considerable experience in the field of work you are applying for and can show what you've covered. Maybe you have served in the Armed Forces and are now moving into civilian life but in a similar field to your original training. Perhaps you were an engineer and are now about to gain a BSc in engineering. You'll want to show that you are building on a strong background:

> A highly motivated engineer with successful experience of leading teams throughout his wide experience of construction gained in the Armed Services. Now looking to take on a management role. Confident, ambitious, diligent and resourceful.

▶ Career objectives

This heading might be used if you are sending out your CV 'on spec' to a number of different employers. In this case, you'll want to show that you have clear goals and lots of determination. Your *Profile* might look like this:

> A language specialist, fluent in both French and German, who has lived and worked in Europe and will shortly have a BA (Hons) in Russian. Planning to work as a translator or interpreter.

ANGLING THE INFORMATION

It's very important not to invent things for your CV or suggest, for example, that your examination results were better than they actually were. It's difficult to remember exactly what you've said in a stressful interview situation, and the truth has a way of surfacing when you least expect it. It's perfectly acceptable, however, to leave things out or to put stress on something that you want to showcase. You can reword things for different applications or change the layout and positioning of particular information in order to either emphasise or diminish it.

REFERENCES

You will need to ask two or three people if they would be prepared to act as your referees. One of these should be someone in a position of authority on your course – probably the head of department or a senior lecturer. If you have been in work recently, another should be your latest employer. Two referees are essential and you may need an extra one, as some employers ask for three.

Your referees need to be able to comment on your abilities and on the way you interact with others. If you're stuck, think about people in authority from somewhere you've done voluntary work or tutors from evening classes you've attended. If the worst comes to the worst, use your bank manager or doctor – but that really is the worst-case scenario because employers want to know what you'll be like in a work or educational situation.

Never include any actual references with your CV. Just give a list of names, job titles, business addresses, e-mails and phone numbers. And do check that you have up-to-date information for these vital contacts. An employer may want to phone or e-mail a referee in a hurry.

LAYOUT

There's a fairly standard format for a CV, and it's best not to be creative on this. Employers want something that is easy to read and that conforms in general to what they expect (see the examples at the end of this chapter). They want to be able to scan it quickly, which means that it mustn't look cramped and that it has to fit on *no more than* two sides of A4.

The sections of your CV will be roughly as follows:

- Personal profile
- Current post (if you are in any work)
- Past employment
- Qualifications
- Education and training
- Personal details – e.g. hobbies, etc.
- Referees

Both the *Past employment* and *Education and training* sections are listed, with the most recent first and then working backwards. Your *Qualifications* section needs to include the name of each award, the awarding body (e.g. RSA, AQA, etc.), your grade and the date of the

award. If you did well in GCSEs, you might decide to note them something like this:

2002   10 GCSEs – including Maths & English at A* –   AQA

A levels, however, would need to be listed separately with your relevant grade for each.

If you're not computer literate or don't have access to a computer,
you'll need to persuade a friend to type your CV for you or pay to have
it done. Whatever happens, make sure that you have a copy on disk or
CD. You will need this CV again and again and again. It's the first
edition of a document that you will use all your life.

THE LANGUAGE OF A CV

The main thing to know about language for CVs is that you will not be
writing full sentences. The whole point of a CV is to give an employer
an easy read. He or she will want to glance through your CV quickly to
get an immediate feel for whether or not to put it on the pile of possible interviewees. If you write in full sentences and paragraphs you
lessen your chances of getting to the next stage of the process. An
employer is very likely to assume that anyone who is unable to sum up
his or her own life experiences simply and clearly will probably be
unable to deal adequately with similar tasks at work. So you will need
to use the fewest words possible and to adopt a really clear layout (see
above).

The other important point concerning language is that you must
write formally and use the correct terms for jobs and their relevant
duties.

HINTS AND TIPS

- use white A4 paper
- use clear type – no italics or fancy fonts
- follow instructions from the job advert/further details exactly
- use no Tipp-Ex, glue, Blu-Tack, etc.
- send a top copy prepared on computer

- stick to the truth
- use appropriate language
- show you are already pursuing your main interest – via hobbies
- show you know about the field of work – via experience/ study/reading/etc.

▶ **Don't include**

- references (only the *names* of referees are wanted at this stage)
- details of your family
- photographs
- pamphlets
- anything not asked for in a job advert

▶ **If the instructions say 'no CVs'**

If the employer has stated that CVs are not wanted, sending one will almost certainly ensure that you are *not* invited to interview. An employer wants staff who can follow instructions. Doing something other than what has been asked gives the suggestion that you might not be capable of the accurate assimilation of information.

EXAMPLES OF CVS

There are obviously different ways of setting out CVs and what you do will depend partly on personal preference and partly on the content of your CV. As suggested above, however, it's wise not to depart too far from what an employer will expect. Remember that when anyone reads your CV, they'll be in a hurry and will want to be able to pick out the relevant information very quickly.

Note: In the examples below, names and some of the data have been changed.

Curriculum Vitae
Tracey Hitchens
6 Hillside Terrace
Newton Abbot
Devon
TQ5 3TH
00000 000000
t.hitchens@telephone.com

PERSONAL PROFILE
A responsible and competent administrator with experience of a variety of organisations, who has particular knowledge of the financial sector and is skilled in dealing with staffing issues.

EMPLOYMENT HISTORY

TCD Ltd Unit 6 Larch Road Plymouth PL3 4AD	March 2003– June 2005 (while studying for my degree)	Cleaning Operative	Responsible for local building society offices
Fiveways Nursing Home Back Road Tavistock Devon	April 2001– August 2002	Administrator/ receptionist	admitted residents dealt with post input wages on computer booked agency staff kept records liaised with doctors carried out secretarial duties for management and staff
National Bank Chertsey Surrey	November 2000– November 2001	Customer Service Officer	oversaw sub-branch handled cash and balanced tills served customers dealt with problems organised security liaised with head office implemented new computer system
Sewing Guild High Street Dartmouth Devon	April 1999– November 2000	Machinist/ shop assistant	manufactured curtains and soft furnishings served customers

The Care Group
Exeter
	August 1998–
	April 1999
		Community
		Care Worker
			provided home care
			  for elderly and sick
			covered: personal care,
			  cleaning, shopping,
			  etc.

Home responsibilities,	1983–1999	Parent	brought up my children
Oxfam,		Volunteer shop assistant	served customers
Air Training Corps		Volunteer treasurer	handled and banked cash kept accounts
Savings Bank Guildford Surrey	1979–1983	Cashier	dealt with customers

QUALIFICATIONS

2005	BA (Hons) Humanities	IIi
1995	Arts Foundation Course, Open University	Pass 73%
1980	RSA Stage 1 Elementary Typewriting	Pass
1979	8 GCE O levels, including English and Maths	Pass

EDUCATION

2002–2005	College of St Mark and St John, Plymouth – BA course in History with English Language and Linguistics
1994–1995	The Open University
1974–1979	Burdock Comprehensive School Guildford

There are various ways that you can deal with the structure and layout of your CV as long as you produce something that looks good and is easy to read. The CV below varies in its layout from the one above, but, because it is very neat and clear, it works well.

Curriculum Vitae
Hilary Crawford
18 Bullers Park
Kingsbridge
Devon
PL8 5PT
00000 000000
h.crawford@telephone.com

Self-motivated, versatile and methodical, with expertise in providing advice and guidance to diverse client groups. Experience in establishing and implementing effective administrative systems in a range of occupational areas including the financial, commercial and educational sectors. Highly motivated to succeed within a demanding environment while complying with operational procedures and maintaining excellent standards of service.

SKILLS PROFILE

ADMINISTRATION

- Established the work-placement programme for a government-funded training organisation: recruiting clients, generating placement opportunities with local employers; matching clients according to employers' specifications, conducting health and safety inspections.
- Developed an industrial placement provision, University of Plymouth.
- Provided administrative support to a team of 4 financial advisers, ensuring compliance with financial services regulations.

COMMUNICATION AND TEAMWORK

- Undertook client assessments to ensure that both employer and employee gained maximum benefit from the placement opportunity.
- Liaised between students and academic staff to ensure effective transmission of information.
- Conducted individual and group presentations for peer and academic review.
- Generated sales leads by cold-call telephoning.
- Provided enhanced directory-enquiry assistance in high-volume call-centre environment.
- Established and retained a base of 400+ home-shopping customers through the provision of exceptional customer service.

INFORMATION TECHNOLOGY

- Devised placement handbook and database to ensure adherence to university guidelines.
- Produced a range of management reports and statistical information using complex spreadsheets to illustrate cash flow, man-hour projections and project spend.
- Extensive use of Internet and e-mail, for both research and communication purposes.
- Rapidly assimilated and implemented new software.

ORGANISATION
- Combined reading for a full-time honours degree with raising a pre-school child and running a successful home shopping franchise.
- Arranged customer appointments and managed diaries for a team of financial advisers.

EMPOYMENT SUMMARY

The Number (UK) Ltd	Customer Service Representative	2005–2006
Kleeneze Europe Ltd	Independent Distributor	2002–2005
University of Plymouth	Industrial Placement Co-ordinator	1999–2002
Wesleyan Financial Services	Customer Service Co-ordinator	1998–1999
CC Training	Placement Co-ordinator	1996–1998
Career break	Independent traveller	1994–1995
British Aerospace	Price Control Analyst	1990–1994
Ministry of Defence	Administrative Officer	1988–1990
Legal and General	Insurance Administrator	1986–1988

EDUCATION

BA (Hons) English Language and Linguistics (1st Class) University College of St Mark and St John University of Exeter	2005
Advanced level English Language and English Literature (B) Stoke Damerel Community College, Plymouth, Devon	1995
9 GCE O levels including English (A) and Maths (B) Cleverham Community College, Battle, East Sussex	1984

HOBBIES AND INTERESTS

In order to keep fit, I regularly play squash and exercise at my local gym. I enjoy writing and contribute to a variety of national magazines. I am an avid reader, with a particular interest in detective novels and thrillers. I have travelled extensively throughout Africa, Asia and Australia and relish the opportunity to experience different cultures.

ADDITIONAL INFORMATION

Date of Birth:	22 April 1966
Driving licence:	Full and clean
Health:	Excellent
References:	Available on request

Here is another CV that differs slightly from the suggested guidelines I've given above.

Curriculum Vitae

Mark Godfrey

18 Preston Villas
Morland Park
Bristol
BS6 8HK

00000 000000
m.godfrey@telephone.com

Personal Profile

An experienced project manager, responsible for the design, planning and construction of a wide variety of products to produce solutions best suited to customer specifications. Industrious, reliable and conscientious, with an outgoing personality and keen sense of humour. Able to work under pressure and adhere to strict deadlines and budgets to ensure maximisation of profit. Highly motivated to work in an environment that will enable existing skills to be fully utilised, whilst allowing new ones to develop.

CAREER SUMMARY

2006–present   Flint Engineering, Bristol
Project Manager/draughtsman

Design, development and construction of a diverse range of engineering projects involving structural steelwork. Responsible for working with clients to ensure the effective implementation and delivery of the project within budgetary constraints.

2001–2003   Various contracts, Bristol and Avon
Fabricator/welder

Involved in the design and production of structural steelwork, sheet-metal work and a wide variety of other components. Operated a range of machinery including guillotine, brake press, drills, saws, oxygen-propane cutting equipment, plasma and all forms of welding equipment. Also worked on the running of lathes and milling machines. All fabrication taken from drawings to strict tolerance.

1998–2001   Motor Accessories, Bristol
Senior Fabricator/welder

Involved in the production of high-quality vehicle accessories. Responsible for the fabrication and welding of bright mild steel and stainless steel accessories.

1991–1998   **Morgan's Precision Engineering, Bristol**
                   Apprentice Fabricator/welder (structural engineering)
Four years' training and gaining proficiency as an apprentice fabricator/ welder.
Following completion of apprenticeship, worked on structural fabrications always
from drawings and to very precise specifications. Highly accomplished in the
processes of MIG, TIG and MMA.

QUALIFICATIONS

2006   BEng – Engineering Design   Ili
                  University of Bristol

2001   City & Guilds level 3D AutoCad

1991–1995   Structural Engineering   BS 4871 & BS 4872
                  Fabrication and welding   Various positions

EDUCATION

1984–1991   Parkdale Comprehensive School, Bristol
                  9 GCSEs grades A–C, including Maths and English

HOBBIES AND INTERESTS

During my spare time, I enjoy vehicle maintenance and socialising with my
friends, playing snooker in a local pub league. I keep fit by regularly visiting the
gym and playing squash.

FURTHER INFORMATION

Date of birth: 05.04.73
Driving licence: Full and clean
Health: Excellent

REFERENCES

Available on request

Note: For a speculative CV, it's fine to say you'll send names of referees on request. When applying for a specific job, it's essential to give
names, addresses, phone and fax numbers (where relevant) and e-mail
addresses for each referee (see above).

Mark's CV looks professional because it's neat, has clear headings,
and uses bold for job dates and titles. His *Personal profile* is a little
lengthy, but it does give a good sense of his background and abilities.
His decision to write prose rather than lists of his responsibilities in
each job is probably the right one because (a) in his case, lists would

have taken up more space and (b) he clearly felt that he needed to include a little explanation in some cases. His sentences are, however, extremely factual. There isn't a wasted word.

SUMMARY

This chapter has covered:

- definitions of a CV
- selling yourself
- materials needed for writing a CV
- lost certificates and addresses
- your duties and key tasks
- your skills and abilities
- your *Personal profile*
- angling the information
- references
- layout
- the language of a CV
- hints and tips
- examples of student CVs

17 Letters and Statements for Job Applications

INTRODUCTION

It's hardly possible to over-stress the importance of anything you write for a job application. Chapter 15 explained that your CV forms 50 per cent of the means whereby you gain an interview. Your covering letter forms the remaining 50 per cent. It's part of the 'sales pitch' by which you persuade an employer to see you.

Constructing a good letter may take several hours and you'll need to write more than one draft. But your time will be well spent, and you will get much quicker at the process after the first few letters you send.

It's sensible to be realistic over job applications. There are a lot of people looking for work, so you'd be extremely lucky to get an offer from the first company your approach. Look on your job hunt as a process. The more professional your covering letters, however, the greater are your chances of finding employment quickly.

THE STATEMENT ON AN APPLICATION FORM

Some employers (for example, local and national government offices) always send out application forms, and in most cases, these have space for you to write a *Personal statement* that stands instead of a covering letter. It is usually clear from the instructions whether or not a letter is needed, but if you are unsure, phone and check. The crucial thing is to do whatever is wanted. If you send material the employer doesn't ask for, you run the risk of having your applications put straight on the 'No' pile. Employers want people who show that they can follow instructions.

If it's a statement that's wanted, the process will be very similar to writing a letter. You'll just leave out the date, addresses, and so on, and may need to write fewer words. Quite often, the application form will state that you can add an extra sheet, in which case, you will not need to cut anything. If there's no possibility of adding an extra sheet, you will need to check exactly how much space you've got and how many words you can get in that space. You also need to be careful over margins. If you are able to photocopy your word-processed statement on to the form, first make a copy of the form and practise on that because it's fatally easy to miscalculate the space and ruin your form.

You will find an example of the statement for an application form at the end of this chapter, but do read the whole chapter if you are new to this process because the information on application letters applies to statements as well.

CHARACTERISTICS OF A GOOD LETTER

You can see how to set out a letter in chapter 6, and many of the points in writing essays from chapter 2 will also be relevant here – such as structure, paragraphing, linking and so on. Your letter needs to be:

- well organised
- clearly expressed
- easy to read
- interesting
- lively
- error-free
- free from negatives

It must show that you are:

- keen
- intelligent
- knowledgeable
- dependable
- sociable
- committed

It needs to cover:

- your interest in the job
- your knowledge of the work

- your relevant experience/abilities
- other relevant achievements
- your career aspirations
- why the employer would benefit from employing you

WHAT ARE MY BEST QUALITIES?

You are going to have to sell yourself, so you need to be clear in your own mind on the qualities you have to offer. Here you may need help from a friend. Start, however, by going back to your CV and to your lists of skills and abilities. Things you've done in the past will help show the kind of person you are. Then think about the obvious things:

- Are you cool in a crisis?
- Are you reliable?
- Do you work well alone?
- Are you a good team player?
- Do you have a pleasant sense of humour?
- Are you ambitious?
- Are you resourceful?
- Are you confident?

Anne, the student referred to in chapter 16 who at first felt she had done nothing with her life, might list her qualities as:

- responsible
- flexible
- adaptable
- reliable
- sensitive
- diplomatic
- self-disciplined
- able to see the big picture
- a good communicator
- a quick thinker

You can probably add to your list by thinking about how you've coped with difficulties and challenges you've come up against in the past. You may feel a little uncomfortable about blowing your own trumpet, but if you don't tell employers what you are like, they won't know and are unlikely to take your application seriously.

You will not need to mention all your qualities in one go. Aim to throw one in every now and then as it relates to different aspects of your experience and to the job you are applying for. In your final paragraph (see 'Your conclusion' below) you might mention a few qualities when summing up the benefits you would bring to the post.

TRANSFERABLE SKILLS

Don't worry too much if there are things on the job specification that you have no experience of. You're going to show how things you've done in the past can be related to the requirements of the job you are applying for. It is always possible to use skills in a different context. For example, if you've run a house, brought up children or organised a fête to raise money for charity, you can show that you have organisational skills. If you have managed an office in a building firm, you can apply the experience gained there to managing one in a totally different field and at a higher level. You might also give examples of how you have adapted to new systems and learnt new skills in the past. This would demonstrate your flexibility.

WRITING YOUR LETTER

▶ Getting started

If you have not been sent a job specification, you will need to phone and ask for one. You can then go through this and highlight key items so that you can be sure to address the most important ones in your letter. If you've been sent a person specification, that's better still because it will help you with the structure of your letter. Anyone reading your application is likely to have a person specification beside them and will be looking to see how you match up. If you cover issues in the order in which they're listed, it can make the reader's task easier and so make it more likely that you will be accepted for interview.

You'll also need to have your CV to hand as you write so that you can refer to key points on it. Your letter needs to point out essential information on your CV that you want the employer to notice. You then need to fill this out with more details and perhaps an example or two.

▶ Your first draft

Just as with an essay, you will need an introduction, a conclusion, and a middle section that contains the meat of your letter. Start with your most important points and put the least important ones near the end of the letter. Remember that whoever reads your letter will be totally focused on the vacant post. Make sure that whatever you write focuses on it too.

Your most important points will be any experience you have in the particular industry or area of work and your relevant skills and qualifications, including any you're studying for. When you refer to points from your CV, explain how these can be related to the job itself. This is your evidence. Just as with an essay, you need to make it really easy for your reader to understand what you're getting at. So don't leave him or her to make the jump between what you've done in the past and how it has prepared you for the new post. Spell it out.

Your language will be fairly formal and your tone needs to demonstrate your enthusiasm for the post and a quiet confidence in your ability to carry out the work. Use active verbs as you did in the 'duties' section of your CV. And here, unlike in essays, you will frequently need to use the word *I*.

▶ Your introduction

Keep your introduction brief. If you are writing a letter, you can begin by saying something like:

> I would like to apply for the above post and I enclose my CV. I am now completing my final year of a BA in Communication Studies and am aiming to work in . . .

If you are writing a statement, it's clear from the fact that you've filled in an application form that you are applying for a job, so you won't want to mention that.

▶ Ways of beginning a paragraph

Aim to use good links as you would in an essay, and try to avoid beginning every paragraph with the word 'I'. If you're stuck for the opening of a particular paragraph, you might consider trying something like this:

- Having always had a great interest in animal husbandry, I am now …
- As a member of the County's athletic team, I was …
- Having recently discovered my ability to design large-scale projects, I …
- It has been my ambition to become a social worker for some years now.
- Teaching is a profession in which all my skills can come into play.

▶ Your conclusion

As in an essay, the conclusion is where you sum up your points. Here, you want to leave the reader with a sense that you have all it takes to do the job. It's often a good place to note that you have a pleasant sense of humour, and, if applicable, that you work well as a member of a team.

▶ Avoiding negatives

It is fatally easy to write yourself out of a job by suggesting that you lack experience in the relevant field, that you don't expect a high class of degree or that you are not quite sure that you have the qualities to undertake the work. As with a CV, omit, wherever possible, to mention things that don't help your case and then turn others into positives. For example, a lack of experience of working with people when applying for a job in personnel might be treated something like this:

> While working as a clerical assistant in a legal firm, I became especially interested in the effect of legal processes on clients. It was this that gave me an interest in the relationship between people and organisations and decided me to pursue a career in

personnel. While at university, I have been lucky enough to gain an insight into personnel work by shadowing personnel officers in two very different industries.

Redundancy can also be made to work in your favour:

> If I had not been made redundant from a firm of insurance brokers where I had worked for ten years, I would not have had the opportunity to undertake part-time work in a residential home. While there, I soon discovered my ability to empathise with residents and their families plus a strong desire to take on a more formal role in assisting at crisis points in people's lives and to become a social worker.

If you have experience of one aspect of a job but not another and the employer wants both, say how keen you are to become proficient in the new area and how quickly you learnt the other one.

▶ Redrafting

You will need to check spelling and grammar especially carefully for a job application as any mistakes will give a bad impression. The employer does not know you at this stage and so will assume that what you send is the best you are capable of. So aim for a professional and polished submission. It's also a good idea to prune your letter of anything that sounds like rambling. Be as concise as you can.

It's essential to use black ink or typescript for your final draft as an employer might want to photocopy your letter for the members of an interviewing panel, and black is the only colour that comes out well. It's also the case that many people have a violent dislike of coloured ink – including blue.

▶ Before posting

If, like most of us, you are up against the clock when getting an application in the post, don't tell yourself you have no time for taking copies of whatever you send. Photocopy the whole of an application form (not just your statement) because you will need to be sure exactly what you put on it before you attend an interview, and make sure you have a hard copy of letters in case your computer goes down at a vital moment.

A copy of your letter or statement may also be useful if you need to make other applications for similar jobs. Having your notes to hand is not really so valuable as having the finished article which you've probably slaved over. A further letter can be quickly constructed by making a few changes, whereas going back to the first draft stage means you'll have hours' more work to do. These copies might also be valuable if you find yourself applying for a job in a different field. You will often find that a sentence or two from an earlier letter can be just what you need to fill a gap.

SPECULATIVE LETTERS

In some cases, you may want to send out what's known as a *spec letter* to various companies to search for jobs that have not been advertised. You might be lucky and land a job that hadn't reached the advertising stage. On the other hand, this can be a way of interesting a company in what you have to offer. The kind of job you want might not be available at once, but you might get an offer of something else or be contacted at a later date when what you want *is* available.

You will need to learn something about each company you approach (use the Internet or your reference library) and then phone to get the name of someone responsible for the area of work you're interested in. Always write to a named individual and always send a top copy – never send photocopies of letters. After a week or two, it's a good idea to follow up with a polite phone call asking the person you wrote to if s/he has had a chance to consider your submission.

Your letter should be less than one page in length and should briefly state your career aims, your knowledge of the particular industry, your interest in the company and your keenness to work in that particular field. Obviously, you'll enclose your CV.

EXAMPLE OF AN APPLICATION LETTER

Your application letter will be sent with a copy of your CV, so the employer will have all your data to hand when reading your letter. Below is Doug's application letter to a housing trust for a job in IT. The employer's job specification for this letter was follows:

- Making sure that the company is optimising its network and systems
- Training staff
- Installing equipment
- Overhauling finance and housing systems
- Advising on design of website
- Making sure the company's IT is secure, efficient, user-friendly

And here's the person specification:

- A relevant degree
- Experience of managing Windows 2003 and a Microsoft Exchange Server 2003
- Experience of supporting systems running on the above
- Experience of developing IT provision to meet the needs of a business
- Ability to communicate complex technical information in layman's terms

44 Riverside
Winchester
Hampshire
WA2 7BB

3 August 2005

Melanie Prior
Personal Officer
Woodleigh Housing Trust
Andover
Hampshire
AN6 5UV

Dear Ms Prior

IT Infrastructure Analyst

I would like to be considered for the above post and enclose my CV. My early career was as a senior mechanic and MOT inspector in the motor trade. Following an industrial accident, however, I retrained as an IT technician. Having now attained a BSc (Hons) in Information Technology, I feel that my new career can move forward.

I have recent successful experience of managing Windows 2003 and of working with a Microsoft Exchange Server 2003. This has been gained in the last two years as I was able to work part-time for the university while studying for my degree. Together with the IT Manager, I set up systems for an expanding communications department and also transferred all data from an outdated system covering food and hospitality on to Windows 2003. Since then, I have been supporting these systems. I feel that this has given me an excellent background for overhauling the Trust's finance and housing systems.

You will note from my CV that, prior to this, I was an IT technician in a large comprehensive school. I was responsible for setting up systems for a complex school timetable as well as revised timetables for examination periods. I was also responsible for managing the databases of pupils and staff. I then became self-employed for a short time, supplying computer packages to individual customers.

During my time at Foxley Comprehensive School, I assisted in installing new computers for the school's IT room, and while working at the university, I played a major part in the installation of a new library cataloguing system, so I feel very competent to install whatever the Trust decides to go ahead with.

The need to be aware of costs and to make full use of a network and its systems in relation to management of an organisation are issues I have had to bear in mind in my work for educational organisations. If appointed, I would look forward to developing the Trust's use of IT and finding ways in which the systems could be optimised whenever possible.

Advising on the design of a website for the Trust would be particularly exciting. I have designed sites for friends and have taken on small commissions which have all been successful. The opportunity to be involved with a more complex site would give me great satisfaction.

As an IT enthusiast, I enjoy helping others to understand and make use of the vast possibilities of ICT. While at Foxley Comprehensive, I assisted staff in adult IT evening classes, and while at university, I was available for queries from both staff and students on an ad hoc basis. In my previous career as a senior mechanic, I trained new recruits and developed simple training materials. So I have the necessary skills to deliver both face-to-face training and printed materials in layman's terms for company staff.

I find myself very much in sympathy with the ethos of Woodleigh Housing Trust and would enjoy being a part of the enterprise. I am dependable, adaptable, quick-thinking and diligent, and I have a good sense of humour. I would be pleased to discuss my application further at interview.

Yours sincerely

Douglas Barford

EXAMPLE OF THE STATEMENT FOR AN APPLICATION FORM

The only real differences between an application letter and a statement are that the statement omits addresses, the date, the salutation and valediction that appear on letters, and any reference to your CV. Below is Sheila's statement for her application form. She was applying for a post as a Key Stage 2 teacher. The job advert said that newly qualified teachers were welcome to apply for the post, and listed the following qualities that the school was looking for:

- good classroom management skills
- an ability to use ICT
- an understanding of child-centred learning
- an ability to use the whole classroom for learning
- adherence to Equal Opportunities legislation

I will qualify as a teacher this summer with a BEd. I believe I am an all-rounder who is ideally suited to Key Stage 2 teaching. As well as being a good classroom manager and having a special interest in local history, I can offer to assist with physical education and drama.

I have just completed my final teaching practice with a year 4 class. This was very successful. The head teacher was especially pleased with the children's work on memories. I had taken them to two residential homes where they were able to talk to elderly residents. This was supplemented with simple questionnaires that they took home to parents and carers.

I also received some excellent comments on my classroom practice. I feel that good classroom management is essential for learning to take place, and I have dealt successfully with cases of challenging behaviour without having to enlist the help of other members of staff or compromise the planned teaching session. I also value structured play as I feel this has the double value of enhancing clear thinking while promoting social skills.

One of the ways I address learning is by making my classroom inviting so that merely being there can be an exciting learning experience for the children. I believe that every child should be interacting in some small way with classroom displays on a daily basis. To this end, I use a response system, where each child can write a comment – or merely place a tick – on items they like. I also encourage the children to bring appropriate items from home to enhance displays.

Putting the child at the centre of learning is an approach that I find really pays off. Having an experienced classroom assistant has been a bonus for me as this has meant that I could spend more time focusing on the children as individuals.

I am highly adaptable and can offer to help out with drama and PE across the Key Stages from Foundation Stage to the top end of Key Stage 2. As a teenager, I was a member of the county athletics team and I now play netball. I have been a member of my college drama group and last year I took part in a local pantomime. I have taken advantage of extra ICT training over the last two years, and am now competent to support children up to Key Stage 3. It goes without saying that I adhere to Equal Opportunities guidelines. I am also flexible, energetic, enthusiastic and self-motivated.

Before having my own children, I worked as a secretary in the planning department of a local authority. So I have good administration skills. I have kept comprehensive records of the children's work during my teaching practice as well as preparing their reports on time. I have had good relationships with parents and I was able to develop these further in discussions of the children's progress at a parents' evening.

At college, I have enjoyed the companionship of other students and I am keen to become a member of a thriving staffroom as well as to give of my best to the children. I would be happy to supply any further information you need and hope to have the opportunity to discuss my application to teach at Marley Head School at an interview.

SUMMARY

This chapter has covered:

- the statement on an application form
- characteristics of a good letter
- assessing your best qualities
- transferable skills
- getting started
- your first draft
- your introduction
- ways of beginning a paragraph
- your conclusion
- avoiding negatives
- redrafting
- speculative letters
- example of an application letter
- example of the statement for an application form

Appendix 1
Spelling Strategies

If you have *severe* problems with spelling, ask one of your tutors to recommend a book that will give you specific help or tell you where to find a drop-in class for English skills. You could try asking in the college library or at Student Services. You might also look at the section on **dyslexia** at the start of this book. If, however, you are like many people and know that your spelling just isn't very good, you'll find some tips here to help you. People learn in different ways, so use the methods that suit you best.

The main thing is to attack the problem consciously. For some years, I think I must have hoped that I would somehow imbibe the correct spellings of words from the atmosphere. Eventually, I realised that I'd have to take positive steps if I wanted to make improvements. There are lots of useful tricks you can use to help you remember how to spell particular words. Memory aids (and they can be used for anything you want to remember) are called **mnemonics** (for pronunciation, ignore the first '*m*').

THE COMPUTER SPELL-CHECK

If you are able to use a computer, you will certainly find its spell-check facility useful. This will pick up a lot of misspellings and so improve the look of your assignments. But there are certain things to beware of. A computer won't recognise many technical words and will change some things you may have spelt correctly to the closest word it knows. It may also be set up for American spelling, which is fine if you live in America, but not much help if you're in Britain. It's usually possible, however, to change the language setting to the one you need.

The main problem with relying solely on a spell-check facility is that you won't be improving your own spelling. This won't matter while you are submitting course work, but can leave you at a serious disadvantage when you come to exams. You'll probably get the best value from a spell-checker by using it *in conjunction with* your own programme of spelling improvement.

MNEMONICS

Mnemonics is the word given to any type of memory aid. Any way of using rhythm, colour, patterns of letters or systems of numbers, including using visual pictures, is a mnemonic. You may already know the mnemonic for remembering whether to put *i* before *e* in the middle of a word:

> *i* before *e* except after *c*

This mnemonic has a strong rhythm to it, and it's this that makes it easy to remember. So we can work out (without having to learn them) how to spell words like

> retrieve ⎱ the *i* does not follow a *c*
> achieve ⎰

and

> conceit ⎱ the *e* must go next to the *c*
> deceive ⎰

There are a few exceptions to this rule, however, such as *eight* and *seize.*

The key to a good mnemonic is to make it:

- simple
- enjoyable
- amusing

If you can add a mental picture that is highly coloured, funny, silly – or even sexy - that's even better. If you want to remember how to spell the word *mnemonic,* for example, try this:

m	n	e	+ monic
mind	**N**ed's	**e**lephant	

You might visualise a tiny man with a huge, ungainly elephant.

It doesn't matter what you choose as long as it will stick in your mind. The more bizarre your mnemonics, the easier they will be to remember.

YOUR PERSONAL SPELLING AID

Another very valuable tool for learning to spell well is a notebook. Divide each page into two down the middle. On the left-hand side, keep a running list of words you have misspelt, and underline the letter or section of each word that has been causing you problems. Then work out and write down in the right-hand column a mnemonic for each one. Finally, have your notebook handy whenever you are writing an assignment. You will need to take especial care over names and technical words related to your own subject. You might use the back of your notebook for these. Be sure to show the correct spelling.

VISUALISING A WORD

Some people find that if they spend a few moments looking at a word and then close their eyes, they can see it clearly in their mind's eye. If this works for you, do use this method for learning. It's quick and simple.

SPOTTING THE PARTS OF A WORD

Sometimes, you can clearly see that a word has several sections to it. So you can remember its spelling more easily by splitting it up. For example:

prom	is	es	promises
fluc	tu	ate	fluctuate
car	til	age	cartilage

SAYING WORDS ALOUD

When you are alone, try saying difficult words aloud, using a sing-song voice and really exaggerating each section of the word. You can devise chants, too. For example, the word *necessary* is often misspelt. Try chanting "One *c* and two *s*'s in *ne - ces - sary*" to help you remember.

SOME TYPICAL PROBLEM AREAS

You will need to know the following terms for this section:

Vowel	a, e, i, o, u
Consonant	any letter *except* those above*
Prefix	an addition to the beginning of a word, e.g. <u>re</u>turn/ <u>un</u>do
Suffix	an addition to the end of a word - e.g. *loud<u>ly</u>/sense<u>less</u>*
Syllable	one section of a word, containing a vowel, that could function as one 'beat'. E.g. in *particularly* there are five beats: *par tic u lar ly*

You might like to reinforce the beats of syllables by banging your hand on the desk or table as you say them.

There are many rules for English spelling, but it's certainly not necessary to remember them all in order to spell well. Sometimes, however, people find them handy, so I'll give two here to start you off. The first one is really easy. You may already know it.

▶ The plural of words ending in y

A word that ends with the letter *y* is made plural by changing the *y* to *ie* before adding *s*. For example:

Singular	*Plural*
city	cities
lady	ladies
body	bodies

---

* The letter *y* can function as both a consonant and a vowel.

Unfortunately, of course, there are one or two exceptions. But, in this case, the *y* are not difficult to remember. Words that have a vowel *before* the *y* don't change. For example:

donkey	donkeys
monkey	monkeys
tray	trays
boy	boys

▶ Double letters

Remembering whether or not to use a double letter can be a real bugbear. For a difficult word where the double letter is somewhere in the middle, the best thing is to copy it out, split it into syllables, and devise a suitable mnemonic.

Other problem areas for knowing whether or not to double a letter are prefixes and suffixes.

Prefixes
These are easy. A prefix is an item made up of a few letters that we put on the front of various words. When adding a prefix, just slot it straight on. Sometimes, this will mean that you end up with a double letter; sometimes it won't. For example:

moderate	immoderate
noticed	unnoticed
marine	submarine
terrestrial	extraterrestrial

Suffixes
A suffix is an addition at the end of a word. The rules are as follows:

- *Don't* double the letter when adding a suffix beginning with a vowel to a two-syllable word where the stress is on the *first* syllable, e.g.:

*mar*ket	marketed
*bud*get	budgeted

- *Do* double the letter when adding a suffix beginning with a vowel to a two-syllable word where the stress is on the *second* syllable, e.g.:

ad*mit*   admitted
de*ter*   deterred

or a one-syllable word that ends in a vowel followed by a consonant, e.g.:

trim   trimmed
spot   spotted

Note: for words of two syllables ending in l, the spelling can depend on where you live, e.g.:

British spelling: travel   travel**ed**
American spelling: travel   travel**ed**

▶ Some commonly misspelt words

Here's a list of some words that are very frequently misspelt. It isn't exhaustive, but should get you thinking. You might like to put them in your spelling notebook.

accommodate	gauge
achieve	independent(ly)
acknowledge	necessary
address	occur(red)
argument	persuade
business	possession
committee	prejudice
definite(ly)	privilege
embarrassed	recommend
existence	receipt
extremely	separate(ly)
February	until
fulfil*(led)	usually

* The American spelling of this word is *fulfill.*

Appendix 2
Common confusions

accept   receive or agree to
except   apart from, with the exception of

affect   change in some way
effect   the result of something

> If I spend less, this will affect my bank balance. Hopefully, the final effect will be that I clear my debts.

practice (noun)   the usual way of doing something or the repetition of an activity (often for improvement)
practise (verb) *   to do (something) repeatedly to gain skill

> John practises the guitar every evening. It's his practice [i.e. habit] to do this after he's had something to eat.

principal   head of a college, director, or most important person in a company
principle   standard by which people behave or a natural law governing the behaviour of a body or system

> The college principal prides himself on his principles

their (possession)   e.g. their essays
there (place)   e.g. over there
they're (contraction)   they are

> Ant and Dec are appearing in Birmingham. They're hosting their show there

---

*The American spelling for this is practice.

to	Mel went *to* France.
two	Mel has *two* cousins.
too	Mel is *too* busy to clean the car.

These two jackets are too old to send to the cleaners.

simple	something that is easy to understand or do or is clearly expressed
simplistic	something that is oversimplified or expressed without taking into account necessary complex issues

The MP gave a rather simplistic explanation of an issue that is in no way simple

where (place)	Tim remembered *where* he'd left the wrench.
were (verb)	Tim and Mick *were* having a drink.

We were having lunch in the pub where I first met Sam.

should've (contraction) – should have
could've (contraction) – could have
would've (contraction) – would have

These last three are very frequently written incorrectly as *should of, could* of and *would of.* The reason this happens is due to what we hear. It can sound as though the word *of* is at the end of *should've, could've* and *would've.*

I should've finished my essay yesterday, and I would've if I could've done.

dependent	something that happens as a consequence of something else
dependant	person who relies on another for some means of support

The size of legacies to Geraldine Smythe's dependants (her five children) will be dependent on the amount of money left after paying inheritance tax.

past   no longer existing
passed   moved by or beyond something

It was ten past three when we passed the accident on the motorway.

Answers

Activity 1

1 wash
2 foretell
3 long
4 migrate
5 sends
6 desire

Activity 2

1 d ate
2 h has
3 d will be crossing
4 d goes
5 b were
6 b is
7 h had
8 h will have
9 d were buzzing
10 b will be

Activity 3

1 past
2 present
3 past
4 future
5 present
6 future
7 present
8 future

Activity 4

1 past perfect
2 present perfect
3 past perfect
4 future perfect
5 present perfect
6 past perfect
7 future perfect
8 present perfect
9 future perfect
10 present perfect

Activity 5

1 present simple
2 past simple
3 future simple
4 future continuous
5 past perfect continuous
6 past perfect
7 future perfect continuous
8 past continuous

9 present continuous
10 future perfect

11 present perfect
12 present perfect continuous

Activity 6

1 A	6 P
2 P	7 P
3 P	8 P
4 A	9 A
5 A	10 P

Activity 7
1 Mrs Steele, letter, Queen
2 Bees, honey
3 Carlos, France, years
4 Mary, bike
5 Julius Caesar, Rome

Activity 8

Concrete	Abstract
1 water	life
2	exercise
	health
3 atmosphere	
bar	
smoke	
4 monk	understanding
5 members	strategy
6 Paul	philosophy

Activity 9

1 beautifully	5 harder, harder
2 slowly, silently	6 high
3 quickly	7 dearly
4 fast	8 rather, rashly

▶ Chapter 13: Writing clear sentences

Activity 1
2, 3, 7

Activity 2

subject	*verb*
1 Jimi Hendrix	died
2 Beatlemania	swept
3 Fraser	plays
4 Duke Ellington	is
5 Mick Jagger	performs
6 Salsa	is becoming

Activity 3

1 Carl	5 a belt of rain, high winds
2 Ron	6 Maxine
3 the cowboy	7 The children, the buns
4 Pam	8 To work at a satisfying job

Activity 4

1 the casino	4 a fight
2 the suspects	5 the events
3 their winnings	6 calm

Activity 5

1 you	4 us
2 class IV	5 me
3 her client	

Activity 6

1 Lucy ran home, crying all the way.
  Lucy ran home. She cried all the way.
2 Ken's dog had been annoying the neighbours, barking all morning.
  Ken's dog had been annoying the neighbours. It had been barking all morning.
3 Brad ran down the road with the cheque, laughing all the way to the bank.
  Brad ran down the road with the cheque. He laughed all the way to the bank.
4 The children came home covered in mud looking absolutely filthy.
  The children came home covered in mud. They looked absolutely filthy.
5 English grammar can be difficult, causing all sorts of problems.
  English grammar can be difficult. It can cause all sorts of problems.

6 I couldn't think how to get the cork out of the bottle. I had tried everything I knew.

 I couldn't think how to get the cork out of the bottle. I had been trying everything I knew.

7 The wolf set off through the forest looking for the cottage belonging to Little Red Riding Hood's grandmother.

 The wolf set off through the forest. He was looking for the cottage belonging to Little Red Riding Hood's grandmother.

Activity 7

1 Nursery schools are places where children learn some of the basic skills they will need for primary school. These include recognising their names, making simple models, and getting along with others.

2 My local school has started a monthly newsletter. Teachers believe that this will help make local people more aware of all the activities available for children and parents. [You might have kept the original wording and put a comma after *newsletter*.]

3 This essay will look at both sides of the argument in order to show the complexity of the issues involved. These are crucial issues, affecting every aspect of our lives.

Activity 8

1 There are fairies at the bottom of my garden where I haven't cut the grass.

2 Although it's freezing, I refuse to wear woolly undies.

3 Place all gallstones in the bucket provided after you have sewn up the patient.

4 As I came out of the supermarket, I bumped into a small horse.

5 A problem shared is a problem halved, as long as the trouble is either legal or is not divulged to a serving police officer.

6 It's hot.

▶ Chapter 14: Punctuation

Activity 1

1 Marian has travelled in France, Spain, Australia, India and the USA. [It is OK to put a comma after *India* if you wish.]

2 We were watched by a lean, ageing kangaroo.

3 After two weeks on buses and trains, it was a relief to smell sea air.

4 Jason, our guide, walked fast and spoke little.

5 Air disasters, it is well known, are fewer than accidents on the roads.
6 Taking a foreign holiday, despite problems with accommodation, currency and language, can be a liberating experience. [It would not be wrong to put a comma after *currency.* Since there is little chance of a misunderstanding, however, it's probably best to omit it.]
7 Day after day, the grey rocks, dotted here and there with small plants, formed a backdrop for our trek. [The first comma marks off extra information at the start. The next two mark off extra information in the middle of the sentence.]
8 Taking a foreign holiday can be a liberating experience. [It would be wrong to put any commas in number 8 because there is no extra information in the sentence. This is similar to the sentence *Maria went for a long walk across the fields to the river.* Everything here is part of the main statement. It's also the case that the phrase *Taking a foreign holiday* is the subject of the sentence, so it mustn't be separated from its verb.]

Activity 2

The full stops after 'freedom' and 'reactionary' could be replaced by semicolons. In the first case, you might decide to keep within one sentence the statements concerning the two views on the motor car. In the second case, you could keep together the explanations of the difficulties in which governments can find themselves.

Activity 3

1 It's only when I laugh that it hurts. (contraction)
2 It's a lovely day today. (contraction)
3 John's father's got his brother's coat. (possession/contraction: father has/possession)
4 When it's raining, that dog always stays in its kennel. (contraction)
5 It's easy to see how the cat shut its paw in the Browns' gate. (contraction/plural possession)
6 The hyenas' eyes were visible in the bushes everywhere we looked. (plural possession)

▶ Chapter 15: Getting conversation on paper

Activity 1
A
1 Jack said, "My partner is expecting a baby."

2 "I was born in Tunis," said Pierre.
3 "Where is the post office?" asked the tourist.
4 The toddler yelled, "I want an ice cream!"
5 "That dog," said John, "always disappears when I want to bath it."
6 "Why," asked Tom, "have you put the beer under my bed?" [Notice that the question mark does not come after the word *Why* because that is not the end of the question.]

B
1 Mary said, "The eggs are in the fridge."
2 "High tide will be at three this afternoon," said the sailor.
3 "Come back here!" yelled the policeman.
4 Sam asked politely, "How much extra will I have to pay?"
5 "I haven't laughed so much," said Ben, "since the chicken coop collapsed."
6 "The main difficulty," explained the leader, "will be getting the tents across the river."

Activity 2
I sense there's an excitement for Bob Crooks in work where he's in dialogue with his material, mixing colours and never being 100% sure of the final outcome because of the speed of the material's reactions.

"I don't want to battle against the material," he says, "so in the final heating, I let the glass do what it wants to do." It is by this means that Bob is able to create the fluid forms he's known for. He's influenced by geometry, architecture and the natural world. "I can't make anything as beautiful as what's in nature," he goes on, "but I like taking elements of different things and turning them into something whole."

Activity 3
2 Kwame said that he was driving a Ford then.
3 Kwame said that he had driven to Italy the previous month.
4 Kwame said that he had driven 500 miles that week.
5 Kwame said that he had been driving for 10 years then.
6 Kwame said that he had been driving at night when the brakes failed.
7 Kwame said that he would drive to Spain the following year.
8 Kwame said that he would be driving a Porsche the following year.
Note that in No. 6, it is not necessary to change the tense of 'failed'.

Bibliography

Blake, William. 'The Chimney Sweeper', in *Songs of Innocence and of Experience*. London: Oxford University Press, 1970.

Buzan, Tony & Buzan, Barry. *The Mind Map Book*, revised edition. London: BBC Active, 2005.

Cottrell, Stella. *The Study Skills Handbook*. Basingstoke: Macmillan, 1999.

Curtin University of Technology. 'Harvard Referencing 2005'. Accessed online 10.1.06   from www.curtin.edu.au

Duffy, Carol Ann. *Rapture*. London: Picador, 2005.

Gill, A. A. *The Angry Island*. London: Weidenfeld & Nicolson, 2005.

Grayling, A. C. 'Why a high society is a free society'. *Observer*, 19.5.02., accessed online 3 June 2005, from http://observer.guardian.co.uk/comment/story/0,,718108,00.html.

Ibsen, Henrik, *A Doll's House*, in *Four Major Plays*. Oxford: Oxford University Press, 1981.

McArthur, Tom. *The Oxford Companion to the English Language*, abridged edition. Oxford: Oxford University Press, 1996.

Shakespeare, William. *Hamlet*, the Arden edition, ed. Harold Jenkins. London & New York: Methuen, 1982.

Vernon, M. D. *The Psychology of Perception*, 2nd edition. Harmondsworth: Penguin Books, 1971.

Williams, Lynn. *Readymade CVs*. London: Kogan Page, 1996.

Note: This bibliography has been prepared in accordance with the British Standard referencing system.

Index